W9-BCX-364

Feasting With Panthers

Feasting With Panthers

A New Consideration of Some Late Victorian Writers

by

RUPERT CROFT-COOKE

HOLT, RINEHART AND WINSTON

New York Chicago San Francisco

Published simultaneously in Canada by Holt, Rinehart and Winston of Canada, Limited.
Library of Congress
Catalog Card Number: 68-11160
First Edition
First published in the United States in 1968
8675050
Printed in Great Britain

DEDICATED
with affection and gratitude
to all those who do not
start the book till they
have read the introduction

Contents

Acknowledgements for Illustrations

Illustrations appear between pages 130–131

The picture of Lord Alfred Douglas and his brother is from a photograph given by Lord Alfred Douglas to Richard Blake Brown, hitherto unreproduced, and included by Mr Blake Brown's kind permission.

The pictures of Reginald Harding and William Ward are reproduced by kind permission of Mr Vyvyan Holland.

The picture of Richard Le Gallienne is reproduced by kind permission of Mrs Hesper Le Gallienne Hutchinson.

The caricature of Oscar Wilde by Max Beerbohm is reproduced by kind permission of Mrs Eva Reichmann.

The picture of Angelo Fusato is reproduced by kind permission of the University of Bristol.

Acknowledgements for Illustrations

The drawing of Oscar Browning by Simeon Solomon is reproduced from the book, *Oscar Browning*, by H. G. Wortham, published by Constable & Co., Ltd.

The picture of William Johnson (Cory) is reproduced from a photograph in *William Cory*, by Faith Compton Mackenzie, published by Constable & Co., Ltd.

The pictures of John Gray and R. H. Sherard are reproduced from the book, *The Letters of Oscar Wilde*, published by Rupert Hart-Davis Ltd.

The picture of Charles Howell is reproduced by permission of the Trustees of the British Museum.

The drawing of Ernest Dowson by Charles Conder is reproduced by permission of the National Portrait Gallery.

The frontispiece picture of Piccadilly Circus, and the pictures of Walter Pater and Oscar Wilde are reproduced by permission of the Mansell Collection.

Ackowledgements for Illustrations

The following pictures are reproduced by permission of the Radio Times Hulton Picture Library: Algernon Charles Swinburne; Simeon Solomon; Sir Edmund Gosse; Swinburne and Adah Menken; John Addington Symonds (at Oxford); J. A. Symonds (with father and sister); J. A. Symonds (in Venice); Edward Fitzgerald; Edward Lear and Chichester Fortescue; Charles Dodgson; Charles Dodgson (with children); Alice Liddell and Young girl.

Other pictures were obtained through the British Museum.

Acknowledgements

I have to express the deepest gratitude to Professor Robert Peters of the University of California and to Harford Montgomery Hyde who most generously gave time to reading the proofs of this book and to Professor John H. Munro of the American University of Beirut who gave me immense encouragement and help in my researches. This does not of course imply that any of them agrees with such opinions as I express. I have also had suggestions or assistance for which I am most grateful from Mr John Betjeman, Lord Kinross, Mr Lionel Lambourne, Mr John S. Mayfield, Mr Alec Waugh and Mr Cecil Woolf.

I owe a great deal to Professor Cecil Y. Lang and the Yale University Press for permission to quote widely from *The Swinburne Letters* and to Mr Vyvyan Holland and Sir Rupert Hart-Davis for quotations from *The Letters of Oscar Wilde*. The editors and publishers of these two remarkable collections of letters have made it possible for me to develop my theme. I thank William Heinemann Ltd for permission to quote from The Bonchurch edition of The Complete Works of Algernon Charles Swinburne. I also express my thanks to Messrs Putnam & Company Ltd for permission to quote from Richard Le Gallienne's *The Romantic 90's* and to all those who have allowed the reproduction of portraits and other pictures. Their names appear in the list of Acknowledgements for Illustrations.

A great deal of work in discovering portraits and arranging their reproduction has been done by Mr Jeffrey Simmons and Miss Frances-M. Blake for which I am also grateful, and the text has been typed, re-typed and scrutinized by my secretary Joseph Susei Mari and Miss Susan Brewer. I am also grateful to Mr A. T. Miller of Frank Hollings Booksellers, for the particular trouble he has taken to discover out-of-print books, and to the librarians of the British Museum and the London Library for their patience and help.

But as any honest writer presenting a new aspect of historical facts must admit, my first debt is to the authors, alive or dead, of works already published, and these will be found in the Bibliography.

Introduction

ALL debauch is ridiculous in enactment or description for it is a sentimental aggrandizement of natural appetite. The glutton, the drunk, the lecher with bizarre proclivities—each is a figure of comedy and should be seen as such. When the writer takes seriously what is no more than excess or eccentricity, greeting it with raptures or exalting it to the status of a satanic evil, his work itself becomes pornographic, morbid or merely silly. This is the literature of Decadence.

Swinburne exploiting his own masochistic nature to produce most of a bad novel called *Lesbia Brandon*, John Addington Symonds writing wistful lyrics to schoolboys, Oscar Wilde humourlessly cataloguing the transgressions of a phony diabolist in *Dorian Gray* become in these exercises funny and disreputable, whatever are the splendours of Swinburne's lyrics, the worth of Symonds's *History of the Renaissance in Italy* or the wit of *The Importance of Being Earnest*. Sincerity alone survives the test of expression, and the only love-poetry that escapes anticlimax, like Sidney's to Stella or Shakespeare's to Mr W. H., comes from a dynamic, uncultivated emotion.

The writers of the later nineteenth century, some of whose lives as they affected their work I propose to examine here, had a self-conscious and literary approach to sex and were aware of the various kinds of isolation it could impose. They were not remarkably dissolute or reckless men, like Villon from whose crimes and depravity poetry ran like blood, but creatures awed by their own notions of sin, infected with a puritanical belief in the evil of pleasure and the pleasures of evil, who trembled ecstatically at the shrine of the pitiless woman, exchanged in whispers their delight in the fatuities of De Sade, were shamefaced or noisily defiant about their love for other men and could speak as Wilde did of his affairs with stable-boys and blackmailers as feasting with panthers.

That was the keynote of their work and the cause of that reputation for wickedness which has followed them in this century. They sought by the power of their not inconsiderable talents to give colour, meaning and beauty to their own sexual idiosyncrasies, to raise the common street-walker to a Salome or, if she had learned to use such tools of her trade as a whip, to a Dolores or Faustine, to make the everyday male whore a Hyacinthus, and moved by the petty stimulus of masturbation to create hinterlands of erotic fantasy and call them Ancient Greece.

Out of their adulteries and intimacies they made a cult; they turned their pederastic hankerings to verse. They spoke with unction of 'strange sins' and 'forbidden pleasures' and they wrote in scarlet ink of all relationships which were not sternly procreative. They made such an infernal din about their wickedness, they abused all workaday morality with such venom, that they passed as lechers or satanists among more philistine Victorians who were doubtless busy with their own erotic warfare undeterred by the barbed-wire defences of beards and whiskers, the balloon barrage of voluminous nightgowns or the poison gases from unwashed feet.

In this book I shall try to treat the so-called Decadent writers as neither heroes nor monsters, but to bring them down to earth and show them as fellow beings, laughable sometimes, more or less gifted, more or less heterodox in their lives and opinions, more or less admirable, pitiful or absurd. Swinburne was a great poet but he was also impotent and a victim of arrested development obsessed with recollections of bloodstained bottoms on the Eton flogging-block. Symonds was a considerable historian and essayist and a doughty fighter for a more sympathetic attitude to those he called Urnings, but he was a fake when he applied 'Greek ideals' to his affairs with gondoliers and Swiss peasants. While Wilde, who allowed his will to become jellified and his good name destroyed by his boozy associations with London renters,• saw himself as a lordly explorer of strange infernos.

It is only in their talents that these men were rare or egregious—their vices and their tastes were not very unusual either in their own time or today. Yet such was the overpowering nature of the puritanism which concealed the proclivities of the mass of Victorians that Swinburne has come to be considered a freak worthy of exhibition, Symonds a great tragic figure, and Wilde, throughout the world, the very type and symbol of the pederast.

So with the other men remembered here, those who influenced these three, those who were their friends or hangers-on or heroes. They are no less warmly credible and I want to remember them without solemnity. In their very heterogeneity they are human and this encourages one to smile at their memory in a friendly and understanding way rather than strike attitudes of reverence or condemnation or babble the respectful phrases of higher criticism. Lord Houghton with his well-thumbed library of pornography, Whitman with his tram-conductors and Fitzgerald with his Norfolk fishermen, the three precipitately dismissed schoolmasters Johnson (Cory), Vaughan and Oscar Browning, sly Walter Pater with his handsome young guests, Dodgson the photographer and his little girl models posing in the nude, Swinburne's friends Howell and Powell, the one bluffing and chiselling, the other listening patiently to the poet's Sadic raptures, Simeon Solomon the darling of the Pre-Raphaelites who was to become a shuffling and drunken pauper, John Thomson with a half-share in a brothel, poor Stella and Fanny the drag queens, Edmund Gosse anxiously concealing his nature till he told Symonds the not very startling truth in a burst of confidence, Edward Cracroft Lefroy the parson whose poems to footballers so impressed Symonds that he wrote an essay on him, the beautiful John Gray who became a priest and his opulent sugar-daddy Raffalovich who fulfilled himself by building a church for him, Count Stenbock who wore a live snake round his neck and wrote stories about werewolves and such, More Adey his friend and Wilde's who was known as the Bearded Lady,

• Male prostitutes.

Bosie Douglas with his fatal impetuosity and Robert Ross who envied his place in Wilde's life, and all that bevy of catamites who surrounded Wilde in spite of both Ross and Douglas, the young poets of the Nineties, Lionel Johnson, Ernest Dowson, hurrying to their graves—they all, it seems to me, need cutting down to size, need stripping of their false colours, need to be discussed in earthier terms and with less wonder and pity. The bogus demonology of some, the obscene growths on the reputations of others, the odium, or worship that many of them have been given—all these have made us blind to their humanity which is funny and sad and altogether natural. They are entertaining figures and there need be no shame in seeing them as such. They do not make a pantheon of grotesques, nor is the entertainment they provide that of a Chamber of Horrors. They are life-sized and correlations for them may be found more easily in the present than in the Castle of Otranto or on the island of Dr Moreau. Their reputations have suffered from several kinds of misinterpretation but chiefly from the literary vice of inflation.

This inflation was largely due to the writers themselves, the lesser of whom claimed a special aura for their times and a distinction for themselves as innovators, experimenters and rebels. But even more responsible are the chroniclers who have insisted that they are dealing with a period apart and, particularly to the last decade of the epoch, have applied distinctive names—the Naughty, the Romantic or the Yellow Nineties, the Beardsley Period and so on. Every episode has been made to seem momentous, every careless aside of one of the men of the time treasured as significant, every commonplace event chronicled with unction.

Examples of this kind of over-writing are many and I quote at random. Ernest Rhys, describing Count Stenbock at the piano, says, 'the steppes of Russia appeared through the darkening window-panes!'• Frances Winwar writes her whole book in these tones, and this is a mild example describing Wilde's last period in Paris which has been shown by Rupert Hart-Davis's edition of his *Letters* to have been a lively and inconsequent time passed riotously with young lovers from the Boulevards, with meals paid for by friends in return for his conversation which had never been more gay and witty: "A lassitude, like a chain of iron, deadened his body, carried ponderously from

• *Everyman Remembers* by Ernest Rhys, 1931.

café to café till his money or his credit gave out and he was forced to return to his cheerless room. He hardly touched food any more and then only when weakened from hunger."•

Perhaps the most flamboyant exponent of this kind of over-writing and disproportionate imagery was Richard Le Gallienne, who described William Sharp thus: "He was probably the handsomest man in London, a large flamboyant 'sun-god' sort of creature, with splendid, vital, curling gold hair and a pointed golden beard, the bluest of Northern eyes, and the complexion of a girl. Laughing energy radiated from his robust frame, and he was all exuberance, enthusiasm, and infectious happiness, a veritable young Dionysus. If only he had been as good a poet as he was good-looking! But it would have been hard for writing to live up to such a victorious appearance."•• His description of the Vale Press is perhaps even more flagrant: "There was a delightful aura of mystery about these early private presses, particularly about the Vale Press. Had Messrs. Ricketts and Shannon been alchemists, their operations could not have been veiled in a more thrilling secrecy, or the results awaited with more hushed expectancy; and specimen pages of any new book on which they were cloistrally engaged were shown privately by Lane to a favoured few as things sacrosanct, and occultly precious, with that reverent solemnity which characterizes the true collector."••• It is Le Gallienne, too, who provides by a conceit of almost metaphysical oddity in one of his lyrics a term for all the sordidness, artificial brilliance and cruelty of late Victorian London when he called the gas-lamps the 'iron lilies of the Strand'. But these are not the only writers who have 'blown up' the period, particularly the last years of it. Everyone who discusses it seems tempted to shout.

Among those of whom I am writing there are no women, for if these men can be said to have created a School or a Movement women had little active part in it, and it would need a woman writer to do justice to Adah Isaacs Menken, Mathilde Blind, 'Vernon Lee', Ada Leverson and 'Michael Field', or to sympathize with those who were connected with it by marriage, like Catherine Symonds or Constance Wilde.

The period I have chosen is from 1857, the year of Swinburne's

• *Oscar Wilde and the Yellow Nineties* by Francis Winwar, 1940.
•• *The Romantic Nineties* by Richard Le Gallienne, 1926.
••• *Ibid.*

meeting with the Pre-Raphaelites at Oxford, to 1895, the year of Wilde's trials. During all but the last few years of this time the outward scene in London, or indeed in all England, changed as little as in any period of similar length in recent history. Though suburbs stretched farther afield and certain unbeautiful but notable buildings rose in the metropolis, the street scene, the way of life of the people, their means of transport (in spite of the coming of bicycles which only became popular in the Nineties), the interiors of their homes and lodgings, their social economy changed scarcely at all. The appearance of men grew somewhat more starched and strait-laced; for women the bustle came and went but trimmings, fringes, flounces remained, and though the use of the bicycle towards the end of the period produced bloomers and Norfolk suits these were adopted only by a *Punch*-derided minority. The attenuated reforms of Gladstone and Disraeli, the coming of compulsory education, the Crimean War, the formation of the Fabian Society had no effect on the outward scene and little, one is tempted to think, on the life of the people. The period, therefore, at least until its last decade, was a more than usually static one and produced an almost unchanging background to the lives here recalled.

It was grim in many ways but vivid and picaresque in detail, a philistine prosperous age with scandalous conditions of poverty unrelieved. The classes were remorselessly defined. There was still an aristocracy and it was for the most part wealthy, its members following a life of uncultivated idleness with their Seasons, their great country houses, their liveried servants, their grouse moors and hunting boxes and their annual migrations to witness or enjoy their various sports. The affluent middle-class followed them respectfully but there was a vast body of professional or near-professional bourgeoisie, carefully distinguished from the tradesmen below them, who had less leisure and perhaps more taste and lived rather magnificently by the domestic dictates of Mrs Beeton, supported by loyal servants not much overworked. Perhaps the figure most revealing of the age was the lower middle-class householder, the Mr Pooter for whom whole suburbs were built, who wore a frock-coat and top hat to work, travelled by horse-drawn bus, ate four gross meals a day, kept a single slavey in close confinement in the attic or basement of his villa, respected his betters but held himself and his family superior to manual workers, attended chapel on Sundays and for a night of abandon went to the music-hall on Saturdays where his wife lifted her veil nose-high to drink her stout.

The manual workers, as yet unstirred by hope or propaganda, laboured for a wage considered sufficient so long as they did not want education, a healthy diet, hygienic plumbing, more than one shoddy suit for Sundays, proper footwear for children, more than a hoarded minimum of fuel or any kind or summer holiday. But below them was yet another class, feckless, hungry, crowded in slum jungles in unspeakable conditions, brutishly criminal, given to drunkenness, street fighting, prostitution and incest, their children bootless and their wives clutching tattered shawls as they begged or pilfered to buy a beery swill or a lean kipper.

These gave to the street scene, even in the West End of London, a touch of what was unforgivably called picturesque poverty; their scarecrow figures seen under the gas-lamps at night were viewed with fear, guilt and loathing by the more prosperous. There were still crossing-sweepers, boot-blacks, match-sellers, occupational cadgers and beggars drawn from this class but they could not aspire to the status of their horsy superiors, cabbies, bus drivers, stablemen or cockneys with their mokes and barrows.

There were street-vendors and street cries, bonnets and billycock hats, Parma violets in buttonholes and an umbrella or walking-stick in every male hand. Railway stations, stinking and cavernous, were not yet overrun by commuters but saw tearful goodbye scenes among families supplied with travelling-rugs and picnic baskets, men and women wrapped in travelling-capes. Smoking among the 'educated classes' was practised in rooms dedicated to the purpose, it being considered offensive to ladies, but among the lower orders a stump of pipe could be enjoyed more freely while cigars—except among the wealthy—were things for special occasions and the cigarette still largely a perquisite of the young. Street lights gave a sickly yellow glow and the pavements were shadowy except when lit by the flaring illuminations of theatres, public houses, music-halls or luxurious restaurants which became fashionable towards the end of the century. ('Eating out' was little known to the early Victorians, except as an all-male occasion.)

London pubs during the 1850s and 60s, almost exclusively patronized by manual labourers and horsy men, acquired a new popularity as vast mahogany erections went up behind their bars, mirrors lined their walls and barmaids, lavishly dressed with splendid coiffures, became 'characters' to the customers. On their solid façades were advertised Wines drawn from the Wood, and port and sherry competed with gin in popularity. Newspapers ceased to be treasures passed round among joint subscribers or club members, but proliferated, gaining unheard-of circulations while ragged newsboys shouted unintelligible promises of their contents including details of the latest murder.

Soldiers were 'redcoats' in fact as well as name, and instead of the antique galleries of today there were curiosity shops. Ragged children played hopscotch on the pavement, muffin-men rang bells through the twilit streets and carried trays on their heads, wagons from the country, some of which had travelled all night, arrived at daybreak at Covent Garden and there was still a certain rusticity about Chelsea and Kensington. But it was during this period that poster advertising ceased to be quaint or daring and forced itself on the people's attention—railway stations, hoardings, gable-ends and warehouse walls displaying their commands and questions, their comic or familiar figures.

It was a busy, on the whole pacific, self-satisfied era which drove the writer in the Decadent, the Aesthetic, the art-above-life tradition to assert himself not only in print but as a person with an acknowledged place in the scheme of things, a period that caused him to feel anomalous but resolved to escape the drabness and monotony about him, a period to make him seek the support of his kind against the forces of Philistia.

For a time it seemed that he would triumph in that struggle and earn the right to a life of his own without the restraints of convention or even, he began fondly to hope, of law. For a time he saw himself as a Sacred Cow, unimpeded in his search for truth, beauty, experience, art for art's sake or what-have-you. Swinburne could get drunk at quite respectable dinner parties on the strength of his fame as a poet, Symonds could bring his gondolier to England and show him off in country houses and Wilde could sit in a box at the theatre or at a table in the Café Royal with a group of his disreputable satellites. Convention and public morality were confounded and all three could defy or deride them in their writings.

But not for long. The prosecution of Wilde was more than a sordid little case under a discreditable law. He himself saw it as the victory of

Caliban but he did not realize its implications for others. In a few months, in three public hearings, it obliterated the kind of individualism he and his literary fellows had claimed as a right. It put the 'artist' (in Wilde's interpretation of the word) back in his place. It was not so much a blow to the homosexual, who was accustomed to such caveats, as one to all men, artists or not, who tried to live without conformity. In itself a commonplace affair of a well-to-do man patronizing male prostitutes, it had at that moment a significance and effect which have never died out.

What the Wildean artist had failed to realize was the strength of the fifth column of writers and painters who faithfully served the cause of what was considered Public Decency. The writings of W. S. Gilbert, most articulate of the Philistines, should have warned him. Ever since the outcry against Swinburne's *Poems and Ballads* the opposition had taken the offensive with ridicule, appeals to outraged morality, well-directed slights, threats of litigation, even a prison sentence• or two as their chief weapons. That fellow writers like W. E. Henley should show themselves on the side of the self-righteous was shocking to the Decadents, but it was the winning side and Wilde and all his works and all his 'artists' went into the wilderness and were superseded by hearty men who wore Norfolk suits and rode bicycles like Shaw and Wells, or writers of good healthy adventure fiction like Rider Haggard and Kipling and many others, or jolly humourists like Jerome and W. W. Jacobs, or outdoor poets like Masefield. It was ten years after the fall of Wilde before anything of his was issued by a reputable publisher and then it was certain extracts from *De Profundis* (for which that title was chosen), and these, in the form in which Ross edited them, appeared to be a long Peccavi. There was such a slump in Decadence that John Lane closed down the once successful *Yellow Book* and the few surviving young poets of the Nineties became unfashionable or even unmentionable so that Arthur Symons went mad, Victor Plarr edited a biographical dictionary, Lionel Johnson drank himself to death, Le Gallienne fled to America and Lord Alfred Douglas spent many years in litigation in defence of his lost reputation.

The Establishment—excellent word, with its present connotation one of the best to emerge in this century—had not had such a victory

• Henry Vizetelly was gaoled for three months for persisting in publishing English translations of Zola's novels.

over all that was foreign, decadent, morbid and unhealthy since Byron and Shelley were driven out of the country. Wordsworth's acceptance of the laureateship, which Browning (who honestly believed himself a rebel) had bemoaned in *The Lost Leader*, was nothing to it. But this, too, was shortlived, and a sequel to this book could, and very likely will, be written describing what might in a rather flighty paradox be called the renaissance of Decadence. If so, there would be plenty to qualify for inclusion for one reason or another—Aleister Crowley, Frederick Rolfe, Edgar Saltus, John Gambril Nicholson, Ronald Firbank, St. John Welles Lucas-Lucas, E. F. Benson, Edward Marsh, Hugh Walpole, perhaps some Americans like Scott Fitzgerald and Carl van Vechten and artists like Alan Odle and Gaudier Brzeska. I write of none of these here though one or two had started to publish within the period.

I have been interested in the lives of the men remembered here rather than in their works, but in their lives only as they were interrelated with their writings. I do not follow Swinburne for long after his retirement to the Pines not only because his life there was uneventful but because he wrote no more of any great consequence after he had sobered up and ceased to undergo flagellation in St John's Wood. Nor of Wilde after his imprisonment for, although this is a spirited and to a biographer a tempting period, Wilde was no longer a practising writer when he reached Paris from Naples.

I have left many biographical matters—highly important though they are for an all-round estimate of any man—to the biographers, and those who seek information have excellent sources, Georges Lafourcade on Swinburne,• Phyllis Grosskurth on Symonds•• and Hesketh Pearson on Wilde••• to name only three. This is particularly true of the three main portraits; with some of the characters less fully discussed I have been content to chronicle. It may seem that I have deliberately chosen the more extraneous creatures of the period, but this is not so; they are those whose abnormalities in their relationship to others are the most surely traceable, whose actions showed them as non-conforming to the laws—potent then—of convention. Could we know the innermost desires of the seemingly most hidebound men of

• *Swinburne: A Literary Biography* by Georges Lafourcade, 1932.
•• *John Addington Symonds: A Biography* by Phyllis Grosskurth, 1964.
••• *The Life of Oscar Wilde* by Hesketh Pearson, 1946.

that age we might find they made Wilde and Swinburne, for example, look like the meekest orthodoxists by comparison.

When we are young we think there is a norm in human behaviour, particularly in sexual behaviour, and that away from its cosy fireside a few adventurous souls reprehensibly stray. We imagine a central mass of humanity following nightly the strictest canons of procreative conduct with equally unimaginative wives, and dreaming of no other. When we grow wiser and have read Havelock Ellis and Doctor Kinsey and received a few score confidences from persons of the most placidly conventional appearance, we realize that there is no such thing but in its place a variety of people who either in practice or in desire, according to their circumstances, qualify for one or another (or maybe more) of the hideous names invented by pathologists to classify them, fetishists, masochists, sadists, pederasts, lesbians, inverts, necrophilists, nymphomaniacs, exhibitionists, coprophilists, transvestists and many others. The central mass unaffected by such things dissolves before us and we know that in the sexual propensities of mankind there is no norm, though there may be repressions, a respect for good manners, ethical or religious restraints or fears of consequence which govern many, or perhaps most, human beings.

Now the artist is notoriously indifferent to these limitations, disliking repressions, having little respect for good manners when they interfere with his work, spurning restraints and fearless of consequences, so that the life of the artist is frequently the most uninhibited. What is more, it receives most attention. No doubt stockbrokers and lawyers attended the sessions in St John's Wood which attracted Swinburne but nobody knows of it now. No doubt at all—indeed it is recorded in the trials—that Wilde was only one of the victims of his gang of blackmailers, but all the others, referred to primly as 'gentlemen' by Counsel, are so much anonymous dust. So that the men who are discussed here took no particular choosing. They are relevant to my central theme—there is no central argument—and their lives seemed to me worth examination. That is all.

PART ONE

Swinburne and *Le Vice Anglais*

CHAPTER ONE

Swinburne and the Pre-Raphaelites

FOR all the narrow conformity of their morals the Victorians, until the sober 1880s at least, allowed themselves a remarkable diversity in their personal appearance, as Dickens and his illustrators as well as the early photographers reveal. Hair grew untamed not only on their heads and upper lips but on cheeks and chins, and there were a score of styles in whiskers which excited no comment, from the sailor's bare lips and fringed chin to the weeping dundrearies of the city. There were few rules for either the material or the cut of clothes and none it seems for headgear. The little excesses in these matters of young people today would have seemed nothing to a Londoner of 1857, who might appear as a colourful loose-clad fop or a buttoned-up undertaker without attracting attention to himself. So it may well be that the appearance of Algernon Charles Swinburne, spending his second year at Balliol College, Oxford, was not remarked on.

It was certainly unusual. A mass of frizzy red hair framing his pale face, usually described as an aureole, emphasized the top-heavy profile and the few forced and feeble hairs trying to grow on the receding chin. In portraits he has been idealized to a Pre-Raphaelite figure with wide eyes, a model for an archangel, but photographs are more merciless and we see the over-hanging upper lip and the emasculated weakness of the face, the long trunk on short legs, and sense the shrill vivaciousness of the young man which has been so often described.

In character he was no less freakish. He had made no friends in his boyhood which had been passed with sisters and girl cousins. He talked a great deal, his conversation running from shrill laughter to fiery arguments and denunciations, but in his talk there was little of the secrecy and sentiment which belong to the confidences of young people. One is tempted to think that in all his long life he never loved another human being and he seems to have detested animals. In his seventeen hundred collected letters there is nothing to suggest that he gave his heart to anyone. There is voluble hero-worship, there are chuckling confidences, there are splendid passages of literary criticism and humour which must have made his letters a delight to recipients, but nothing warmer or more human. Nor was he in love with himself. His is not the egotist's indifference to others but the hermaphrodite's.

When he met the Pre-Raphaelites in his second year at Oxford, they found him excellent company, garrulous, funny and learned. They laughed at him a little, called him 'dear little Carrots' and adopted him. He remained on amicable terms with several of them for years but he was incapable of responding to those warm-hearted men with anything but intellect and humour.

No poet ever had kinder, more understanding or more generous parents. His father was a widely travelled retired admiral. His mother was his father's cousin, a peer's daughter. Admiral Swinburne accepted the fact that Algernon conformed to none of his standards and though he was disappointed in his son's choice of a career he did nothing to discourage it, gave him an income and paid for the publication of his first book. Again and again during Swinburne's years of alcoholism the elderly admiral travelled up to London to rescue his son and bring him down to his home for months of recuperation. Yet no reader of his letters or careful student of his life could suppose that Swinburne loved his parents.

His nature was not frigid or unresponsive, it was shallow, however profound his powers of thought, however intense his creativity. He was sensitive and easily hurt but in a mercurial, superficial way. Because vital emotions were not involved in his human relationships he woke no deep response in others, and though many pitied him as a man and revered his genius no one except his parents loved him.

This was revealed in his relations with Dante Gabriel Rossetti and the later Pre-Raphaelites when he met them at Oxford in 1857. He gave them his ready hero-worship, he responded to their amused affection and encouragement and it was in emulation of their will to work and create that he turned seriously to writing. He read his poetry to them, delighting in their praise. But he could not join in their communalism more than airily and briefly.

Nor was this meeting quite the gay wild happy occasion that so many writers have described, nor were the men Swinburne met the roistering carefree jokers that we have been asked by Lafourcade,• William Gaunt•• and others to suppose. The false impression comes partly from the recollections of Val Prinsep and partly from a much-quoted dithyramb from Burne-Jones—"There was a year in which I think it never rained, nor clouded, but was blue summer from Christmas to Christmas, and London streets glittered, and it was always morning, and the air was sweet and full of bells." But Val Prinsep (portrayed as Taffy in *Trilby*) was nineteen years old at the time and thrilled to be in tne circle, while Burne-Jones was not writing of the Oxford year at all, but of 1856 in which he had first met Rossetti, helped to produce (financed by William Morris) *The Oxford and Cambridge Magazine*, established himself with Morris in London in the rooms Rossetti had shared with Deverell five years earlier, *anno mirabilis* in which hc had won the painter's friendship and told a fellow-caller on his way to Rossetti's "We shall be seeing the greatest man in Europe."

The Pre-Raphaelites had been commissioned to cover the walls of the debating hall of the Oxford Union with frescoes and Lafourcade••• says, "In the whole history of English literature I can think of no more picturesque scene than the meeting of Swinburne and the Pre-Raphaelites in the Union Hall." Picturesque perhaps—all those bearded Bohemians in odd clothes painting scenes from *Morte d'Arthur*—and important in Swinburne's poetic life, but clouded with futility and approaching tragedy. The original Pre-Raphaelite Brotherhood which

• *Swinburne: A Literary Biography* by Georges Lafourcade, 1932.
•• *The Pre-Raphaelite Tragedy* by William Gaunt.
••• *Swinburne: A Literary Biography* by Georges Lafourcade, 1932.

had set out with brave ideals eight years earlier was no more—all its adherents scattered, and what little of a creed they had in common no longer recognizable in the work of any of them. To Holman Hunt, Millais and the rest the nebulous faith which had given them a name had been no more than a stepping-stone, and the men round Rossetti now were young newcomers for whom Pre-Raphaelitism meant a cult of the medieval, a devotion to Malory, Tennyson and Round Table themes steeped in romanticism—in fact whatever Rossetti decided it should mean at the moment. The future Sir Edward Burne-Jones was Ned Jones a picture-framer's son from Birmingham, William Morris the thickset bespectacled son of a prosperous bill-broker, a poet with a large leonine head who had thrown up his job in an architect's office; these were Rossetti's new disciples and Val Prinsep, R. S. Stanhope, J. H. Pollen and some younger men were to help. They received no payment but their living expenses in Oxford were paid and the whole scheme was intended to be something of a lark for Rossetti and his young followers, and was called by him, with purposeful jocularity, the Jovial Campaign. The later Pre-Raphaelites, like the original Brotherhood, used popular slang and nicknames profusely. Pleasant men and lovely women were 'stunners', lodgings were 'cribs', watches were 'tickers', works of art, particularly in words, were 'grinds', money was 'tin', and Morris was 'Topsy' from some obscure reference to *Uncle Tom's Cabin*.

"What fun we had in that Union!" wrote Prinsep embarrassingly, years later. "What jokes! What roars of laughter!" But they were painting in tempera on an unprepared newly built whitewashed wall and nothing would remain of their knights and ladies, Lancelot, Guinevere and the rest. Rossetti had a sick, neurotic and extravagant woman on his hands in Lizzie Siddals whom he eventually married shortly before she committed suicide. He was having an affair with Annie Miller, Hunt's particular model who had been left in his care while Hunt was abroad. He was also quarrelling with Ruskin over work and money, for Lizzie spent rashly in Paris and sent constant demands for funds. He was seriously in debt and found Lizzie's determination that he should marry her a perpetual strain, for his love for her, at times oppressive, fluctuated almost to hatred. The work at Oxford was something of an escape but it earned him no money and he was—as he remained throughout his life—a tormented man with bursts of erratic happiness and periods of gloom. The slang, the jokes and the chaos while the members of the group painted their murals had little contentment or pride of achievement in them.

But Swinburne was captivated. These men with their noisy adoration of the 'stunners' among women they knew, their rather self-conscious camaraderie and above all their consuming love of art, of all art and of all the arts, seemed to him splendid. He, too, became involved in the Arthurian cycle, and his *Queen Yseult* appeared in the December (1857) number of *Undergraduate Papers*. "I read it one evening to Morris and the others, and they seemed to agree with me. They all, however, praise the poem far more than I (seriously speaking) believe it deserves. Morris says it is much better than his own poem, which opinion I took the liberty to tell him was absurd." Morris repeated this a few months later. "Such however is the invincible absurdity of all poets", Swinburne wrote to his friend Edwin Hatch, "that he ventured to prefer *Rosamond* to *Peter Harpdon* in a repeatedly rebuked and resolutely argued statement. It appears to me simple mania; but certainly I am glad of his words, for *Rosamond* is about my favourite poem, and is now verging on a satisfactory completion."

Work on the Union walls which was supposed to be finished during the Long Vacation, dragged on till the February of the following year. Swinburne wrote to Hatch: "One evening—when the *Union* was just finished—Jones and I had a great talk. Stanhope and Swan attacked, and we defended, our idea of Heaven, viz a rose-garden full of stunners. Atrocities of an appalling nature were uttered on the other side. We became so fierce that two respectable members of the University—entering to see the pictures—stood mute and looked at us. We spoke just then of kisses in Paradise, and expounded our ideas on the celestial development of that necessity of life; and after listening five minutes to our language, they literally fled from the room! Conceive our mutual ecstasy of delight."

But with all this gamesome and speculative talk, and Swinburne's delight at being accepted in that virile group as 'dear little Carrots', there began to form in his mind that conception which dominated his work thereafter, the super-stunner, the cruel and beautiful woman of destiny whose breath is poison to her worshippers, the creature whom Mario Praz,• after Keats, calls La Belle Dame Sans Merci. Her first

• *The Romantic Agony* by Mario Praz.

appearance was in a mock Elizabethan drama which Swinburne wrote in the year after he met the Pre-Raphaelites and called *Laugh and Lie Down.* She is named appropriately enough 'Imperia' and she has her page-boy Frank whipped to death after he has made such speeches as

What makes you sigh still? You are now
So kind the sweetness in you stabs mine eyes
With sharp tears through. I would so fain be hurt
But really hurt, hurt deadly, to do good
To your most sudden fancy.

The merciless and cruel spirit of Imperia would be born again and again in Swinburne's work, as Lucrezia, Rosamond, Mary Stuart, as Tannhauser's Venus in *Laus Veneris,* as Faustine, as Dolores, and finally in real life in the kindly American body of 'The Naked Mazeppa' Adah Isaacs Menken.

It seemed that this many-headed goddess dominated Swinburne as his alcoholism dominated him in the following years. And soon the two would be joined in the temples of his mind by the crazy and preposterous Marquis de Sade. When once in the grip of this trio Swinburne, while developing his true poetic genius, became a masochist who would stop at nothing as he sought the means to sacrifice himself, a drunk who ceased to be *sortable* and was repeatedly rescued by his anxious father to recuperate from paroxysms of dipsomania, and an obsessed pornographer writing sad sick absurdities like *The Whippingham Papers.*

For a time, in free converse with the adult and lusty Pre-Raphaelites he attempted at least to ape a hearty normality and adored Jane Burden with the rest of them. But after he had been injected with hormones of de Sade's creation he abandoned himself to the dreams and realities of his vice. For nearly twenty years, till he was finally sequestered in suburbia by Watts-Dunton, his life was disorderly, a fevered sequence of alcoholic and masochistic excesses ruinous to his health and productive of his greatest poetry.

If Swinburne had an obsession he also had a fetish, and it was a very curious one—the flogging-block at Eton. It is difficult to suppose that his masochistic instincts were alive in boyhood, but in his recollections of boyhood, which remained vivid to the end of his life, they dominated everything else. If he actually took pleasure in being flogged or watching others flogged while he was still at Eton he must have been a most unnatural young horror; it is more probable that his fixation with the flogging-block and the scenes he remembered there developed later in his life. He was still writing verses about it as late as 1880 when he turned out an unofficial ode on the 450th anniversary of the school:

> Dawn smiles on the fields of Eton, and wakes from slumber
> her youthful flock,
> Lad by lad, whether good or bad: alas for those who at
> nine o'clock
> Seek the room of disgraceful doom, to smart like fun on
> the flogging block.
>
> Swish, swish, swish! O I wish, I wish I'd not been late
> for lock-up last night!
> Swish, that mill I'm bruised from still (I couldn't help
> it—I had to fight)
> Makes the beast (I suppose at least) who flogs me flog me
> with all his might.
>
> 'Tell me, S——e, does shame within burn as hot (Swish!
> Swish!) as your stripes my lad,
> Burn outside, have I tamed your pride? I'm glad to see
> how it hurts you—glad—
> Swish! I wish it may cure you. Swish! Get up.' By Jove,
> what a dose I've had.

In 1867, then a man of thirty, Swinburne wrote facetiously to his friend George Powell (himself an old Etonian though of a later generation than that of Swinburne) about that block.

> I should like to see two things there again, the river—and the block. Can you tell me any news of the latter institution or any of its present habitués among our successors? the topic is always most tenderly interesting—with an interest, I may say, based upon a common bottom of sympathy.

Two months later he acknowledges a photograph of the thing in these words:

> Many thanks for the photograph, which is most interesting. I should like of all things to have a large one, but what a pity the scene is imperfect, a stage without actors, a hearth without fire, a harp without chords, a church without worshippers, a song without music, a day without sunlight, a garden without flowers, a tree without fruit! I would give anything for a good photograph taken at the right minute—say the tenth cut or so—and doing justice to

> *all sides* of the question. As it is the block is just at the right angle for such a representation. If I were but a painter!—I would do dozens of different fellows diversely suffering. There *can* be no subject fuller of incident, character, interest—realistic, modern, dramatic, intense, and vividly pictorial, palpitant d'actualité. Do get some fellow with a turn for drawing to try it.

He lent this photograph, apparently, for reproduction in the *Art Journal* and in the following year is writing wildly to his publisher J. C. Hotten: "Thanks for the Art Journal extract. Will you get back and send me *at once* the photograph I lent long ago of the 'Eton block' etc.? *today if possible* I want it."

Six years later Swinburne reproached Powell: "*How* could you be at Eton and not remember to invest for me in at least two of the large photographs of the flogging-block, when you knew how I wanted them and was shy of writing to order them?"

Lord Houghton hears of this when Swinburne writes to him that Powell has taken a small house near Eton where he has boy cousins. "He has culled for me some newly-budded 'blossoms of the block', as one may call the narratives of swished youth, which are neither fruitless nor unfragrant. 'I think' he says 'I can procure a genuine birch which has been used.' " Powell obtained the birch and Swinburne wrote ecstatically:

> I long to thank you in person and to enjoy the sight and touch of the birch that has been used. I don't think I ever more dreaded the entrance of the swishing room than I now desire a sight of it. To assist unseen at the holy ceremony some time after twelve I would give *any* of my poems. How on earth did Giles manage to procure you the latter? it must have been a mysterious adventure of knight errantry. What fun it would be to enact (I did once with another fellow—) the whole process, exchanging the parts of active and passive in turn. The Russians with their daily use of it at meals and baths are more delicately civilized than we. Do let us some day get up the scene. I dream of it and wake to laugh. I should like to have seen your cousin and heard his account. How often has he been swished? In the words once addressed to me when at school by a younger cousin at home, 'Please write again soon and tell me a Lot more about a lott more swishings, it's such a *joly* spree' (*sic*). I *did* with a vengeance, and the seed fell on good ground. I wish you could send me a representation of the ceremony with text appended as in a realistic romance.

In 1870 in a letter to Charles Augustus Howell, Swinburne, who has invented an imaginary cousin at Eton, writes what purports to be a letter from him but is clearly invention on Swinburne's part and shows that his obsessed and nostalgic memories of the Eton flogging-block continued to preoccupy him even in correspondence with a man who only feigned interest in order to pander to Swinburne's proclivities. The letter runs

> My dear Algie—I must tell you about the young un—it's worse than ever this half—He was swished 3 times last Friday, & once every day the week before. His bottom is like a plum pudding—every bit of flesh is a bloody red weal where it isn't a long slicing cut. He played in the football match yesterday which was rather plucky as he was awfully sore still as you may suppose. He's just come into my room & by Jove it's to say he's complained of again & to be swished this after four. (Etonian for 3-3/4—one of the four flogging times in a school day.) He was caught up town again & was late for school too. I bet he catches it—I wouldn't have his bottom for something. Charlie has been swished 9 times this half too which is pretty well but nothing to Herbert. My tutor told him the other day he'd be turned into a birch some day at this rate—he says he shall give the subject for verses to our division next week—Ovid's Metamorph: you know & that style of thing—I wish you'd do some for me & I'll make Herbert give me a list of his floggings since last summer & send you. He says the birch does sting so awfully these cold mornings at the first cut.

What a bore Swinburne must have been about it in conversation as well as in letters! As late as 1894 when he was three years short of sixty he demonstrated this form of arrested development in a letter to Watts-Dunton by speaking of himself as 'your minor'.

> The day before your minor had (he must confess) broken bounds and played truant in very Etonian fashion, and came home so torn with brambles and stung with nettles that he felt rather as if he were returning from a subsequent and consequent interview with the Head Master (the birch itself could hardly have stung more, or lacerated the flesh quite so severely—I can feel, while I write, one long jagged cut or scratch on the fleshy hinder part of my right thigh: quite appropriate as the truant's doom, and vividly suggestive of vivid reminiscences.)

It will be seen that Swinburne's policy in writing to his friends was to turn the whole ugly obsession into a joke, but he cannot disguise the craving and anxiety with which he sought for satisfaction of his macabre hunger. Pictures, verbal descriptions, anecdotes he demanded; it was all a lark, he said, in which his friends must share. Perhaps he even supposed that there was nothing unusual in the nature of his fetishism but that anyone would naturally understand and sympathize with him for wanting to see boys birched.

Not that the boys had anything to do with it. Swinburne was no pederast. It was the scene which haunted his mind until he tired of looking at mere reproductions of it on paper and desired the actions to be repeated on his own person.

2

After Edmund Gosse had written his white-washing biography of Swinburne,• largely to the specification allowed by the poet's family, he seems to have felt conscience pricks about his duty to truth and to posterity and left some manuscript notes with the British Museum dealing with this agitated period in Swinburne's life. The fact that Gosse had 'passed vaguely, and in terms which left all detail to be conjectured, over the moral irregularities of the poet' was 'animadverted upon severely by some of the reviewers'—a matter of concern to the touchy and pompous biographer which set him to write some livelier details about the middle period for the benefit of 'serious persons' trusting that 'all who read these words will consider that they are presented to them in confidence'.

The 'persons' could scarcely remain 'serious' after reading some of Gosse's details which run to fifteen pages of text into which he contrives to drop the names of eight peers. But he does tell us something about Swinburne's drunkenness which no one else has ventured to reveal though others have described his person in these years, his agitated manner, his rust-coloured hair thinning, his wild eyes, his weak attempts at a beard.

Swinburne had no more sense of decor than other Victorians and one can picture the hideous sets of rooms in which he lived, quarrelling with his landladies and tradespeople, carried to bed from cabs, swigging brandy, no more personally clean than others in those days of difficult

• *The Life of Algernon Charles Swinburne* by Edmund Gosse, 1917.

ablutions but frequently with a drunkard's repentant care of his morning's toilet.

He drank spasmodically but uncontrollably, impatient for the effect of the alcohol he swallowed. Gosse describes him unforgettably:

> It was important, at meals, to keep the wine or beer or spirits out of Swinburne's reach. If this were not done, as often by host or hostesses not aware of his weakness, he would gradually fix his stare upon the bottle as if he wished to fascinate it, and then, in a moment, flash or pounce upon it, like a mongoose on a snake, drawing it towards him as though it resisted and had to be struggled with. Then, if no one had the presence of mind to interfere, a tumbler was filled in a moment, and Swinburne had drained it to the last drop, sucking-in the liquid with a sort of fiery gluttony, tilting the glass into his shaking lips, and violently opening and shutting his eyelids. It was an extraordinary sight, and one which never failed to fill me with alarm, for after that the Bacchic transition might come at any moment.

Once intoxicated he skipped, shouted, recited, screamed, was picked up by policemen, stamped in rage on the hats of his fellow club members, fell flat on his face as he left a hansom-cab with Walter Pater, danced like a faery-maenad, became 'unfit for decent society' and developed delirium tremens—all according to Gosse or his informants.

Yet he never, says the same authority, recognized that he was a drunkard and after each occasion on which his long-suffering father, the Admiral, came to rescue him from his London rooms and take him home to recuperate, he would speak of the 'illness' from which he had recently suffered. When already tipsy he whispered to Gosse's wife (Gosse having pretended there was no more liquor in the house) "Does Edmund really think it is *possible* that I could ever be so little of a gentleman as to drink more than was good for me?"

Gosse was no psychologist and was completely at a loss when he tried to understand Swinburne's masochism, believing that 'the generative instinct was very feebly developed in Swinburne' because when he 'walked about London with him by day and night, I was struck with the fact that he never seemed to observe the faces or figures of people whom we met, or to receive from them any of those electric shocks which are the torment and ecstacy of youth'. Later he writes of Swinburne's undergoing pain—"I cannot help believing that these scourgings were in some extraordinary way a mode by which the excessive tension of Swinburne's nerves was relieved. I do not know whether the medical authorities would admit this possibility."

It seems certain that Swinburne was sexually impotent, occasionally seeking gratification from the crudest forms of masochism but chiefly finding cerebral excitation in imagining, or seeing, or seeing in reproduction, or reading or hearing of flagellation. The matrix of all this was the Eton flogging-block but in time the tutor's place was taken by the 'merciless woman' of his poetry. Gosse proceeds to another kind of blindness.

> Extravagant, even vicious, as might be some sides of Swinburne's conduct, they were not essential, but accidental: that is to say, they might have been entirely absent without the nature of his genius being affected by that absence. I do not say that they did not influence some portion of his early work, but they might have done so exactly as much as if they had been, so far as the world could judge, entirely interior and not visible to the closest observer. They were no part of his genius, and scarcely an excrescence upon it.

Without accepting Freudian, or post-Freudian theories of the nature of inspiration, it is evident again that the 'merciless woman', whose personality represented for Swinburne the sublimation of all his erotic fancies and practices was his supreme if not his only muse. She drew from him all the astonishing paeons, all the screams of agony, all the verbose beauties of his verse, with the beat of its rhythm like that of a primeval drum, its haunted chanting as beautiful and as empty of articulate meaning as a great symphony. She was Dolores and Faustine but like some terrible idol she was greedy for blood and music, incense and sacrifice, and there is little in all Swinburne's poetry more than these. He made garlands for her of the roses which so frequently scent his lines and he threw cold lilies at her feet. He painted pictures of forsaken gardens and scorched landscapes but only as a background for his own passionate cries under her domination. He identified her sometimes with the sea which—he was never tired of exulting—had whipped his flesh and salted his wounds in boyhood. When he tried to escape her voracity to exalt Mazzini and red revolution, all the intoxicated syncopation of his *Poems and Ballads* grew stale and became mechanical. 'Nice' was the word he used for his interest in revolution and though its results were long-winded and melodious enough they lacked the hectic glory of his earlier poems.

It has been suggested that Swinburne's attempts to love were mighty and obsessive strivings because they were given such megaphonic expression in poems like *The Triumph of Time*. The contrary is more likely to be true. He was seeking some cerebral ejaculation, some poetic coition, to compensate for his physical failure. What great poetry has ever come from simple and satisfied desire?

3

Neither in his own letters nor in those written about him is there much to show Swinburne in his everyday life in those years. But there are written recollections and portraits which enable us, remembering the times in which he lived, to catch glimpses of him in the harsh and vital atmosphere of London in the 1860s and 1870s.

One can see him in dingy lodgings, known always as 'my chambers', surrounded by antimacassars, festooned mantelpieces, heavy pieces of furniture, alert on a horsehair sofa declaiming to his friends, while the only things of any beauty in sight were his books. He did not collect the paintings of the artists he knew as he might so easily have done, but was in his private life without much taste in furniture, food, dress, music or the lesser arts. He does not seem to have cared about typography or binding. So there he would squat perkily in his ill-tailored long-wearing suits, proclaiming in uncontrolled ecstasy the glories of de Sade, Mazzini, Landor, Blake—any of his heroes.

Or emerging after nightfall into a London scarcely changed from that, a freakish figure with his red hair and skipping walk, he would make his way perhaps a little uncertainly to the house of one of his friends from which he would have to be brought home in a cab. Even in the harsh gas-light he would be noticeable, his short legs, his violent tic, his wasted haunted look, while sometimes on that mass of hair a tall hat was balanced.

He would be invited to 'breakfast' somewhere and would be either taciturn at table or far too talkative. The telegraph system had not yet (till 1870) been taken over by the post office and everything was done by messages sent by hand, invitations replied to while the bearer waited. All too often Swinburne would fail to appear after accepting, and write repentant letters next day explaining the 'illness' which had prevented him. He subscribed to most of the important reviews and weeklies and scoured the pages of the daily press for items which tickled his erotic fancy, being rewarded in April 1860 by an account of a pupil being beaten to death by a schoolmaster.• He would trip round to the British Museum Reading Room for some piece of research and write long letters full of facetious references to flagellation. Most grotesquely of all he would walk from his rooms in Dorset Street through Regent's Park, stopping at a bench occasionally to scribble, on his way to St John's Wood where in a discreet house two obliging women, described as 'golden-haired and rouge-cheeked' were paid to chastise him. He spoke of this as a '*maison de supplices à la Rodin*' (a reference to de Sade's *Justine*), as 'the Grove of the Beloved Disciple', and as 'the Sadice-Paphian spring of St John's Wood'. The picture of Swinburne, in frock coat and top hat, attending there is tragi-comic, but his visits came to an end after a monetary dispute with the two ladies.

• This was a particularly nasty case which Swinburne remembered in a letter to Monckton Milnes nearly three years later. According to the Annual Register for 1860 the owner of a high-class Eastbourne school, a Mr Hopley, was tried at Lewes for causing the death of a half-witted boy Reginald Cancellor, the son of a Master of the Court of Common Pleas who paid £180 a year for the boy's board and instruction. "One morning young Cancellor was found dead in his bed. The body was carefully covered over. It had white kid gloves upon its hands, and long stockings drawn far up over the thighs; nothing was visible but the face." Hopley suggested that the boy had died of disease of the heart and wished a certificate from the surgeon and immediate burial. At one moment it appeared likely that the whole affair would be hushed up. But mysterious stories of midnight shrieks and blood-stained instruments of punishment began to be whispered about. The servants had seen blood upon the linen in Mrs Hopley's room, and had heard sounds which convinced them that the miserable wife had spent the night in the frightful task of preparing the body to pass a superficial investigation, and in getting rid of the traces of violence which would testify against her husband. Then came the real investigation. The gloves and stockings were stripped off, and the legs and the arms of the corpse were found to be coated with extravasated blood, 'the cellular membranes under the skin of the thighs were reduced to a perfect jelly; in fact, all torn to pieces and lacerated by the blows that had been inflicted'. There were two holes in the right leg about the size of a sixpence, and an inch deep, which appeared to have been made by jabbing a thick stick into the flesh. The appearance was that of a human creature who had been mangled by an infuriated and merciless assailant. All these appearances coincided but too faithfully with what was now learnt of the conduct of the schoolmaster. A servant girl who slept next to the pupil-room heard the boy crying and screaming under blows, and her master talking and beating. She listened at 10 o'clock, when the torture was going on, and she awoke at 12, and it was still proceeding.

CHAPTER TWO

Swinburne, Lord Houghton and Simeon Solomon

AT least nine men were very much aware of Swinburne's proclivities and varied as they are, and interesting in themselves, they provide a curious cross-section of Victorian society. There was Lord Houghton (Richard Monckton Milnes) whose large library of erotica provided Swinburne with copies of de Sade's works, Simeon Solomon an artist of considerable ability whose life-story was in itself dramatic, Charles Augustus Howell an Anglo-Portuguese 'Mr. Norris', George Powell a dissolute Welsh squire, John Thomson an unusual pimp with half-share in a brothel, Richard Burton the explorer and translator of the *Arabian Nights*, Edmund Gosse, not yet the arch-snob and would-be literary bigwig of later years, Theodore Watts who would become Theodore Watts-Dunton and Swinburne's better half in his last years, and Dante Gabriel Rossetti the painter and poet, the only one amongst them whose work apart from his personality arouses any interest today.

Most of these have been the subjects of later biographies; Houghton in James Pope-Hennessy's *Monckton Milnes: The Years of Promise* and

The Flight of Youth, Howell in *Pre-Raphaelite Twilight* by Helen Rossetti Angeli, Burton in at least two recent studies, Gosse in *The Life and Letters of Edmund Gosse* by Evan Charteris, and Rossetti, most fortunately of all, in Oswald Doughty's *A Victorian Romantic*. But all of them appear and re-appear in memoirs and critical studies of the age, as mere shadows like John Thomson, as slightly comic figures like Gosse and Watts-Dunton, a trifle enigmatically like Monckton Milnes, vividly but fleetingly like Solomon. All of them, except perhaps Burton and Rossetti who have been over-biographized, will repay a fresh if brief and irreverent re-examination in the light of their influence on Swinburne and his eccentricities.

2

Richard Monckton Milnes (1809–1885) was a man born greedy for all the minor satisfactions he could find in life, mental as well as physical; greedy for experience, for the pleasures of sight and sound and taste, greedy for possessions though not for power, for friendship though not for love. Born rich enough to enjoy the interesting pastime of politics, he was an undistinguished Member of Parliament for twenty-six years before obtaining the peerage which befitted him. A poet and critic of quick if not profound perceptions, as a young man he was hailed by Landor as 'the greatest poet now living in England' and in middle age, having put away such illusions about himself, he continued to write, befriend writers and love literature, keeping a quick curiosity for everything new and valid in three languages. A passionate bibliophile and book-collector, he helped to found the Philobiblon Society in 1853 and was its most active member and the editor of its *Miscellanies* for the thirty-one years of its existence. During that time he amassed one of the most interesting private libraries of the last century which, with its inscribed copies, its books with bound-in personal letters, its unique collection of erotica, overflowed the large library of his country house and filled wall space in almost every room and passage of it. Both as a bachelor and after his successful marriage at the age of forty-two to the rich daughter of a peer, he made a cult of friendship and was said to have known every interesting contemporary at home and abroad, giving his generous affection and often his practical help to men and women for their own sakes, although he had a collector's discrimination in people as well as in books.

He was a genial and lavish host in his bachelor home in London, later in his great house in Yorkshire and at the house his wife inherited in Upper Brook Street. He broke out of the tightly closed circle of mid-Victorian society—a few score families who visited one another—in which he had a place, to entertain writers, artists and foreigners, an almost unprecedented social liberalism. His bachelor breakfasts were famous for many years for the daring contrasts between the guests—it was no small thing in 1856 to confront 'old Lord Lansdowne' with the American Nathaniel Hawthorne and the Comte de Polignac with Elizabeth Barrett Browning. As good a guest as he was host he moved from one great country house to another, and between the homes of his continental friends, welcome everywhere for his bonhomie, his intelligent and often witty conversation and, when the ladies had left the room, for what was considered the brilliant bawdry of his talk.

He loved food and wine and it is a weakness in Mr Pope-Hennessy's excellent biography, or in the family papers from which much of his information is derived, that so little is known of Houghton's tastes in these. What did they eat and drink at those breakfasts and at the formal dinner-parties which Houghton and his wife gave in London and at Fryston? Did he keep a cellar to compare with his library? We know only that he grew red-cheeked, stout and gouty with the years. Although his wife meticulously noted the names of her guests on every occasion, she did not (unless Mr Pope-Hennessy has not thought it worthwhile to reproduce them) leave a record of her menus.

Houghton was an inveterate traveller, not like his friend Burton an explorer, but a persistent wanderer in Europe who visited America and was only prevented, by doctor's orders when he was in his seventies, from making a visit to India. He knew France, Germany and Italy as few Victorians did and went to Egypt for the opening of the Suez Canal and to Holland to stay with Queen Sophie. He collected what were not yet known as 'antiques' wherever he went—a habit most uncommon at the time. "How can one furnish", he asked his wife in a letter, "without damask or Dresden, or Sêvres or porphyry, or marble, or three clocks all going in one room, or *anything*?"

There seems to have been no great depth in his liking for music—he was an opera-goer and when in Vienna went to hear Strauss's band in the Volks-Garten. He was a tireless observer of natural scenery, architecture and art. He wanted to miss nothing that others had enjoyed before him and to find new things to see and to remember. He was a sensualist in every concept of the word, interested in vice rather than vicious, a lover of all things that titillated his humour, his taste or his senses. Mundane, knowledgeable, experienced and gossipy, he inspired admiration, envy, gratitude in his fellows rather than love.

Having himself nothing more than an unarticulated working philosophy of kindness and helpfulness to other people and a pleasant if sometimes complacent outlook on life, he was an immensely tolerant man. A German fellow student Fritz Windischmann wrote to him when they were both young men. "You see the world and all its beauty, you are now here now there on the earth, now here now there in science, now here now there amidst the pleasures of life: you mean to attain peace, you arrive at some belief, you discover some new thought that fills your soul, you are inspired, encouraged—and then, again, cold, cast down: and the highest philosophy with which you console yourself is still 'vanitatum vanitas'." A remarkable piece of character reading.

Houghton met Swinburne in London in 1861 and at once added him to his collection. Henry Adams then an American *attaché* who met him at that time describes Swinburne as at first appearing like a boy. "He resembled in action . . . a tropical bird, high-crested, long-beaked, quick-moving, with rapid utterance and screams of humor, quite unlike any English lark or nightingale. One could hardly call him a crimson macaw among owls, and yet no ordinary contrast availed." Others in the party, Adams said, found Swinburne 'quite original, wildly eccentric, astonishingly gifted and convulsively droll'.

It was not likely that Houghton would let one like this get away, yet it was not only the singularity of Swinburne's manner and appearance which intrigued him, or his gifts as an entertainer, for Houghton was one of the first to realize that the 'crimson macaw' had genius, and in his good-natured way gave practical expression to his faith by arranging for Swinburne to contribute to *The Spectator* and encouraging him to read his not highly recitable poems at gatherings in his own house.

He also, after much pleading from Swinburne, unwillingly lent him copies of de Sade's novels, and this act of his has caused a good deal of literary twittering. Was it a deliberate piece of corruption? Or of self-indulgent cynicism? Was Houghton, as Lafourcade in his *La*

Jeunesse de Swinburne and Mario Praz in *The Romantic Agony* would have us believe, a cruel and designing monster who used his guests as chessmen in a game set for his own amusement? The smallest study of the man would have demonstrated the absurdity of this. He liked to show off his erotica as other collectors have done, he may have thought casually that de Sade would be 'bad for' Swinburne, as legislators believe pornography to be 'bad for' people today. He may even have waited with a slightly mischievous curiosity to hear what were the poet's reactions to *Justine*. On the other hand he may have mistaken Swinburne's habit of burlesque for a genuine sense of humour and proportion, and thought that he would find de Sade laughable, as any dispassionate reader must. He had read *Charenton* the poem which Swinburne had written about the 'martyred' Marquis before he had read his works, and may have thought that acquaintance with the silly obscenity of the novels would cure his intelligent young friend of his interest. (This is borne out by Swinburne's letter to Houghton of August 18th, 1862 after he had first examined *Justine*. "You retain my Charenton and desire me to clear my head of the subject. I am in a very fair way to do so.") Or he may have lent the book as he would lend any other with only a mild and idle curiosity about Swinburne's opinion of it. Whatever the truth it is impossible to see Houghton as an intriguing Mephistopholes, determined to bring ruin to a young man of genius. It would be easier to believe—though this too seems grossly improbable—that he saw the necessity of feeding Swinburne's genius on alcohol and masochism, and supplied the first by introducing the poet to the hard-drinking Burton and the second by lending him de Sade.

At first it seemed that Swinburne, a man of taste, would dismiss *Justine* as a preposterous farrago of disgusting horrors, and the long letter to Houghton in which he reported his first reactions must have encouraged Houghton to believe this.

"At first", he writes rather too emphatically, "I really thought I must have died or split open or choked with laughing. I never laughed so much in my life: I couldn't have stopped to save the said life. I went from text to illustrations and back again, till I literally doubled up and fell down with laughter—I regret to add that all the friends to whom I have lent or shown the book were affected in just the same way. One scene between M. De Verneuil and Mme. d'Esterval I never thought to survive. I read it out and the auditors rolled and roared.

Then Rossetti read out the dissection of the interesting Rosalie and her infant, and the rest of that refreshing episode: and I wonder to this minute that we did not raise the whole house by our screams of laughter."

Judging the book on its own grounds, by which he presumably means *as* pornography, he finds it 'a most outrageous fiasco'. His chief disappointment is that de Sade, 'like a Hindoo mythologist' takes bulk and number for greatness, 'as if a crime of great extent was necessarily a great crime, as if a number of pleasures piled one on another made up the value of a great and perfect sensation of pleasure'. The rigmarole of cruelty and death had failed, in other words to excite Swinburne and this he considered its first purpose. "I boast not of myself; but I do say that a schoolboy, set to write on his own stock of experience, and having a real gusto and appetite for the subject in him, may make and has made more of a sharp short school flogging of two or three dozen cuts than you of your enormous interminable inflictions; more of the simple common birch rod and daily whipping-block than you of your loaded iron whips and elaborately ingenious racks and horses." Swinburne, at this stage therefore, would rather be back witnessing scenes at his old flogging-block than have all the smashed-in heads and torn-off breasts of de Sade. To everyone his own obsession. He goes on to address de Sade. "We took you for a sort of burlesque Prometheus; you are only a very serious Simeon Stylites—in an inverted posture. You worship the phallus as those first ascetics worshipped the cross; you seek your heaven by the very same road as they sought theirs. That is all." Whether *Justine* 'drives curates and curates' pupils' to madness and death or not, Swinburne continues, it has done decidedly little damage to his brain and nerves.

He boasted too soon. Within three months he had begun to write that long series of letters to Houghton (whom he frequently addressed as 'M. Rodin' after the character in *Justine*) which continued for eighteen years to contain references to de Sade. These are always facetiously worded, as though the Marquis was a joke shared by the two of them, nevertheless it is evident that Swinburne had read and reread de Sade's novels till he had reached a nauseating familiarity with them. Three years later on the publication of *Atalanta in Calydon* he wrote a long metaphorical letter to Houghton—he, the author, is the much-whipped schoolboy who has 'shown up' his verses and been chastised by various critics, not for false quantities since Tennyson has written to envy him his gifts but for 'shirking chapel and profane swearing', in other words for the blasphemy which reviewers saw in the book. He will tell his publisher to send a copy of the book to Houghton, or as he puts it: "I will tell Payne (pretty name for an usher) to send you the material of flagellation at once. It is rather hard to have to supply the twigs destined to make my own posteriors writhe and bleed, but I know it's the way of the school. I have been well flogged and some four or five times already for the same fault. Tennyson and Jowett, the Athenaeum and the Spectator have each had their innings. Twice I have been swished in private, and twice in public before the whole school—for 'irreverence'. My skin has the marks of the birch still on it."

It has been suggested that Watts-Dunton discouraged the friendship, but there is no evidence of this for the two corresponded until Houghton's death in 1885, though Swinburne had gone to live with Watts-Dunton in Putney in 1879. The last Sadic reference was in a letter from Swinburne to Houghton from The Pines, Putney Hill on October 12th, 1880 and it is, ironically, '*Non, Rodin n'est pas mort*'.

Much of the correspondence with its smirking passages about de Sade and sadism is frankly inane. Though Houghton's letters to Swinburne have not survived—or at least have not been published—it may be assumed that in them Houghton tried to keep the thing on a jocular level as though he were a man of the world indulging a smutty-minded schoolboy, and Swinburne responded readily to this. So long as he could giggle about swishings he was happy enough and showed Houghton in his letters no intensity on the subject. That the joke was in poor taste and intolerably prolonged over the years does not seem to have occurred to either of them. After all it was during those years that Swinburne wrote all the best of his poetry and if Houghton's letters could be read it is safe to assume they would show him to have been far more interested in this.

There were of course many other sides to the friendship. Perhaps the nearest to a genuine passion in Houghton's life was his love of literature. He continued to write till he was an old man and his contributions to the *Edinburgh Review* in later years were intelligent and balanced. He was an omnivorous reader and gave his whole keenest attention to Swinburne's work which he sometimes found obscure but which he never underrated. Between such a man and the volatile poet there was more to discuss than de Sade. Swinburne's letters to Houghton have more in them of literary discussion, acceptances of invitations, apologies for non-appearances and references to mutual friends than of the flogging-block.

Swinburne breakfasted and dined frequently in Upper Brook Street, meeting there most literary and political figures of the time. But it is easier to imagine him at Fryston Hall, Houghton's great Yorkshire home, for there, to many of his fellow guests, he seemed exotic and vociferous against the traditional background of an English country home.

Not that Fryston was typical of the many thousands of rich men's houses which were maintained rather splendidly in every English county throughout the last century. The library, the absence of trophies, gun-rooms, a billiard room, or any sign of country sports, made it singular, quite apart from the extraordinary variety of its guests. Lord Houghton did not hunt or shoot and though a most active man who travelled widely he detested exercise for its own sake. He had inherited the large eighteenth-century house on the banks of the River Aire, redecorated it and kept it warm and cheerful in spite of its bleak situation, but took no very keen interest in the park or the farms around it. He left the great woods unspoiled, cutting an avenue or two for grassy rides through them, and let his gardeners keep up the exceptionally large fruit and vegetable gardens, vineries and glass-houses for which it was famous in the county, while his wife added flower gardens and ran the house extravagantly well with a large staff of servants whose manners were 'homely and outspoken' rather than obsequious. His father would have been quite satisfied with a cook, a kitchen-maid and a page-boy if it had not been for visitors who rode over from Pontefract and were surprised to find that their horses' heads were held by the kitchen-maid. When Lord Houghton had spent two thousand pounds on redecorating his home and making it comfortable his wife organized the staff to entertain their large house-parties at which fourteen or sixteen people might sit down to dinner. The life of the place is suggested by a group photographed in front of the house in 1873, two women in bowlers upright in a trap while a whiskered groom wearing a cockade in his top hat, stiff and solemn, holds the horse's head. Other members of the family and servants stand behind them on the steps which lead between pillars to the glass-fronted doors.

Swinburne coming by train from London would be met at the station and driven, with his valise, to the house. It would be pleasant to know a dozen trivial things about this which would tell us more of Swinburne and of Victorian domestic life. What did he wear for the journey? Did he startle or entertain his fellow travellers? What did the Yorkshire servants think of him when they unpacked his modest—or perhaps in some details immodest—belongings? We know what other guests thought—'a sort of pseudo-Shelley' (Matthew Arnold), 'a cross between the devil and the Duke of Argyll' (William Stirling), while the Archbishop of York who was present when Swinburne read some of his less discreet poetry to him and Thackeray and Thackeray's daughters, 'made so shocked a face that Thackeray smiled and whispered to Lord Houghton, while the two young ladies, who had never heard such sentiments expressed before, giggled aloud in their excitement'.

His fellow guests knew who he was, at first a protégé of Houghton's with bundles of unpublished poetry to read, later an established if erratic genius who must be excused the eloquent obscenity of his conversation after dinner and his tendency to swallow wine and later brandy with evident eagerness. But what was said in the servants' hall about him? Were his tips adequate? Did he insist on his daily tub? Perhaps they treated him, as so many kind and simple people did all his life, as an inspired child who had to be looked after, forgiven and nursed.

Certainly that is how Houghton saw him, though he must have been aware that Swinburne had a child's spitefulness, too. He put up with much for the sake of Swinburne's confidence and never became so exasperated with him that he forgot his worth as a poet. That Houghton's influence on Swinburne was regrettable is an opinion which can only be held by those who think the physical and moral welfare of the man more important than his work. Swinburne was both a ludicrous figure and a genius and only while he boozed and talked nonsense about flagellation and even submitted to it could he release the extraordinary flow, like a wild verbal river, of his poetry. Houghton was a true friend of the poet if not always of the weak intemperate man.

3

Lord Houghton indulged Swinburne's idiosyncrasies, Simeon Solomon played up to them and was perhaps somewhat amused by them. He was amused by most things at the time they met, a gay, talented young man, as a painter something of a prodigy, handsome, vivacious, happy.

Not many of the facts of Solomon's life are known* but the few that have come to light are tediously repeated by all who have written of him. His father, for instance, manufactured or imported (accounts differ) 'Leghorn hats'. What 'Leghorn hats' were or are nobody seems to know but they reappear in every account of the painter. He was born in 1840 at 3, Sandys Street, Bishopsgate Without, the eighth and youngest child of Michael Solomon and his wife, born Kate Levy. Both his elder brother Abraham (b. 1822) and his sister Rebecca (b. 1832) became painters, and Abraham was a Royal Academician who painted such favourite genre pictures of the period as *Waiting for the Verdict.*

Simeon was sent to Cory's Academy** in Bloomsbury but at the age of fifteen he was entered as an art student at the Royal Academy Schools where he became friendly with Henry Holiday, who was only a year older than he was, and Marcus Stone. By this time his father had sold his hat business and started a factory for embossing paper doilies—a nice period touch—which in those days of paper frills and lace-paper was understandably more profitable. Abraham was married and independent and Holiday was asked to visit Simeon's parental home and his brother's studio while he took the sparkling and voluble young Jewish cockney to his own home.

Marcus was the son of the artist Frank Stone, a friend and illustrator of Dickens who had become an A.R.A. four years earlier. Marcus had a brother and two sisters, these with Holiday and Simeon formed a cheerful group of companions who visited one another's homes frequently, and 'specially cultivated charades'. But the three youthful artists, Holiday, Marcus and Simeon, took their work seriously and founded a Sketching Club which met once a week, being joined by Albert Moore.

* A full-length biography by Mr Lionel Lambourne is to appear shortly.
** Or Carey's? Again accounts differ.

Two years later, when still only seventeen, Simeon exhibited one of the biblical pictures on which at this time he chiefly worked, *Isaac Offered*, at the Academy summer show. He had been brought up in the orthodox Jewish faith and for years (though later there were several exotic influences in his life and art) he continued to paint scenes from the Old Testament and remained devoted to the Jewish Liturgy. His older sister Rebecca who afterwards gained a reputation in the studios as a woman of 'loose life', whatever that may have meant eighty years ago, and something of a drunk, was in Simeon's childhood a devoted 'little mother' and teacher who took him to the synagogue and imparted to him her own highly coloured version of Hebraic lore. Sir William Richmond• wrote: "When I first knew Simeon in 1858, his art was at its zenith. It was about this time that he made a noble series of designs wholly inspired by the Hebrew Bible, which were indescribably ancient-looking and strangely imbued with the semi-barbaric life it tells of in the Book of Kings and in the Psalter of David. So strongly was this the case that they seemed to be written in Hebrew characters; no one but a Jew could have conceived or expressed the depth of natural feeling which lay under the strange, remote forms of the archaic people whom he depicted, and whose passions he told with a genius entirely unique. Most of the early designs were in pen and ink, others in sepia used very dryly; later Simeon used water colour with magical skill, but he never mastered oil pigments. Unfortunately, Solomon departed from his simple genius to accept an artificial and neurotic vein of late and debased Roman Art; the result was, he was no longer sincere; whereas when he consented to be a Jew, to think out designs and dream as a Jew, no more highly interesting personal work has ever been done."

So in his late teens he had the world before him. Precocious in the manner of a young homosexual free on the London streets, already a professional artist, with little parental interference, he developed the sophisticated wit and gift of repartee, the sharpness and exhibitionism to be expected from such a young man. He was taken up by his elders, in some cases for his good looks and ready passions, in others for his talent, his humour, his vitality. Several who knew him spoke afterwards of his humour but among them there seem to have been none who recognized it as the natural campness of his kind.

• *The Richmond Papers* edited by A. M. W. Stirling.

Henry Holiday may or may not have enjoyed with Simeon something more physical than the companionship which in later life he pompously recalled with many a 'sorrowful digression' on the 'melancholy topic' of the 'heavy cloud' under which Simeon's life ended. (It was, he said in his Reminiscences, published when he was seventy-five, 'an aberration, a morbid growth, inexplicable to me, and at variance with all I knew of him when he was in his right mind'.) His own paintings such as *Joseph Sold to Potiphar*, quite apart from his somewhat self-righteous accounts of his early friendships, suggest that if he himself had no 'aberration' or 'morbid growth' he had rather more than the detached artist's interest in his own sex posed voluptuously.

What he certainly had not was that particular bright sense of fun which belongs to the cockney queer. He makes blundering attempts to reproduce the things Simeon said which 'made them all laugh', but the kind of rippling humour, taking quick advantage of words and events to drop a frivolous comment, sometimes silly, sometimes rewarding but rarely memorable, simply cannot be reproduced on paper. It is gone with the moment and attempts to revive it end in bathos. It is more spontaneous than wit and more superficial than humour. To hear it today one must go to a queer bar or club and listen to a group sending one another up. Here are some of poor Holiday's attempts:

> Simeon joined [the Artists' Corps] soon after and asked me to coach him a little in the drill. I did what I could, but his demands were not always reasonable. He wanted me, for instance, to 'fall into a hollow square' to show him how it was done. Of course we all had to take the oath of allegiance, and a day was appointed when we were all to go and swear. I went with Simeon and he asked me gravely if I thought the sergeant would be satisfied if he said 'Drat it', as he had a conscientious objection to using stronger language.
>
> Simeon was given to imparting fragments of scientific information of doubtful value in our walks; as, for instance, when, as we passed Brother's Water, he said with an air of a professor, 'I don't know whether you are aware that this is the only lake in the district which finds its own level.' It was quite news to me, and we wondered if the others had mislaid their levels or how they got on. Another time, having made an excursion to Borrowdale, where we stayed at a little inn in Rosthwaite for two or three nights, he wished to light a cigarette and priding himself on having put matches in his waistcoat pocket, he tried to light them on the window-sill; but alas!

> they were safety-matches which only ignite on the box, a new invention. He was disgusted and took a solemn oath that he would himself invent some matches which would only ignite on window-sills. [After their ascent of Snowdon] Simeon, who had a happy knack of parodying the little hackneyed idioms of common conversation by using them exactly in the wrong place, said, 'You might be a hundred miles in the country'.
>
> He opened the natural history of the Rhinoceros thus: 'It chiefly frequents the tropic of Capricorn and other secluded spots'; and closed it with the statement that—'It lives to a great age and has no young.'
>
> Simeon Solomon was of the party, and entertained by us by reading a treatise he had just written on astronomy. He opens in a strictly practical manner by treating of the use of the telescope. He explains, for instance, that an opera-glass is not sufficiently powerful for astronomical purposes and 'a stethoscope is well-nigh useless'. He recommends the student not to close the eye which he applies to the instrument, and points out that a telescope is useless if a friend, applies his eye or the palm of his hand to the other end, adding, 'I lost much time once through this absurd behaviour on the part of a friend whom I now no longer regard as such.' Again, 'I do not consider the earth to be included in astronomy as I cannot find it in the celestial globe.' He explains the fact that the earth is further from the sun in summer than in winter by the expansion of the orbit with the heat. He says, 'I do not think much of perihelions and the like; I have some in a bottle but do not find them interesting.'

From these, unfunny though they are, it is possible to gather something of Simeon's spirited habit of chit-chat, but Sir William Richmond's• description of his humour tells us more than all Holiday's quotations of his quips: "Simeon Solomon was a fair little Hebrew, a Jew of the Jews, who seemed to have inherited a great spirit, an Eastern of the Easterns, facile and spasmodically intense, sensitive to extreme touchiness, conscious of his great abilities, proud of his race, but with something of the mystic about him which was pagan, not Christian. Quaint was his humour. He touched all subjects lightly, and with so much brilliancy, that the follies he uttered and wrote seemed to be spontaneously wise and witty sayings. He twisted ideas, had a genius for paradox, and when in a humourous vein, speaking with assumed seriousness, he convulsed his friends by his strange weird imagination."

• *The Richmond Papers*, edited by A. M. W. Stirling.

Before reaching manhood he was already successful and popular. He met Dante Gabriel Rossetti in 1857 and in the following year was commissioned by William Burges the architect to design panels for some of his painted furniture. Rossetti's disciples Burne-Jones and William Morris began to make much of him. He struck Burne-Jones as sophisticated—"We are mere schoolboys compared with you", said the Birmingham man enviously, though he was Simeon's senior by seven years. He went about much with Henry Holiday—they used to visit Dante Gabriel Rossetti and went for a long walking holiday together in the Lake District.

In 1860 Simeon exhibited the best-known of his early pictures at the Academy—*Moses in his Mother's Arms*, often miscalled *The Finding of Moses*. Thackeray in *Roundabout Papers* praised it and mildly ridiculed a hostile critic by giving a much-quoted, and often misquoted, dictum: "For example, one of the pictures I admired most at the Royal Academy is by a gentleman on whom I never, to my knowledge, set eyes. The picture is (346) 'Moses', by S. Solomon. I thought it finely drawn and composed. It nobly represented to my mind the dark children of the Egyptian bondage. . . . My newspaper says: 'Two ludicrously ugly women, looking at a dingy baby, do not form a pleasing object', and so good-bye, Mr. S.S."

It was some years after this (there is no evidence of how many) that Solomon and Swinburne met, probably at Rossetti's, and at once there began a relationship which shocked the associates of both, stimulated their respective creativities, gave release to Swinburne's lewdest impulses, and helped to bring Solomon to prison and the gutter. There is a story, the origin of which is unrevealed, repeated by Bernard Falk in his somewhat sensational and unreliable account of Solomon,• in which Swinburne and Solomon, both stark naked, chased one another about Rossetti's house in Cheyne Walk. It does not seem to have impressed Rossetti who shouted to them to stop jumping about like wild cats but apparently considered their antics as nothing more than an irritating disturbance of his work. He was probably right, but in Solomon's letters to Swinburne, which have miraculously

• *Five Years Dead* by Bernard Falk, 1937. This is a collection of stories covered by Falk as a journalist. Not long before Solomon's death Falk was sent by the *Evening News* to get a story from him and the account in *Five Years Dead* is a re-hash of this.

survived while Swinburne's replies are lost, a more dangerous aspect of their friendship is evident.

Neither was a party to the other's predilections. Solomon was neither masochist nor sadist and Swinburne was not homosexual, or any other sexual in a physical sense, but a neuter who found excitation in thoughts and occasionally the practice of masochism. But Solomon, who even in young manhood was not without a certain wiliness, was quite willing to play up to his more distinguished friend. He was more worldly than Swinburne, knew more of metropolitan depravity and was fully and healthily sexed. But he was without academic education and was enormously impressed by his friend's knowledge of the classics and by his aristocratic background and acquaintance.

Moreover it was through Swinburne that Solomon met a number of distinguished and hospitable people, including the two dons Walter Pater and Oscar Browning. He did one of the few existing portraits of the first and stayed with him in Oxford, on what terms it is not difficult to guess. The second was still an assistant master at Eton when he met Solomon, but he was dismissed later after various indiscretions had come to light. He took Solomon to Italy with him. Swinburne also introduced him to Lord Houghton who invited him to Fryston, to George Powell a wealthy homosexual and to other friends more or less distinguished in ways other than those of the painters he already knew.

No letters survive from the first few years of the friendship during which both the young men were having lively rather than substantial success. Swinburne published *Atalanta in Calydon* in 1865 and the first series of *Poems and Ballads* in the following year and they gave him a place, however hotly debated by some critics, in the literature of the age, or as many thought, of all the ages. Solomon exhibited at the Royal Academy his controversial *Habet* in 1865 and in 1868, after his visit to Italy with Oscar Browning, his beautiful but in popular opinion degenerate *Bacchus*. He also drew a series of illustrations for Swinburne's novel *Lesbia Brandon*. They seem to have spent much time together in Swinburne's rooms in Dorset Street and at Solomon's in John Street, Bedford Row and later in Fitzroy Street. It is certain that Swinburne converted Solomon to at least a show of appreciation of the Marquis de Sade for in Solomon's first extant letter written in September 1869 he writes: "Have you heard that Capell is going to publish a popular *Justine*? We are coming to a sense of what is right."

Solomon's letters are curiously stilted and sometimes naive and one gets the impression that he is trying to keep up with the erudite and studiously witty squibs of Swinburne. Though the first ends 'With love, ever yours' it is signed 'S. Solomon' and addressed to 'Dear Swinburne'. A subtle piece of flattery is introduced in a jocular manner: "What do you think? a model called Miss Blake who is one of your most devoted admirers ran off with the copy of 'Poems and Ballads' that you gave me, and nothing has been heard of her or it: I fear that she has changed her mode of life for the worse, but I hope against fear."

From Solomon's next letter it may be seen that Swinburne had written one of those twittering screeds about flagellation to which his friends were accustomed, covering his obsession as usual with joviality. "I assure you that I wept at the recital of the boyish agonies you depicted in your last, I was doubled up with grief at the idea of so many tender posteriors quivering under the pitiless strokes of the rod, swayed, doubtless, by a man not wholly free from faults himself, but enough of a subject from which I avert my mental and physical eyes." He goes on to speak of an architect named Nesfield who had described his sufferings at school. "He is a fat, jolly hearty fellow, genuinely good natured, very fond of smoking, and I deeply grieve to say of women; although doubtless bearing the marks of the many Etonian rods I mentioned, feels no more the *real* merit and meaning of that instrument of delight than my pen does; I should unhesitatingly pronounce him to be not at all of a sensual temperament in your and my conception of the term." Solomon had shown him a pornographic drawing of 'the disgraceful act of flagellation' in a penny paper called *Peter Spy* and it had reminded him of his own experiences but when he had shown it to Albert Moore and "when he read it he asked me with open mouth and eyes what it meant; he was entirely ignorant of [the] whole subject, and I sighed to think how I was in his happy, innocent condition before I knew a certain poet whom I will forbear to mention, but, I warrant you, I quickly enlightened him". Solomon then goes on, evidently to amuse Swinburne, to quote some extracts from the imaginary autobiography of 'a man of irregular affection'. He ends with a drawing of the Queen presenting rods to the schoolmasters of Great Britain and a promise, the significance of which is important for an understanding of the Swinburne/Solomon relationship: "On my return I will make you many drawings".

In November Solomon writes from the Arts Club a letter on things that interest *him*, with only one reference to a French model whom he has taught to ask people for *Justine* as a palliation to Swinburne's insatiable demands. He has sold a picture to Powell, has been to see Pater at Oxford and read his article in the *Fortnightly*, is painting (for 'a most charming little clergyman who unites religious unction with the broadest aesthetic views') a picture called *Summer Twilight.* There is to be a new art magazine called the *Portfolio* and has Swinburne read the article about him, Solomon, in the *Saturday*?

Four months later from the New Club in Fitzroy Street Solomon thanks Swinburne for a parody of Gilbert's *The Bishop and the Busman.* ("It also was a Jew: It couldn't well be wuss.") In the following year Solomon writes from c/o Colonel Brine at Teignmouth. He has been staying at Torquay with the novelist Mrs Pender Cudlip—"I beg to state that I did not pend her cudlip."

Ten days later he is back in his rooms in Fitzroy Street and writes to ask Swinburne a favour. He has published a prose poem called *A Vision of Love Revealed in Sleep* and wants Swinburne to review it for an Oxford magazine called *The Dark Blue.* He pleads for this eloquently and Swinburne agreed.

The review, when it was published, left Solomon with very mixed feelings. Swinburne, as was his custom in criticism, overstated his case both in praise and blame. "Since the first years of his early and brilliant celebrity", he wrote, "he has been at work long enough to enable us to define at least certain salient and dominant points of his genius. . . . I have heard him likened to Heine as a kindred Hellenist of the Hebrews; Grecian form and beauty divide the allegiance of his spirit with Hebrew shadow and majesty." But later, after admitting that two of the poems in *Poems and Ballads* 'Erotion' and 'The End of the Month' were written to accompany designs of Solomon's, he says of the prose poem: "Dim and vague as the atmosphere of such work should be, this vision would be more significant and not less suggestive of things hidden in secret places of spiritual reserve, if it had more body of drawing, more shapeliness of thought and fixity of outline", and of Solomon's paintings that in the faces of the fair feminine youths he creates there was 'a mixture of utmost delicacy with a fine cruelty'.

Solomon seems to have protested and Swinburne to have rejected the protest for Solomon writes apologetically:

> I received your letter of yesterday and I am very sorry to find from its tone that what I said in mine must have been very awkwardly and ungraciously done. It is very difficult for me to know what to say to you but I am quite sure that whatever I may say will not imply a want of gratitude for and acknowledgment of your kindness in writing the article in the 'Dark Blue'. And you must promise to forgive me if I speak the whole truth about it. When you sent the MS and I read it, I saw and appreciated the full beauty of the paper and the great honour that had been done me by the most brilliant of our writers, but I saw that there were certain parts which I could have desired to be omitted but I dared not ask you to eliminate or even to modify them, for I thought it would have been a liberty, and, as a beggar who had so large a boon conferred upon him, I felt it would have been unjustifiable: when the article appeared in print one or two very intimate friends said 'eloquent and beautiful as it is, I think it will do you harm'. You know, of course, my dear Algernon, that, by many, my designs and pictures executed during the last three or four years have been looked upon with suspicion, and, as I have been a false friend to myself, I have not sought to remove the impression, but I have gone on following my own sweet will; in pecuniary and some other ways I have had to suffer for it, and shall probably have to suffer still. I really hardly know how to say any more, but I wish to make you feel that what I said in my last letter and what I repeat in this arises from no want of gratitude for the honor you did me and the kindness you showed me and I hope you will send me a letter absolving me from such an imputation in your mind.

Shortly after he wrote again:

> I was so pleased and relieved by your last letter and the kind manner in which you so completely exonerated me from the charge of ingratitude and ungraciousness; I saw by it that you entirely understood what I meant although it was awkwardly conveyed.

Though the thing was thus patched up it may have had a lasting effect on their relationship. It could be a coincidence that no more intimate letters from Solomon have come to light and Swinburne certainly continued to send messages to him through George Powell, but the great warmth of their friendship during the 1860s seems to have been somewhat chilled by a few revealing sentences in Swinburne's long and laudatory review of Solomon's work. The Victorians took seriously every criticism printed in their multifarious quarterly, monthly and weekly reviews and bitter quarrels followed many of these. Solomon's anxiety about the public attitude to his work may have been increased, in fact, by the inclusion of his name in an attack on *The Fleshly School in Poetry* which piece of lumpish mud-slinging in the *Contemporary Review*, the outcome of jealousy and malice, has had the odd effect of immortalizing the man who wrote it, a disappointed hedgehog named Robert Buchanan, for both Swinburne and Rossetti replied scathingly to it. Of Solomon's work Buchanan spoke in a way which would please a modern artist but scared Solomon in 1870. "English society goes into ecstasy over Mr. Solomon's pictures—pretty pieces of morality such as 'Love Dying by the Breath of Lust' . . . Painters like Mr. Solomon lend actual genius to worthless subjects, and thereby produce monsters—like the lovely devils that danced round St. Anthony."

But when Swinburne first agreed to write the review, as if to reward him Solomon gave him an account of an interesting trial he had just attended at the invitation of Counsel to one of a number of transvestists charged with 'conspiracy to commit a felony', the Queen v. Boulton and Others. "Boulton", wrote Solomon, "is very remarkable, he is not quite beautiful but supremely pretty, a perfect figure, manner and voice. Altogether I was agreeably surprised at him. Of course they will be acquitted."

4

The story leading to this appearance in court is an interesting period piece full of low comedy and curious detail, and shows how little in essentials the behaviour of transvestists varies from period to period or from one country to another. It gives a squalid but colourful picture of one unfamiliar aspect of London life in the 1870s. But it is included here for a better reason—in its judicial aspects it is in contrast with the case against Oscar Wilde twenty-four years later and lawyers can judge how far the change had come from the passing of the Criminal Law Amendment Act in 1885. The prosecution was half-hearted and the court seemed anxious to believe the best of the four men in the dock, any one of whom, if subjected to the kind of cross-examination which Wilde faced, would have gone to prison in 1895. There was no suggestion of blackmail here for the Blackmailer's Charter was not yet law. The police were totally inexperienced in what methods to use to obtain convictions in cases of this kind—they had not even learned to threaten and cajole one party to inform on the other. The details may be found in *The Trial of Boulton and Park, with Hurt and Fiske*, 1871, *The Annual Register for* 1871, 1872, newspaper reports of the time and *Bad Companions* by William Roughead, 1930.

The young men here were of a different type from those who were to give evidence against Oscar. They were both pathological inverts who dressed as women, sang in falsetto and used women's names. They were not professionals, though they were not above asking their lovers for 'some coin', and they came of respectable parents. Ernest Boulton, known as Stella, was the son of a stockbroker, twenty-two and good-looking in an effeminate way while his friend Frederick Park, known as Fanny, was articled to a solicitor, and no less obvious. A simple surgical operation today would put them out of reach of the law, but in 1870 the poor wretches, having lived as women, sweated to grow whiskers and moustaches in time for their trial.

Stella under the name of Mrs Graham frequently hired a private brougham to take her and Fanny to theatres, restaurants, even to the Oxford and Cambridge Boat Race and the driver giving evidence later, said 'he had no idea they were not women'. No one joined them at the Boat Race and they spoke to no one. They were less discreet one night at the Alhambra for John Reeves, the manager, had his attention called to them while they were in a box.

> They were hanging over, lighting cigarettes from the gas jets below the box. All the people in the auditorium below were looking up at them; they were making stupid noises, chirruping to each other with their lips; they were chucking each other under the chin, and playing at frivolous games. A third person was with them; he was Gibbins. They were turned out, and the price of the box returned to them.

At the Lyceum Theatre, according to an attendant in the 'grand saloon', they occupied the box 'opposite to the Prince of Wales's' and in the interval drank brandy-and-soda. They asked for the 'ladies' retiring room' and when they were led to it Stella entered while Fanny waited at the door. They were taken for 'fast women'.

It was outside the Strand Theatre that they were arrested after they had seen the performance on April 28th, 1870. Stella was wearing a scarlet satin dress with a muslin shawl over it, false hair and a chignon, bracelets, rings and lockets. 'It was a very low dress and the arms were bare', but he had white kid gloves. It was discovered later that he wore petticoats and stays, and ladies' white boots, while his 'bosom was padded to make it appear very full'. Fanny wore a satin dress of dark green or blue, low-necked and trimmed with black lace. He had a black lace shawl and white kid gloves.

When the police approached, two men were with them, one of whom lived in the apartment under theirs in Wakefield Street. His name was Thomas and although he wore male clothes it could be seen at once that he was one of their circle, so not surprisingly, with considerable presence of mind, he dived into the crowd and disappeared. The other, Mundell, a recent recruit, was not prepared for anything of this sort and was taken to Bow Street with Stella and Fanny.

In the morning, still in women's dress, they were brought before a Magistrate charged with frequenting the Strand Theatre with intent to commit a felony. This would be changed later in the proceedings to 'conspiracy to commit a felony', a very different matter, but any stick is good enough to beat a dog with and the police wanted them out of the way while they searched their rooms. This they began to do early next morning but after they had seen 'female jewellery and dress' it was time (presumably) for a tea break and they locked the door of the room, intending to continue their search and inventory later.

But Detective Chamberlain, who was in charge, had forgotten Thomas, the one that got away. A resourceful queen this, for with two others, Cumming and Gibbins, he broke down the door of the room and removed all the drag. It was found again before the trial and produced, but not categorically as having been found in Stella's and Fanny's rooms. The inventory produced in Court has a quaint, dated and irresistible interest today, for, although any history of fashions will tell us what men and women wore in 1870, the wardrobe of a transvestist is not so open to research. Here are the items shared between Stella and Fanny:

> There were sixteen dresses, satin, rep and glacé; green cord silk (estimated at £9. 9s); violet glace silk, trimmed with white lace (estimated price £10. 10s); black satin, trimmed with mauve satin (estimated at £6); blue and white satin, piped with white satin (put at £7); a mauve rep silk (put at £8); a gray moiré antique

(put at £10. 10s); a white glacé, trimmed with blue satin and lace (£8. 8s), and a white corded silk (£6. 6s). Then there were a dozen petticoats, ten cloaks and jackets, half-a-dozen bodices, several bonnets and hats, twenty chignons, and a host of miscellaneous articles—stays, drawers, stockings, boots, curling-irons, gloves, boxes of violet powder and bloom of roses, etc. The estimated value was about £170.

But more important to the police than the drag were the letters they hoped to discover in the apartments, and here they were luckier. What they found soon set moving one of those hound-like investigations that were to become a feature of police activity eighty years later during the Home Secretaryship of Maxwell Fyfe. Opening the letters, sniffing round the urinals of their suspects, bullying potential witnesses for information, searching homes without a warrant and (as they did in this case) persuading doctors to examine their prisoners' private parts without an order from a Magistrate,• the police hoped to show their prowess and integrity. They forgot only one thing. They had no proof at all, no direct evidence, to support their charge, which failed ignominiously.

But in the meantime, those letters. Detective Chamberlain must have wondered at his luck when he discovered that two years earlier Stella had enjoyed a wild affair with Lord Arthur Pelham Clinton, the third son of the Duke of Newcastle, and that Lord Arthur, then only twenty-eight years old had encouraged Stella to have cards printed as 'Lady Clinton' and sign herself as such. There were tender little notes from Stella—"Just off to Chelmsford with Fanny. Not sent me any money, wretch!" "Write at once and if you have any coin I could do with a little." "My dear Arthur,—We were very drunk last night, and consequently I forgot to write . . . And now, dear, I must shut up, and remain affectionately yours,—STELLA." "My dear Arthur,—I have waited two hours for you, and do not like to be treated with such rudeness . . . I shall not return tonight—not at all, if I am to be treated with such rudeness." Fanny, on the other hand, signing herself

• "Of the eight 'medical gentlemen' who examined the prisoners in Newgate, the prosecution called four. Dr Paul, the police surgeon, admitted that he did so without an order from a magistrate. He was reprimanded by the Lord Chief Justice, who warned him that if he acted in such a manner again he might find himself involved 'in very unpleasant consequences'." (*Bad Companions* by William Roughead, 1930.)

'your affectionate sister-in-law' was more articulate when writing to Lord Arthur. "My dearest Arthur,—How very kind of you to think of me on my birthday! I had no idea that you would do so. It was very good of you to write, and I am really very grateful for it. I require no remembrances of my sister's husband, as the many kindnesses he has bestowed upon me will make me remember him for many a year, and the birthday present he is so kind as to promise me will only be one addition to the heap of little favours I already treasure up."

Hearing that he was to appear in the dock with Boulton and Park, Lord Arthur did what was expected of a gentleman in those days—he discreetly committed suicide. (There was no inquest, two doctors obligingly stating that he had died from exhaustion resulting from scarlet fever aggravated by anxiety caused by the charge.)

As a consolation for this loss of a titled defendant Mr John Safford Fiske, American Consul at Leith but living in Edinburgh, was readily accepted, particularly since his letters to Stella seemed to be written to titillate a jury. They were sickly and mooning love letters addressed to 'darling Ernie'.

> I had a letter last night from Louis which was charming in every respect except the information it bore that he is to be kept a week or so longer in the North. He tells me you are living in drag. What a wonderful child it is! I have three minds to come to London and see your magnificence with my own eyes. Would you welcome me? Probably it is better I should stay at home and dream of you. But the thought of you–Lais and Antinous in one–is ravishing.

When Fiske's rooms were searched there was found behind the grate in his bedroom an album of photographs which his sentimental nature had not let him destroy. The photographs 'beautifully executed' were of young Boulton 'in female attire' in one of which Stella was discovered 'in an attitude of prayer'.

After these tit-bits for the prosecution, the letters to Stella of a young Edinburgh surveyor named Louis Hurt were of less importance but they were sufficient in the eyes of the police to justify a charge against Hurt which put him in the dock with the rest of them. He wanted to take Stella to stay with him and his mother in France. "I have told my mother that you are coming, but have not yet had time to receive her answer. I thought it well to tell her that you were very effeminate, but I hope you will do your best to appear as manly as you can—at any rate in the face. I therefore beg of you to let your moustache grow at once."

A more priggish and discreet character than his friend the American Consul, he disapproved of Stella's wearing women's clothes in public. "Even if in town I would not go to the Derby with you in drag", he wrote sharply. "I am sorry to hear of your going about in drag so much. I know the moustache has no chance while this kind of thing goes on."

It was almost entirely on these letters that the Prosecution relied. The case, which had received enormous publicity, came up in the Court of Queen's Bench before the Lord Chief Justice on May 9th, 1871, more than a year after the arrest, so that the defendants had presumably been in gaol for thirteen months and there had been time for Fanny to grow 'whiskers' and even Stella had 'a slight moustache'. The Prosecution witnesses were not impressive. There was Mundell who had been released after the first hearing in the Magistrate's court on condition that he would give evidence for the Prosecution. He had met Stella and Fanny in men's attire at the Surrey Theatre, followed them to a pub in the interval and 'entered into conversation' believing them to be women dressed as men. They had met four days later at the Strand Theatre when he had bought roses for them. They were then in women's dress. 'He had treated Boulton as a gay woman but she had kept him at arm's length.' Thomas (who was called 'another gentleman') was with them and had told Mundell that the two 'did it for a bit of fun'. Theirs was 'the finest get-up in London'. After Mundell came Detective Chamberlain and other policemen one of whom said that Stella and Fanny had tried to bribe him. Then appeared a blackmailing beadle from the Burlington Arcade who admitted taking money from the whores who paraded there. He had been dismissed, and had worked since as a ticket-collector, a policeman and a bus conductor. There followed a coachman, a few landladies and servants none of whom said anything in the least incriminating. Finally the Prosecution called its medical evidence and made the most of the letters.

The defence was a brave and as it proved effective one. The whole thing was a lark, one huge rollicking joke. Boys will be girls and if they like dressing up and writing to one another as 'darling' and generally behaving with exaggerated effeminacy, who was to say that any 'felony' was behind it? Not one shred of evidence had been produced of anything more than silliness and indiscretion. Were they to be sentenced for these?

Besides, a lot of evidence was produced about their appearance on the stage. Lord Arthur and Stella had appeared in the Spa Rooms at Scarborough in plays called *A Morning Call* and *Love and Rain* (characters: Lady Jane Desmond, a young widow—Ernest Boulton Esq.: Captain Charles Lumley—Lord Arthur Pelham Clinton M.P.). Sometimes Boulton had as many as fourteen bouquets at one performance. The two often went to parties after the performances in their professional costumes.

The evidence which swayed the jury, one feels, was that of Stella's mother. "She stated that he was twenty-two years old, and had dressed up as a girl from the age of six. As a child his favourite role was that of a parlourmaid, in which he deceived even his own relations. He was constantly occupied with private theatricals either at home or with friends, and always played female parts. She knew Lord Arthur Clinton as a friend of her son; they used to act together. Ernest stayed with him with her consent, and she and her husband visited them at Lord Arthur's rooms in Southampton Street. They had performed together at the Egyptian Hall, at Chelmsford, Brentwood, Scarborough and Southend. Ernest used to send her his press notices and all his photographs in character. 'His success was something wonderful; bouquets were thrown on the stage.' "•

Evidence of character was given for both Hurt and Fiske as being of high moral character and in his summing up the Lord Chief Justice said of them: "I must emphatically say that I am of opinion that Mr. Hurt and Mr. Fiske ought never to have been put upon their trial in this country at all. In the first place gross injustice is done them, as they are mixed up with matters with which they had nothing at all to do, but which are calculated to excite great prejudice; and the administration of justice is most seriously embarrassed by the proceeding."

William Roughead gives a neat account of the end of the case.

The jury then retired to consider their verdict, and when fifty-three minutes later they returned to Court, they found the four defendants

• *Bad Companions* by William Roughead. (Edinburgh 1930.)

Not Guilty on all counts. The verdict was received with applause—'Loud cheers, and cries of "Bravo!"' Ernest, to the shame of his moustache, fainted in the dock and had to be revived with water: it was a last tribute to the shade of Stella. Fanny, fortified by whiskers, never turned a hair.

The odd thing is that Counsel for Stella and Fanny may even have been speaking the truth when they called it all a lark. Inverts they were but it is not uncommon to find cases where the limit of effeminacy is passed and the girl-boy becomes almost sexless, expecting the attentions given to a woman, the clothes and jewels and scents in an exaggerated form, but not demanding any categorically sexual act. There was something so extremely exhibitionistic about these two, their appearances in drag in the boxes of theatres, in 'Mrs Graham's brougham', at the Boat Race and the Derby, that one wonders, particularly in the case of Stella, whether they were not merely exhibitionists. They did not prink themselves, it would seem from the evidence, to get off with men, but to show themselves, be admired, simper and bow and ape or even exceed the social antics of women. It is hard not to believe that if anyone ought to have been found guilty of conspiring to commit a felony it was those 'high moral characters' Fiske and Hurt who aroused so much popular sympathy because, according to Lord Chief Justice, they were mixed with matters with which they had nothing at all to do. It must be remembered that 'a felony' meant sodomy and nothing else, and the case had been built up by the police without their taking the precaution to provide evidence of this, or what might be made to appear to the jury as evidence. Stellas and Fannies in our time would be given the benefit of no such doubt. A compact in a pocket, a smile bestowed in Coventry Street, a chance meeting in a public house are considered evidence enough of those indictable offences which became popular with prosecutors after 1885.

Simeon Solomon's comments on the case are enlightening and it is a pity that Swinburne's reaction to them is unknown. He may not have been much interested for there was nothing to appeal to his tastes. Solomon on the other hand was fascinated. "There were some very funny things said but nothing improper except the disgusting and silly medical evidence of which I heard but very little. Reynolds publishes everything (they say) and the D.T. does nearly the same.

I think the public interest has quite died away. I saw the writer of those highly effusive letters he looks rather humdrum." Fiske certainly did not consider himself humdrum and if his letters to Boulton are to be believed he had recently turned down an heiress with £30,000 a year for the sake of his 'darling Stella'.

Solomon met them by chance in a neighbouring restaurant with their solicitors and sat down with them to study them better. He, like the Chief Justice, thought it hard for Hurt and Fiske 'to be mixed up with the others'. There is some irony in the reflection that within three years he would stand where they did.

5

Now, at thirty Simeon Solomon allowed success to go to his head. He had friends like Pater who gave him not only lavish praise for his work but hospitality in Oxford where he received the heady flattery of young men. Pater had used some stimulating phrases about Solomon's *Bacchus* in 1868 as a complete realization of Dionysus Zagreus, 'the god of the bitterness of wine', 'of things too sweet', 'the sea water of the Lesbian grape become somewhat brackish in the cup', and remained an enthusiast even when Solomon attempted in his paintings not altogether successfully to recapture his early Hebraic enthusiasms. Oscar Browning, too, gave Solomon the adulation of an ageing queen for a handsome young man who was also an artist. By taking him to Italy he had given him the opportunity to study the works of Luini and Sodoma and other painters of the Lombard School, and this had powerfully affected his work and broadened his scope. He went again to Italy in 1870 and at this time began to be attracted, pictorially, to Catholicism. His poem was being talked about and Frances Winwar• in her usual ecstatic manner describes him—from imagination—at Pater's rooms in Oxford.

> Sometimes Simeon Solomon himself, their close disciple and the bosom friend of Swinburne, visited Pater. A small graceful man with a face deep-eyed with reverie like one of his own drawings, Solomon would sit before a hushed group and read to them his poetical allegory, *A Vision of Love Revealed in Sleep*. It was a disturbing tale, the account of a pagan calvary wherein Love beautiful

• *Oscar Wilde and the Yellow Nineties* by Frances Winwar, 1940.

> as Eros yet like Christ cognizant of pain, walked the stages of his passion—Hellenism borrowing the mysteries of the Church.

Bernard Falk• is scarcely less inventive in describing (it would be hard to guess from what source) the bodeful and shocking behaviour of Solomon in public.

> Nothing amiss was noticeable until the autumn of 1872, when his peculiarly affected behaviour attracted the attention of his less frivolous friends. As he went about, he was seen to lean on the shoulders of youthful male models, much in the manner of Julius Caesar when in the company of favourite courtiers of tender years.

It may not be without significance, remembering the importance attached by the Victorians to facial growths of all kinds, that Solomon shaved his beard at this time. "I think S.S. minus his Jewish *barbiche* must be an obscene spectacle" wrote Swinburne to George Powell.

It is certainly safe to guess that Solomon was behaving indiscreetly from the sequel to all this which came in 1873. He was convicted and sentenced on February 11th.

The thing in itself—a sordid affair in a public lavatory—might have been easily outlived and forgotten if Solomon had not felt himself betrayed. He was treated by the Magistrate with leniency considering the period and the charge, which was such that no paper reported it and no account appeared in public print. The charge sheet, however, still exists and one is surprised to learn that Solomon only suffered six weeks' confinement in Clerkenwell House of Correction, a term of 'police supervision' being substituted for a suspended sentence of eighteen months' imprisonment.

There seems to be no truth in the story, repeated by Robert Ross in his essay on Solomon and Bernard Falk who drew on this, that Solomon was put in an asylum. On the contrary, before the year was out he was staying with his friends in Devonshire and giving widely advertised public readings from Dickens. But from this time on he ceased to be 'respectable' and it is impossible to know now who, if anyone but himself, is to blame for what is invariably and unctuously called his downfall.

Swinburne was disturbed. His reactions may be judged accurately from his letters to Powell and Watts-Dunton which must be quoted

• *Five Years Dead*, op. cit.

at length. The first rumours which reached him did not perturb him very deeply for he wrote of Solomon with some of his usual facetiousness just a month after the conviction.

> Have you any news good or bad of Our Wandering Jew? The aberrations of that too erratic vagrant from the narrow way are a subject of real uneasiness and regret to me, who have a regard for his genuine good qualities of character and genius. Let us, my brethren, while we drop a tear over the sheep now astray from the true fold of the Good Shepherd, if not indeed irrevocably classed among the goats to be ultimately found on the left hand of the G.S., give thanks to a merciful Providence that we are not as this Israelite, in whom if we have not been mistaken as to his character I fear there must be a good deal of guile.

Swinburne's remarks, already showing the self-righteous attitude he later adopted, would be more acceptable if he had not, in the same letter, said that he would be charmed when he saw Powell to read the full history (in French periodicals which Powell had bought at his suggestion) 'of the accomplished youth Master Gélignier'. This refers to a matter raised in his previous letter.

> Have you seen anything beyond the wretchedly curtailed announcement in Saturday's Times of the apprehension in the suburbs of Paris of a band of Sadists, disciples of the excellent M. Dolmance, headed by a captain aged fourteen and a half (Gélignier by name), which dear child, who among us would be in the fourth form, has taken part in eighty robberies with *Sadique* violence, several murders and other *attentats*, to say nothing of the daily bread of diversions unnecessary to specify, and has maintained his ascendancy over comrades of 27 and upwards? Surely this sweet bud of 'vice' must be a blossom from the chance-sown seed of the Marquis. It seems that the 'Gaulois' has given 'deplorably' full details of the matter, as well as other French papers to the scandal of virtuous journalism. Could you I wonder find any number of a newspaper containing such at Roques, where we went together, in High Holborn, close to Bedford Row?

Le Gaulois printed on February 22 an account of the case quoted by Cecil Y. Lang:

> There were eleven men and three women in the gang, which, except for arson, had committed 'tous les actes qui tombent sous l'application du Code pénal'. Their commander-in-chief, Albert Gaston Gélignier, a swaggering, handsome 14-year-old who looked

20, dominated men nearly twice his age partly by blackmail and partly by force of character. His lieutenant, Eugène Renault, aged 17, who had 'des liens plus intimes avec son chef, liens horribles, hors nature', was (appropriately) nicknamed 'le Môme Marin'.

That he should be showing a gloating interest in Gélignier while poor Solomon, just then in gaol, is dismissed with fatuous mock-quotations leaves an unpleasant taste in the mouth.

Three months later, while still not fully cognizant of the details of the case he wrote to Powell more sympathetically, but with a suggestion of prudery which did not come very amiably from a self-confessed disciple of de Sade.

I had often been going to write to you, especially on the wretched subject to which you refer, and as often had put off on that very account. I have been spending a fortnight in Oxford where I saw and spoke with a great friend of poor Simeon's, Pater of Brasenose, who has seen Miss Solomon, and appeared to have more hope of his ultimate recovery and rehabilitation than from the horrid version I had heard of the form of his insanity I had ventured to retain. I spoke also with another common friend, Bywater (who is *Proctor* for this year!!) who was much distressed about it. I suppose there is no doubt the poor unhappy little fellow has really been out of his mind and *done* things amenable to law such as done by a sane man would make it impossible for any one to keep up his acquaintance and not be cut by the rest of the world as an accomplice? I have been seriously unhappy about it for I had a real affection and regard for him—and besides his genius he had such genuinely amiable qualities. It is the simple truth that the distress of it has haunted and broken my sleep. It is hideous to lose a friend by madness of any kind, let alone this.

By December of the same year (that of Solomon's conviction) he had become flatly disapproving, unable to forgive Solomon's poor little success in Devonshire where the artist was probably staying with Miss Annie Thomas (Mrs Pender Cudlip the novelist) at Torquay as he had done in 1871 and recovering from the shock of his imprisonment. Swinburne began to be circumspect and anxious about the effects of Solomon's fall on his own reputation. He not only wanted no further communication with Solomon but had adjured Powell to have nothing more to do with him. His letter was to Watts-Dunton (still at that time Theodore Watts).

I had heard before that Simeon Solomon was in Devonshire staying with some old friends; also that he had been giving *public readings*

> in his own name from (I think) Dickens in the neighbouring town with great success; and I have just heard from Powell that it appears from his own account that he is living in a round of balls and private theatricals. Everything connected with him is so extraordinary that nothing can be expected to happen in his case except that which seems unlikeliest, and I suppose we shall hear next of his presentation at court with a promise of the rever[sio]n of Sir F. Grant's vacant president[ial] chair; but in the meantime I h[ave wri]tten to Powell a long letter of eld[erbr]otherly advice not to be led away by any kindly and generous feeling towards an unfortunate man whom he has been used to regard as a friend, into a renewal of intimacy by correspondence or otherwise which might appear to involve him in equivocal or questionable relations with a person who has deliberately chosen to do what makes a man and all who associate with him infamous in the eyes of the world. It is something new for me to come forward as the representative of worldly wisdom; but as I said to P. I do not think I need fear to be accused of lukewarmness in friendship or pers[on]al timidity in the face of public op[ini]on; it is not exactly for turning tai[l or dese]rting my friends when out of favour [with] the world or any part of it that I have exposed myself hitherto to attack; only in such a case as this I do think a man is bound to consider the consequence to all his friends and to every one who cares for him in the world of allowing his name to be mixed up with that of a —— let us say, a Platonist; the term is at once accurate as a definition and unobjectionable as an euphemism.

A month later he emphasized to Watts-Dunton that he intended to avoid Solomon.

> At the end of next week I am going into Cornwall for ten days with Prof. Jowett who has just paid us a new year's visit here. Between this and then the Master of Balliol will be at Torquay, where I am not sorry that I do not join him, as I have no wish, especially in his company, to encounter that of a Platonist of another sort than the translator of Plato—'translator he too' as Carlyle might say, of Platonic theory into Socratic practice—should he still figure in that neighbourhood as the glass of fashion and the mould of form, if not (as I sincerely hope not) 'the glass wherein the noble youth' of the West country 'do dress themselves'. Powell has answered to my little fraternal lecture on caution in that quarter very nicely, in two or three sensible and grateful words.

Little is known of Solomon's movements for the next seven years until in 1880 he was admitted into hospital in a pitiful condition, suffering it would seem from exposure, barefoot and in rags. There is some hearsay evidence of his unfulfilled promises to dealers from whom he may have extracted small sums, of his drunkenness and exploitation of those who tried to help him. Falk who saw some members of his family in after years says that they did everything possible to rehabilitate him, but in vain. It is said that he became a pavement artist in the Brompton Road and sold matches and shoelaces in the Mile End Road and led the life of a down-and-out, a gruesome existence in London in the 1870s when every vagrant was considered to be a diseased criminal.

In 1877 Swinburne in a letter to Watts-Dunton spoke of 'that poor wretch Solomon', and two years later wrote to Edmund Gosse of him 'now a thing unmentionable alike by men and women, as equally abhorrent to either—nay, to the very beasts—raising money by the sale of my letters to him in past years, which must doubtless contain much foolish burlesque and now regrettable nonsense never meant for any stranger's eye who would not understand the mere childishness of the silly chaff indulged in long ago'. This is the only reference so far traced to this unfortunate episode, though every detail of Swinburne's life has been exhaustively investigated by a series of indefatigable scholars including Dr Cecil Y. Lang whose notes to his monumental edition of the letters leave almost nothing undiscovered. It may or may not be true that Solomon tried to sell some of Swinburne's letters; it is certain that he had long been released by Swinburne's behaviour towards him from any obligation to loyalty. Selling the compromising letters of living people is never pretty conduct but in all the circumstances and considering the condition to which Solomon had been brought, the wonder is that he had not parted with them years before.

In 1894 the records of St Giles Workhouse show that a 'broken down artist' named Simeon Solomon was admitted and for the remaining eleven years of his life he was in and out of this institution where he was allowed facilities to paint when he could bring himself to it. He died there in 1905 of heart failure, aggravated by bronchitis and alcoholism and was buried in Willesden Jewish Cemetery.

There are two fallacies about his last years which have been widely accepted. One is that he was reduced to a state of utter misery by his sufferings. To Robert Ross, who sought him out in 1893, he was 'a small red man with keen laughing eyes' who thoroughly enjoyed himself in his own particular way, and rejected fiercely all attempts at rescue or reform. "He was extremely cheerful and not aggressively alcoholic. Unlike most spoilt wastrels with the artistic temperament, he seemed to have no grievances, and had no bitter stories or complaints about former friends, no scandalous tales about contemporaries who had remained reputable; no indignant feeling towards those who assisted him. This was an amiable, inartistic trait in his character, though it may be a trifle negative; and for a positive virtue, as I say, he enjoyed his drink, his overpowering dirt, and his vicious life. He was full of delightful and racy stories about poets and painters, policemen and prisons, of which he had wide experience. He might have written a far more diverting book of memoirs than the average Pre-Raphaelite volume to which we look forward every year, though it is usually silent about poor Simeon Solomon." This is a convincing picture because it has about it the curious quality of uninventability.

The other fallacy is that he did no work of any value after 1873. This is very far from true. His work became erratic and many of his pictures were tawdry pot-boilers, turned out for the odd guinea from a dealer. Of his work in his last years Arthur Symons wrote vividly in 1911.

> In late years Solomon restricted himself to single heads drawn in coloured chalks, sometimes two heads facing one another, the Saviour and Mary Magdalen, the Virgin and the Angel of the Annunciation. The drawing becomes more and more nerveless, the expression loses delicacy and hardens into the caricature of an emotion, the faint suggestions of colour become more pronounced, more crudely asserted. In the latest drawings of all we see no more than the splintering wreck of a painter's technique. But as lately as ten years ago he could still produce, with an almost mechanical ease, sitting at a crowded table in a Clerkenwell news-room, those drawings which we see reproduced by some cheap process of facsimile in pink or in black. . . . They have legends under them out of the Bible, in Latin, or out of Dante in Italian; or they have the names of the Seven Virtues, or of the Seven Deadly Sins; or are images of Sleep and Death and Twilight. 'A void and wonderfully vague desire' fills all these faces, as water fills the hollow pools of the sand; they have the sorrow of those who have no cause for sorrow except that they are in a world not made after their pattern. . . . These faces are without sex; they have brooded among ghosts of passions till they have become the ghosts of themselves; the energy of virtue or of sin has gone out of them, and they hang in space, dry, rattling, the husks of desire.

This description arouses curiosity and it is not surprising to find that in April 1966 Durlacher Brothers of New York held an exhibition of Solomon's work and among the paintings and drawings shown were many from Solomon's work-house period, including a magnificent painting called *Night and Day*, dated about 1900, and many water-colours from the Nineties. His talent could not be utterly extinguished, of course, and emerged triumphantly on occasions to the end. No more exotic or controversial figure exists among British artists.

CHAPTER THREE

Swinburne, Howell and Powell

THERE is a memorable short passage in Helen Rossetti Angeli's book about Charles Augustus Howell which is a just tribute to its subject. Writing of an act of benevolence by Howell on Ruskin's behalf she says it "takes us back into an extinct past, with all its fond hopes as dead as the anoplethyrion: to the 'socialistic' philanthropic struggles of the Victorian conscience, such as gave rise to the preposterous unrealities of an *Aurora Leigh*—so pregnant with good feeling so full of poetry, so *dead*. Howell is alive in the midst of it all."•

He is. Among the stories of the Pre-Raphaelites which have been appearing at intervals during the last century there are accounts of him which contradict one another in almost everything, yet from them emerges a far more vital and vivid figure than the tired spectres of the Pre-Raphaelites themselves. He lied about himself and myths have grown round him but the essential man is 'alive in the midst of it all', a person one comes to know as one can never know that brooding mysterious man Rossetti. Reading of one of his exploits or impostures one says—yes, of course Howell *would* do that; one almost hears his voice and one soon comes to anticipate his reactions.

• *Pre-Raphaelite Twilight: The Story of Charles Augustus Howell*, 1954.

He was one of those men whose character and manner are seen in their portraits. Tall, with curly almost frizzy brown hair, a long heavy chin, large teeth and thick lips hidden by a straggling thick moustache, he had hooded yet somewhat protuberant brown eyes and an opaque yellow complexion. One knows at once that this was a voluble talker with that worst kind of dishonesty, self-deception. One knows that he was energetic, alert and inwardly unsure of himself though outwardly over-confident. One knows that he had zeal and persuasiveness and one guesses that one would end by being exasperated by him, angered by the ingenious duplicity that he never admitted even to himself. Those self-righteous explanations of how the deficit was due to someone else's dishonesty, or to an extraordinary piece of misfortune, or to illness, or to circumstances that could never have been anticipated—looking into the eyes in his photograph one can hear him explain, promise, exculpate. One might even guess (correctly) that he was an inveterate, reputedly continuous, cigarette smoker.

Almost every epithet applied to human beings of authentic individuality has been thrown at him—remarkable, puzzling, attractive, zealous, flamboyant, sinister, vicious, dishonest, a cunning rogue and an arrant rascal are but a few of them. He *was* a rogue, capable of chicanery and even misappropriation from his friends, but he never saw himself as anything but a romantic adventurer who gave his whole heart to those he cared for, and he could never believe that those transactions for artists over which he worked so hard and lied so readily were anything but kind acts. He lived among artists but had no creative skill, and among dealers but without either the business capacity or the knowledge to compete with them, so that he leapt about seeking commissions, doing little deals, fiddling here and there, taking away things to sell which never reappeared but for which the money would be balanced by some obscure service, a charlatan who believed himself misjudged, a bit of a cheat but not a common one, a man whose instincts were kind, even generous, but so fenced-in by self-pity and frustration that with the years the charm and good nature were hard to find. To read his correspondence with the Rossetti brothers, apologetic, bragging, adulatory, proud and servile in turns, to hear him say 'but you can't think *me* capable of any dishonesty, surely?' is to come to know a rare and engaging character who saw himself as maligned, unlucky and deserving of riches and success. He failed, but this may have been because he set his sights too high. Uncreative himself he tried to be one of a group of people to whom creation was second nature, and he could only exploit and oblige them in turns.

Perhaps it is because Howell in essentials was a figure of this age as much as of his own that we know him so well. He carted pictures about in hansom cabs or four-wheelers and made his appointments by letter or messenger; his dress was that of a Bohemian of the 1860s with a large cornelian tie-ring at his neck and high-buttoning waistcoats with lapels, but as an artist's tout and dealer's runner under the alias of a distinguished man who entertained important people he is alive today. A con man who convinced himself first, who never made a promise to pay which he did not intend to fulfil or an illicit profit which he did not believe his right, he passed on the precedents of living on his wits to others and now, too, we find charming liars who always know everyone just then in the news, as Howell at different times claimed to be an intimate with Orton the Tichbourne claimant and Disraeli. They belong to romantic royalist causes like the Order of the White Rose, as Howell did; they surround themselves with pickings from junk shops, every item of which has a story, often topical, just as Howell claimed of some silver he was flogging that the real Tichbourne heir had given it to his mother.

Such men are forced to imagine brilliant backgrounds for themselves, circumstances remote and romantic from which they derive their extraneous personalities, and in this Howell succeeded. His birthplace and upbringing certainly were beyond the knowledge of most of his associates and it happens that not one of those who have written about him has had any experience of them. If one of them had, he would have known that Howell's origins were not mysterious but merely obscure. For he was born into that small community, the British in Oporto, which has been established in the wine business for three and a half centuries and has its own traditions and its own rigid caste system.

Howell was the son of a humble member of that community who worked in one of the Lodges and gave drawing lessons in his free time. This Alfred William Howell had married a Portuguese wife which cut him off from most of the British, for the men who met at the

Factory House—which had been opened as stock-market club and gossip-shop fifty-odd years before Howell's birth—made up one of the narrowest and most aggressively British colonies to be found anywhere in that age of cantonments from which all 'natives' were excluded. (Even today the Portuguese shippers do not attend the weekly lunch at the Factory House.) Howell senior, unprosperous and married to a Portuguese woman, had the status of a 'poor white' and Charles himself that of a Cape Coloured or a Eurasian youth growing up at Simla. This left him with a roaring inferiority complex that lasted his lifetime and was the key to much that was unamiable in his character.

Sent at sixteen or seventeen to an uncle in Darlington, he went back to Portugal after two years and turned up in England, this time to stay, in 1863, that is when he was twenty-three. London then as now more tolerant in matters of race or of foreign residents than other parts of England and the Empire, received him well and he soon managed to ingratiate himself with John Ruskin and for five years was some kind of amanuensis to him. Ruskin at that time believed himself a minor prophet and was lecturing the world indefatigably on its art, morals and politics.

Nagging memories of humiliations as a boy perhaps turned Howell into a mighty liar and by the time he had met the Rossettis he had acquired a descent from the Marquis de Pombal, mysterious associations with high unnameable people in Portugal and a heroic part in the Orsini conspiracy for which he had been forced to fly for his life across the Channel. He claimed descent from Boabdil el Chico, and said he had been apprenticed to 'the great engineer Stephenson' and therefore (at the age of eighteen) employed to construct the Porto and Badajos railway. After the Orsini plot he had lived with brigands in the fortresses of the Serras da Estrella and gone straight from this retreat to Rome where he was an *attaché* in the Portuguese Embassy. Later he had earned his living by diving for the gold hidden in a sunken galleon which he had purchased and for a long time was the sheik of a tribe of outlaws in Morocco. He claimed to be heir to a baronetcy and at the drop of a hat would wear the sash of a Portuguese Order 'hereditary in his family'. He sought for and obtained permission to pay the funeral expenses of a tramp providently named Howell Murray who had died in a Paddington Hospital in 1878 and, having done so, buried him in a recently purchased family vault as Sir Murray Howell Murray, Bart, 'My wife's father'.

Yet it would not be wise to dismiss too categorically all Howell's pretensions, for he certainly attracted to himself some highly peculiar events. If among his stories had been one that he undertook to recover from the coffin of a woman seven years dead a roll of manuscript poems which her distracted husband, a great poet, had buried with her in the agony of his loss, and that he had carried this out, no one unconversant with the facts would surely have believed him—yet this is just what he did for Dante Gabriel Rossetti. And if one was told that the only details about his death given by any contemporary had been that he was found dead outside a Chelsea pub, with his throat cut and a half sovereign inexplicably gripped between his teeth, one would say that Howell himself could scarcely have done better. Yet T. J. Wise thus chronicles it. Moreover even during Howell's lifetime now and again one of his more fantastic Munchausen stories was proved true to the irritation of his circle.

In matters of sexual morality he himself was something of a puritan, though this may be thought to make his pandering to Swinburne's eccentricities more reprehensible. At the age of twenty-seven he married his cousin Frances Catherine Howell and for the next twenty-one years till 'Kitty's' death in 1888 he was a devoted husband. There is nothing to show that he was interested in vice of any kind and his letters even to Dante Gabriel Rossetti who had a taste for smut and venery are proper to the point of primness. One gets the impression that he had too much to explain to his correspondents, too much to justify, or to deplore in others, to have time or energy to write bawdry or even gossip. The keynote of his correspondence is that it is ridiculous for a man like him to be hard up. "The King of Portugal", he writes, "has proposed me as resident (London) first secretary to the Portuguese Embassy, and that the Government is stirring in it. If the thing is carried through I must meet it as much out of debt as possible and be quite ready for it. Once in my hands everything is all right, and then I will make swells by the right thing, I shall deal—of course—but others will do the work, and I will only advise both buyer and seller. It is damned nonsense being hard up at all. I am tired of it and will stand it no longer if I can help it." He boasts, but of social rather than sexual prowess, and of his efficiency as a salesman, not as a libertine: "So many people come here now, such as Baron Stern, Rothschilds, and other coves with mountains of tin, that I have been thinking it would be wise for you to send 3 or 4 of your finest chalk drawings for me to hang up in the drawing room." Most of us have known once or twice in our lives a liar if not of Howell's scope at least of his audacity and it is noteworthy that few if any of these inventive persons are given to any kind of excess but verbal.

How, then, to account for Swinburne's letters to the man? In the very first extant of these, dated June 1865, after catch-phrases from de Sade, *cela mène a tout* and *Oh, monsieur*, words that occur in all Swinburne's correspondence with those initiated in the de Sade cult, and the quotation of a newly finished stanza of *Dolores*, not to mention a command that Howell should communicate to the ink in his reply '*une odeur mélangée de sang et de sperme*,' we find this revealing postscript:

> P.P.S. (*private*) I want you to compose for me a little dialogue (imaginary) between schoolmaster and boy—from the first summons 'Now Arthur (or Frank—or Harry) what does *this* mean, sir? Come here'—to the last *cut* and painful buttoning up—a rebuke or threat at every lash (and *plenty* of them) and a shriek of agonized appeal from the boy in reply. I want to see how like real life you will make it. Write me this—and you shall have more of my verses—a fair bargain.
> Describe also the effect of each stripe on the boy's flesh—its appearance between the cuts.

Fourteen months later, after several other Sadic letters and hysterical demands to 'dear Charlie' that he should come at once to Swinburne's rooms, there is another, similar, postscript:

> (PPS) If you *have* heard of any boy being *swished* lately in our schools, let me hear of the distressing circumstances. Ecris-moi quelque chose de piquant, by way of *salt* to all this business.

It seems that Swinburne, as a *quid pro quo* for Howell's descriptions and drawings of flagellation, was in the habit of sending him notes, manuscript verses and other odds and ends which Howell studiously pasted into albums and later sold.

> I hope that will do as M. de Gernande said when he dug his wife's eyes out. There's a note for you which deserves a *lovely* sketch of switching by return of post. Send one, and make a day to call soon.

As late as 1870 Swinburne was writing to Howell a long imaginary account of floggings suffered by a 'schoolboy acquaintance' of his. This letter more than others by its ghastly affectation of levity reads like something salvaged from the wastepaper basket of a lunatic asylum but Howell apparently expressed approval, for Swinburne wrote, "I am glad you liked the P.S." and continued in the same drooling vein.

There seems to be no evidence anywhere in the correspondence for a suggestion made by Mr Randolph Hughes (editor of an edition of *Lesbia Brandon*) in a note to Miss Helen Rossetti Angeli that "Howell was at least occasionally one of those who played the part of a flagellant school-master to him, and thus gratified a *penchant* acquired by the poet during his troublous Eton days" unless it may be thought to lie in some words used in a letter of September 9th, 1867 after an apology from Swinburne to Howell: "What I deserve you must judge; I leave it to the Marquis (not Townshend) to decide!" On the whole it seems unlikely, though in realms of such improbability as the masochistic fantasies of Swinburne nothing can be called impossible.

It is far likelier that Howell thought the whole thing a macabre and in some way profitable joke. He was a gifted *raconteur* and could keep companies of his friends—particularly the Pre-Raphaelites—amused by exaggerated stories of his own and others' escapades and he seems to have made narrative capital of his service to Rossetti in recovering his poems from his wife's coffin. (Rossetti wrote to his brother a few days after the event, "I have begged Howell to hold his tongue for the future, but if he does not I cannot help it".) Howell was inhibited by no sense of loyalty—anything for a good story—and even if it were not proved by the sequel it could be deduced pretty certainly from his character and habits that he could not resist the opportunity for ogreish fun which little Swinburne, with his obsessions and *outré* desires, provided.

Perhaps Howell cannot be blamed too severely for this for Swinburne invariably moved behind a screen of banter and self-ridicule, and though he spoke of 'the martyred Marquis' did so as if he found de Sade and the Eton flogging-block the most riotous of absurdities. That Howell found Swinburne no less seems natural enough and the cream of the jest for him must have been that he was describing not a dull nonentity, not a mere anonymous figure in a sexual case-book, but a man he believed to be one of the greatest of poets. Swinburne at the Grove of The Beloved Disciple, Swinburne inventing cousins at Eton and writing imaginary letters from them full of sadistic description, Swinburne sitting on the knee of the Amazonian Adah Menken, Swinburne at the mercy of his own arrested development, must have been irresistible to Howell and long after the friendship ceased, from a letter written by Swinburne to Edmund Gosse (December 15th, 1879) from The Pines, Putney Hill (the same letter in which Simeon Solomon was castigated for selling Swinburne's letters), we learn that indeed he was so: "I will not for very shame's sake so far forget or forego my own claim to a sense of self-respect as to fret my heartstrings by day or by night over such disgusting facts as that I hear of one person who was once my friend and is yet my debtor habitually amusing mixed companies of total strangers by obscene false anecdotes about my private eccentricities of indecent indulgence as exhibited in real or imaginary *lupanaria.*"

When Swinburne discovered in 1885 that Howell had disposed of his letters and that a bookseller named George Redway had become possessed of them it excited in him, he told Redway, 'merely a feeling of disgust towards the person who offers them for sale'. Watts-Dunton secured them in return for the copyright of a Swinburne poem, but he too, after Swinburne's death, let them fall into the hands of the extraordinary bibliophile and forger T. J. Wise, so that Dr Cecil Y. Lang is able to print them, for the first time, in his six-volume edition. Howell, for all his nervous activity, his gift for recognizing a good thing and his unscrupulous behaviour to his friends and benefactors, got very little out of it all, just as from his industry, imaginative persuasiveness and dishonesty on behalf of Rossetti he obtained nothing but poverty and at last the contempt of friends, enemies and those who came after them.

Nor does he seem to have gained anything by his attempt to intervene on Swinburne's behalf in the poet's disputes with his publisher, John Camden Hotten, though he has been most bitterly abused for this. The story is a complicated one and need be told only briefly.

Hotten, the son of a Cornish carpenter and undertaker, came to London as apprentice to a London bookseller and in time became a clever publisher. He collected and dealt in pornographic books but most of his business was respectable and he introduced several American writers to English readers, James Russell Lowell and Oliver Wendell Holmes among them. When Edward Moxon, who was about to publish Swinburne's *Poems and Ballads* in 1866, fell into a sudden panic and withdrew the book, Hotten courageously took it over.

It is doubtful whether Swinburne, who was inclined to treat his publishers as inferior tradesmen, ever fully recognized his obligations to Hotten and there were soon serious differences between them which Howell, among others, tried to patch up. It is not impossible that Howell received some consideration for this from one or both parties but there is no justification for asserting as Dr G. C. Williamson does in *Murray Marks and His Friends* that Howell committed Swinburne to an oral contract by which he (Howell) was the gainer.

Later, when Swinburne wanted to leave Hotten and go to another publisher, he remembered with embarrassment some material he had sent Hotten for a book called *Flagellation and the Flagellants, a History of the Rod in All Countries from the earliest period to the present time* by the Rev. Wm. Cooper, B.A. Swinburne may have known that 'The Rev. Wm. Cooper, B.A.' was in fact a man named James G. Bertram. In any case he had also sent Hotten a list of subjects he wanted illustrated of which he gives a specimen in a letter to Howell after he has warned him to say *nothing to anyone, least of all to Watts* (Watts-Dunton).

(1) Charlie on the whipping-block;
Algie holds his shirt up;
Dr. Birch giving the first cut with a fresh rod on Charlie's bottom.
(2) Algie horsed on Charlie's back for his first flogging—his bottom covered with blood;
(3) Study of Algie's bottom before flogging and after;
(4) Small boys watching their big brother whipped;—and such like—

There is no reason to think that Hotten tried to blackmail Swinburne with these but the knowledge that he had them was worrying to Swinburne when Watts-Dunton (from whom he remained determined to keep all knowledge of the matter) was trying to extricate him from his commitments with Hotten. So Swinburne, in February 1873 (the very month of Simeon Solomon's commitment to prison), called on Howell for his assistance.

Whether Howell obtained possession of this material or not is unknown, for a month or two later Hotten conveniently died and Andrew Chatto, a reputable publisher, took over his firm and with it Swinburne's books. But it is not without significance that Swinburne, after seven years of friendship with Howell, was prepared to entrust him with such a delicate matter.

It does not blur the portrait of Howell that has been painted by others, perhaps more suspicious of 'foreigners' or perhaps with less fortunate experiences. This is so clear-cut that the details surrounding it are teasingly vague and there are many small things about him, as about most of his contemporaries, which will never be known. What, for instance, did his neighbours in Brixton and afterwards Fulham think of the tall foreign-looking man who left his sensible wife on the doorstep to travel up to town at such irregular intervals? He could scarcely be something in the city for he seemed to associate with odd-looking people, probably painters or writers, whom he occasionally entertained to dinner, though the local tradesmen were always grumbling about his unpaid bills. And what were all those parcels and portfolios he brought home? Someone claimed to have seen the notorious poet Swinburne arriving dead drunk at the house and someone else had heard that Mr Howell called himself a member of the Royal Society and heir to a baronetcy. Miss Someone, who was very artistic, had heard from Mrs Howell that her husband had a picture by Botticelli to sell and it would bring them a lot of money and that he was expecting the Japanese Ambassador to dinner as he was going to Japan. A man who lived near them had actually seen the large collection of testimonials from important people which Mr Howell had collected in order to obtain for himself a very important post. He had also seen an oil painting of a boy which Mr Howell said represented young Shelley. And what extraordinary stories Mr Howell told! He claimed to have met two dog-headed men in Leicester Square and to have seen a mouse eating a haddock in his own cellar!

But such speculations and anecdotes must have seemed unimportant compared with the news which spread about in the winter of 1873 that the District Railway Company wanted to demolish Mr Howell's house in order to extend their line, and that Mr Howell was demanding compensation. When he claimed to have been paid £4,000 there may have been as much envy as doubt or wonder, and he certainly moved away soon after.

He died two years after his wife, in 1890, after one or more 'deaths' faked by false announcements to raise the price of items in his collections. There was no obituary in any daily newspaper but a very curious one appeared in *The Royalist*, the organ of The Order of the White Rose to which he belonged. It is impossible to resist the conviction that Howell himself had supplied the information for this or even written most of it himself in anticipation of his own demise, so faithfully does it echo his most extravagant claims, including his Knighthood of the Portuguese Order of Christ, apprenticeship to 'the great engineer Stephenson', construction of the Badajos Railway and his wife's being the daughter of 'Sir John Murray, last of the Baronets of Stanhope'. "After spending some time in hiding among Portuguese brigands he was appointed *attaché* to the Embassy in Rome", it continued. Howell is not the only man to have written his own obituary in advance of his death, but perhaps no one has done it more audaciously. But it was left to Swinburne to speak the last unforgiving word:

> But if it was necessary to pollute any page by mention of that polecat Howell, I think you might or rather should have spoken more plainly about the character of the vilest wretch that I, at all events, ever came across. Watts said to me once—'Howell ought to be flayed alive' (not with reference to any matter concerning Gabriel). And, by God, if I could have sentenced him to be whipped to death I would have done so. I am not sure that I would not now, if he were not (happily) in that particular circle of Malebolge where the coating of eternal excrement makes it impossible to see whether the damned dog's head is or is not tonsured.

2

A less substantial figure, indeed little more than a ghost compared with Howell, is that of Swinburne's fellow-Etonian George E. J. Powell. Even Dr Cecil Y. Lang, the indefatigable editor of Swinburne's letters, admits that very little is known of him 'beyond what can be inferred from Swinburne's letters', yet since over a hundred frank letters exist the inferences are not so inconsiderable.

Powell was five years younger than Swinburne, a victim of various diseases, one of which may have been—perhaps hereditary—syphilis. He was homosexual and literary, and at war throughout his adult life with his father Colonel William Thomas Rowland Powell, who died only four years before his son, so that Powell enjoyed his long-awaited inheritance of the family home briefly. Powell seems to have been a kind and generous man and, unlike many of Swinburne's friends, was presentable at Swinburne's home and apparently a favourite with the Admiral and Lady Jane and Swinburne's sisters.

Something may be learned of him and his background from a book entitled *The South Wales Squires: A Welsh Picture of Social Life* by Hubert M. Vaughan. His home, Nant-Eos, or Nanteos, is described as 'a stately Georgian mansion' and Powell himself in a letter to Watts-Dunton called it 'a splendid old place, with surroundings of the most wonderful loveliness'. It was four miles from Aberystwyth and considered by many the most notable house in Cardiganshire.

Powell's father, the Colonel, seems to have been a hard-riding country squire given to rural sports and cattle-breeding, wholly contemptuous of his artistically minded son who collected pictures and 'objects of virtu'. George Powell disliked shooting and his father in exasperation gave him a gun and cartridges and told him not to return to the house until he had shot something. George responded by shooting the first animal he met—a valuable bullock. (The incident was told in *Peter Ibbetson* by George du Maurier who knew Swinburne and probably Powell.)

George was thirty-eight when his father died and he inherited his 'beautiful but unhappy home'. He found himself obliged to 'take his place in the county' or as he explained 'receive and return visits—a dreary farce in my eyes'.

It was perhaps his distaste for this which led him to marry Dinah Harris, a girl of humble life in Fishguard. He died a year after his wedding leaving his books and papers to University College, Aberystwyth. In all Swinburne's letters to Powell there is no reference to any woman in Powell's life but there are a good many enquiries after his male friends. Powell seems to have indulged Swinburne in his taste for Sadic literature and practices without much enthusiasm for Swinburne is less rapturous about them in his letters to Powell than in the wearisomely tautological letters he wrote to Howell and Houghton. Swinburne introduced Powell to Simeon Solomon and the two associated for several years, but it would seem not to Houghton or any of the Pre-Raphaelites except Burne-Jones. One gains the impression that the Swinburne-Powell friendship was a thing apart, a cosy and natural relationship with a good deal of give and take in it. Swinburne sympathized with Powell's idiosyncrasies though he did not share them and Powell with Swinburne's. Powell was impressed by Swinburne's pre-eminence as a poet and Swinburne accepted and often demanded favours from Powell in finding rooms, subscribing to periodicals and clearing up the small worries of his disorderly life. They stayed with one another, Powell going to Swinburne's parental home and Swinburne staying at Nant-Eos, though not, it may be guessed, while the Colonel was in residence. While here, according to Vaughan, they 'especially loved to haunt a certain low-class inn in Aberystwyth, kept by a disreputable old woman whose Rabelaisian talk owned a special attraction for Swinburne'. From this, and from certain later references in Swinburne's letters to Powell, it would seem that the Welshman liked what his prototypes today would call 'rough trade'.

This genuine and in many ways conventional friendship between the two men lasted some seventeen years, and though towards the end in Swinburne's most hectic and alcoholic period he neglected Powell, so that Powell had to write anxiously to Watts-Dunton for news of him, Powell's death brought Swinburne as near to grief as his egocentric nature allowed him to go and he wrote three of his *Century of Roundels* to his friend's memory.

The correspondence was started by Powell in November 1865 when he wrote to Swinburne, just then having his first real success with *Atalanta in Calydon*, to ask if he might make him joint dedicatee with Lord Dufferin of a volume of Icelandic legends in which he had collaborated with a Danish author. Swinburne agreed and when the book was delivered to him, with a photograph of the author, sent Powell a copy of *Chastelard* which had just been published. They planned to meet but as so often with Swinburne arrangements went wrong and it was not until April 1866 that they met, and even after doing so missed one another again and again in spite of letters and messages carried by page-boys. Their correspondence was on literary matters, the villainy of publishers and such, until after Swinburne's many-times-proposed visit to Powell in Wales in October. At Nant-Eos Powell's father was in possession for they stayed at a hotel and a nice period touch comes in a letter Swinburne wrote after his return to Henley: "Could you let Stephen inquire at the Queen's whether or not I left a shirt and collar behind me, which I know was packed by him, and unpacked, but the repacking in the morning was left to the waiter while I breakfasted in a fearful hurry—thanks to the inattention on the attendant's part—and on arriving here I found none? Per contra, I believe I did the busman out of his fare—6d—which he only came for when the train was starting and I could not get at it." After that they grew more intimate; Swinburne became 'always yours affectionately' and sent messages and a letter to a young man named George Butler O'Halloran, a friend of Powell's who was living with him at that time. Before the year was out Swinburne was on terms which enabled him to join his friend in maledictions on Powell's father whom he compared to Le Fanu's villainous character.

> As to your father, forget his existence—especially during an English November. It is clear to me that Uncle Silas was a comparatively desirable relative. Certainly during his too long life I think in your place I would *not* set foot in grounds which are his—until they become yours and regain their native attraction.

It was now that Powell's ruling passion for the music of Wagner began to be heard of and Swinburne wanted him to meet his brother Edward who was also, it seemed, a Wagnerian. Swinburne, who had no feeling for music except in his poetry, was certainly not. De Sade made his baleful entry in the correspondence, at first casually but later more seriously.

> I think your remarks on Justine the most sensible I ever heard. They quite give my own feelings, with which I never found any one to agree before. Usually that work is either a stimulant for an old beast or an emetic to a young man, instead of a valuable study to rational curiosity.

In the spring of 1867 there was a piece of hero-worshipping gush from Swinburne:

> I was most sorry to miss you *and* Mme. Schumann yesterday, but it could not be helped. (1) Your note only came that morning (2) I did not get it till about two P.M. (3) I had (and kept) an engagement for the evening which might have been risked by my starting so late for the Crystal Palace. You will not wonder at the care I took to keep it, when I tell you that it was an engagement to meet Mazzini. I did; I unworthy spent much of last night sitting at my beloved

chief's feet. He was angelically good to me. I read him my Italian poem all through and he accepted it in words I can't trust myself to try and write down.

This was part of Swinburne's not very convincing passion for revolution, anti-royalism, risings in Europe and particularly Italy. It is impossible to take for more than a kind of elaborate exhibitionism the revolutionary faith of a man who said it was *nice* to have something to love and believe in as he did in Italy. But he convinced himself that as a republican he was a terror and enjoyed shocking the Victorians with the passionate exuberance of his politics.

Before May, Powell seems to have taken into his care a chronic invalid named Charner who suffered throughout the year and died just before Christmas. No one has discovered who 'Charner' was—some beautiful phthisical youth, perhaps, with wide eyes already looking on eternity, or an ageing wasted one-time athlete who had been a hero of Powell's youth. Swinburne sent his best wishes for Charner's recovery—'between you and the sea he ought to get on well'. In his next letter, "I hope you both keep well, and that you will both pull on together for years yet."

In August, Powell, who was staying in Windsor to be near his (real) young cousin at Eton, obtained for Swinburne the birch mentioned on page 22, and received 'a thousand thanks' for it. But Charner was ill again and Swinburne sent 'all his wishes' for his better health. In September Swinburne wanted to run down for a few days and hoped Charner would 'keep up', but in November some mysterious circumstances arose the nature of which we are free to guess from Swinburne's note:

Very sorry to have missed you and to hear of the reason. I have just come from Mornington Crescent where I went for news and was glad to hear *you* were all right as of course I was rather alarmed by *possibilities.*

Then came Swinburne's letter of sympathy on the death of Charner.

In the next year Swinburne made a passing reference to his 'present possessor known to Britannia as Miss Menken', to him as Dolores, but he was soon back to a quotation from de Sade and showed his confidence in Powell by telling him of the house in St John's Wood: "My life has been enlivened of late by a fair friend who keeps a maison de supplices à la Rodin—There is occasional balm in Gilead!"

In August 1868 Swinburne went to stay with Powell at Entretat where he had a narrow escape from drowning, but in November he wrote, "I hope if you have to come we may meet and have a little fun before the year is out. I have found far from dry or chilling the Sadice-Paphian spring of St John's Wood whereof I once spoke to you."

Powell, in Paris, got a request from Swinburne to buy him a hair restorer recommended by Rossetti. "My hair was always so proverbially thick and curly that I don't want it thinned before its time." There is a not too ambiguous footnote to a letter from Swinburne after he had stayed with Powell in Wales again which may explain the attraction, for Powell at least, of that certain low-class inn in Aberystwyth—"Give my remembrances to my sailors." More revealing of Powell than of Swinburne is a passage from a letter in 1871:

> I wish you well through your bother about that wretched boy, whom I would commend to the notice of Father Clément did I know his address. Dean Buggeridge, I hear, is now in town—he has taken lodgings for the season in Quimlico. His work on the Cities of the Plain, their site, history, and remains, is now in the press. I regret to hear that his sermon on 'The Angels in Sodom' (Gen. xix. 4–10) is considered heretical in some quarters—too Broad (in fact) in its tone. It seems he condemns the conduct of Lot in offering his daughters to the men of Sodom as substitutes for his guests, as selfish and unfeeling, utterly wanting in social and patriotic spirit. 'Which of you my brethren,' he exclaims, 'would have taken a woman for a man—not to say, an angel?' The English Church Union intends to bring the matter before Convocation. Please tell Simeon of this when you next see him.

Throughout 1872 Swinburne was repeatedly asking Powell for small favours, to find him rooms, to recover an ivory paper-knife lost in a move, to investigate a carpenter's charges and arrange for the removal of a patent filter. Powell seems to have been patient and helpful.

When Simeon Solomon was sent to prison in 1873 Swinburne, as we have seen, counselled Powell against further association with him. Powell still had O'Halloran with him and another unidentified friend named Arnotts. He drew Swinburne's attention to an interview with Emerson in an American paper. In this Emerson "condemned Swinburne severely as a perfect leper and a mere sodomite, which criticism recalls Carlyle's scathing description of that poet—as a man standing up to his neck in a cesspool, and adding to its contents". Powell suggested a way of replying to this which would not show Swinburne as losing face. Swinburne turned out one of the most violent pieces of invective ever written and Powell had this transcribed, writing:

> Herewith the original and transcript, which I propose,—if you agree to it—to send to Woodroffe in N. York as an *extract from a letter*, to a friend, which you are quite willing to have published there. He will see to this, and your dignity will be in no way compromised.

In 1874 as the correspondence began to tail away into mere requests from Swinburne to Powell to order books and newspapers and do other small commissions; an accident to Powell startled Swinburne, for the first time, into using his friend's Christian name. But he was back to 'my dear Powell' again in the following year and in the few letters that remain. Swinburne enquired after Powell's father in the quaintest terms.

> I shall be anxious to know the upshot of your honoured parent's illness. If an all-wise Providence should see fit to remove him from this vale of tears to Abraham's bosom, I presume you will make a clean sweep of 'the cousinhood' and celebrate your accession by such orgies as shall make Nant Eos a worthy rival in reputation to the Château de Lacoste—seat of the noble house of Sade.

A sprained ankle kept Swinburne in bed for many weeks.

> I want some diversion as much as Nero ever did—and after the manner of that imperial Poet. I would give worlds for something—though it were but a drawing of my favourite school subject—to titillate my weary spirits.

When Powell had inherited Nant-Eos in August 1878 without having heard from Swinburne for many months, he wrote to Watts-Dunton:

> I am about to trouble you again—as in last Autumn—with a question or two of a confidential nature, concerning our dear Bard. *Where* is he, and *how* is he? Thrice have I written to Great James Street, and in all these cases quite without response. Nothing since Pickering (of Piccadilly), deposited at his door, from me, two portraits—Henry VIII and Elizabeth—forming exact pendants to his Mary Stuart.—Not a word of even the simplest acknowledgment! And Pickering assured me that he was then in town, and (like a canon of

the church) 'in residence'. Observe, my Dear Watts, that I am not *complaining*, but only seriously anxious about our friend. Has the old tempter seized him? Has—but let me group the crowd of questions that flash to my nibs, into one—what, in fact, is the matter with him?

Powell said in this letter that two doctors had given him up but that he was 'superior to the eternally quoted bay-tree'.

He died four years later. Swinburne's notice of this fact in a letter to Watts is somewhat flat and philosophical but it was now fifteen years or more since they had enjoyed that 'low inn' together and Swinburne, though staying with his mother just then, had been firmly under Watts-Dunton's care in Putney for three years now. His letter ran:

I am really very much grieved as well as startled by the news of poor George Powell's death. I can hardly realize the idea that I shall never see him again with whom I have spent so many days and weeks together and exchanged so many signs of friendship in past years. I had no notion that his health was seriously shaken, much less that his life was endangered. The poor fellow was one of the most obliging and kind-hearted of men, and wonderfully bright-spirited under severe trial and trouble. I shall always have a very tender and regretful remembrance of him. However, it is no use wailing.

But he wrote more feelingly to his sister in the following year.

. . . In reading 'Autumn and Winter' you will remember that my poor dear friend George Powell, the most unselfish, generous, gentle and kind and affectionate of men, died last year just about three months before Wagner—the man who was to him what Victor Hugo is to me. As soon as I heard of the latter's death, the fancy crossed me that poor George had gone before to announce his coming—one of the fancies that cross one's mind even when the heart is really and deeply moved—at least it is so with me.

Cecil Y. Lang thinks Powell was "by no means the best possible influence on Swinburne during the sixties and seventies, and it is fair to surmise that if Powell's premature death had not terminated the friendship, Watts would have intervened, tactfully, firmly, finally". This last may be true for Watts-Dunton discouraged many old associates. But it is equally arguable that Powell was one of the sincerest, least demanding and kindliest friends the poet had, and earned Swinburne's never very readily given gratitude again and again.

CHAPTER FOUR

Swinburne, Menken, Gosse and Watts-Dunton

JOHN THOMSON has been described as one of the mysteries of Swinburne's life and certainly the little information we have about this character is odd and contradictory. The sources for it are four. George R. Sims in his *Sixty Years of Recollections of Bohemian London* gives some small account of him, Edmund Gosse in the essay on Swinburne which he deposited in the British Museum quotes Sims and adds to his information, Swinburne makes a number of brief references to him in letters and addresses two letters to him, while his name occurs in letters from the publisher Hotten and in documents in the British Museum concerning Swinburne's transactions with Hotten.

From these the following pieces of information emerge and the reader is entitled to take his pick according to his own standards of credulity: (1) That he was son of the keeper of a lodging house near Dorset Square, in which Savile Clark lived, and was discovered by Clark and Swinburne reciting Milton in the basement. (2) That Swinburne stayed in the lodging house of Thomson's mother in Bloomsbury and took an interest in the boy and had him constantly with him. (3) That Thomson was a 'big-hearted young fellow with a fat baby face and large spectacles'. (4) That he became Swinburne's secretary. (5) That he introduced Swinburne to the house in St John's Wood in a street known to Swinburne as The Grove of the Evangelist in which the two 'golden-haired and rouge-cheeked ladies' flagellated the poet. (6) That he was part-proprietor of the establishment. (7) That his mother was the 'elder lady, very respectable' who according to Gosse 'welcomed the guests and took the money'. (It has been established by Cecil Y. Lang that, according to the Post Office Directory of 1876, Thomson's address was 7 Circus Road, St John's Wood.) (8) That Thomson introduced Swinburne to Adah Isaacs Menken. (9) That Swinburne introduced Thompson to Adah Isaacs Menken. (10) That Thomson intervened in Swinburne's disputes with Hotten and collected money for Swinburne from the publisher. (11) That he was asked, as Powell was, to obtain or send on books and undertake like missions to lodgings and shops. (12) That on one occasion Swinburne stayed with him, or at least told his parents he was doing so. (13) That Thomson's brothel in St John's Wood was a side-line while he was dramatic critic of the *Weekly Dispatch*, or *vice versa*. (14) That Thomson was acquainted with George Augustus Sala whom Swinburne greatly admired.

Beyond these nothing has been traced and it seems unlikely now that more will be heard of Thomson though he was certainly on terms of some intimacy with Swinburne, whatever the nature of those terms may have been.

If we could accept him as a cynical bawdy-house keeper there would be no difficulty about believing that he introduced Swinburne to Adah Isaacs Menken and so eliminate an improbable story that the meeting between Swinburne and the circus rider was the result of an earnest family conference called by Dante Rossetti who thought it would 'make a man' of Swinburne.

Menken was a grand creature physically, no longer very young and never very beautiful but with limbs called by her admirers statuesque. She was born Dolores McCord but the first of her five marriages was to a Jewish music-master Alexander Isaacs Menken and she kept his name which she used on the title-page of the pamphlets of verse she had printed. She had been actress, model and provincial *salonnière* but never openly a prostitute, and had travelled a great deal in the States and Europe. She had a special predilection for writers and in 1866 had a notorious affair with Alexandre Dumas the elder.

At the time she met Swinburne she was working a profitable racket in both the theatre and circus. Billed as The Naked Mazeppa she wore pink tights and had herself strapped to the back of a horse which ambled round circus ring or stage. The link with Byron—the act had originally started as a melodrama adapted from Byron by H. M. Milnes—was not appreciated by most of the audience, but its name caught the Victorians in their thousands and suggestive posters did the rest. The Americans had accorded Menken resounding and profitable applause for her daring—not so much in being jolted round a ring upside down but in using that title and appearing in flesh-coloured tights, and she had been encouraged to bring her act to Europe. She appeared in London at Astley's in 1864 and 1865, crossed several times to Paris, returned to the States and appeared in London again in 1866 and 1867, always repeating her performance. It was in the autumn of this last year that Swinburne met her, perhaps through the Pre-Raphaelites who thought her a 'stunner', perhaps through John Thomson, or perhaps by his own volition.

She appears to have been a kindly, vulgar, not unintelligent creature with a passion—the contemporary and it seems now the only word—for literature and literary men. Her own verse was lachrymose and deplorable but she was proud of it and felt her noisy reputation as a circus rider robbed her of the eminence due to her as a poetess. Swinburne was just what she wanted, a famous man of letters who appeared to adore her.

Perhaps he did, in some mystical totemistic way of his own. For here she was in person, his Belle Dame Sans Merci, his super-woman, his Dolores. With her lavish physique and her acceptance of the applause of multitudes she must have seemed to him his pitiless goddess.

Besides, he was proud of his achievement in attracting her attention. A photograph was taken of them together, the circus lady in costume sitting and little Swinburne standing beside her wearing a frock-coat and trying not to look diminutive. It is irresistibly funny, but both were proud of their association and circulated the picture so much among their friends that it was mentioned in the press and caused perturbation to Admiral Swinburne and his wife. Poet and equestrienne seem to have spent a good deal of time together, including several whole nights, but without any satisfactory result, Menken reporting to Dante Rossetti that she 'hadn't been able to get him up to scratch', and adding plaintively, "I can't make him understand that biting's no good."

It is improbable that she spoke in these earthy terms to Swinburne himself, for when he had one of his falls from a hansom cab and damaged his face so much that he kept away from her, Thomas Purnell reported to Swinburne:

> To-day I have had a letter from Dolores—such a letter! She fears you are ill; she is unable to think of anything but you; she wishes me to telegraph to her if you are in danger, and she will fly on the wings of the wind to nurse you. She has become a soft-throated serpent, strangling prayers on her white lips to kiss the poet, whose absence leaves her with ghosts and shadows. She concludes:
> 'Tell him all—say out my despairing nature to him—take care of his precious life. Write at once; believe in me and my holy love for him. Let him write one word in your letter. He will, for he is so good!'

Swinburne, on the other hand, spoke of her in letters as he spoke of other obsessions, like the flogging-block, with facetious humour.

"I must send you in a day or two", he wrote with cock-a-hoop satisfaction to Powell, "a photograph of my present possessor—known to Britannia as Miss Menken, to me as Dolores (her real Christian name)—and myself taken together." The 'present' possessor, with its naive attempt at the blasé, is revealing.

Menken died in Paris in the following year and Swinburne's words (in a letter to Powell) have been frequently quoted: "I am sure you were sorry on my account to hear of the death of my poor dear Menken—it was a great shock to me and a real grief—I was ill for some days. She was most lovable as a friend as well as a mistress." To read too much into the last word would be to gain a false impression. It may have been inserted for bravado, or 'mistress' may have had some special meaning for Swinburne derived from his obsessions. The whole abortive affair lasted only a few weeks and, although Menken has been foolishly called 'the only woman in Swinburne's life', and romanticized with other turgid phrases such as might have been quoted from her own verse, she was in fact a strip-tease artist a century before her time, the ex-wife of a number of sordid characters including a booth boxer, and her sentimental yearning after literature and poets bored

Swinburne who told Gosse that she woke him up early in the morning and insisted on reading her poetry to him, swinging her handsome legs on the edge of the bed. She may have obliged him by some Sadic pantomime; she certainly could not obtain—as she complained to Rossetti—any normal response from him.

2

If Swinburne could offer no rewards to women he could put literary snobs in fevers of jealousy by the unguarded improvidence of his bachelor life, and two men competed for his possession (though not of course in any physical sense). Here was a poet of mixed but clamorous reputation, a publicized and controversial figure, the sort of man whom any literary hanger-on would like to introduce as 'my friend Swinburne'. He lived unprotected by any proprietary female, an alcoholic, an eccentric and a genius who demanded to be looked after by his friends and repaid it by the scintillating hysteria of his conversation. Small wonder that Edmund Gosse and Theodore Watts-Dunton both wanted in some sense to appropriate him.

The warfare between them was mortal and undecisive, going to and fro with victories and defeats though no fire was openly exchanged between them. At first it was Gosse, the young literary aspirant who sent Swinburne his poems to criticize and flattered him in the most fulsome terms, who held the stronger position, then Watts-Dunton, no less devoted but more practical who extricated Swinburne by his prowess as a lawyer from the intolerable situation into which he had fallen with a difficult publisher and made Swinburne call him 'last in date among my closest friends but certainly not least in my love and trust and gratitude'. Gosse retaliated by throwing his house open to Swinburne who came to regard Delamere Terrace where Gosse lived with his young wife as a second home. "He would call and remain for hours at a time", wrote Evan Charteris in his *Life and Letters of Sir Edmund Gosse*. "On one occasion he arrived obviously unwell, complaining that he was suffering from a surfeit of mineral waters. He remained for three days desperately ill, watched over by Gosse and Mrs Gosse in turns. He was completely at ease in the Gosses' home, sometimes gentle, exhausted, silent, sometimes ecstatic, or voluble and inspired as the mood drove him. Of an evening spent at Delamere

Terrace, Gosse wrote: 'When he and I were alone he closed up to the fire: his great head bowed, his knees held tight together and his finger-tips pressed to his chest, in what I call his "penitential" attitude, and he began a long tale, plaintive and rather vague, about his loneliness, the sadness of his life, the suffering he experiences from the slanders of others.' He was privileged, he was under no social compulsion; humoured by Gosse, he became domesticated, his ways were understood, his whims catered for."•

This was ended by a master-stroke from Watts-Dunton who, finding Swinburne almost at the point of death from alcoholism and other ills, carried him off to his sister's house at Putney and later, after Swinburne had somewhat recovered and spent some time with his mother, made a home for himself and the poet at Putney in which Swinburne stayed for the remaining thirty years of his life, undisturbed by Watts-Dunton's marriage at the age of seventy-three and four years before Swinburne's death.

At this 'incarceration' of Swinburne at Putney Gosse raged, particularly when he found himself excluded, without open rudeness but firmly, from the poet's presence. He revenged himself by creating a picture of life at Number Two, The Pines, which endures to this day. Swinburne, a singing-bird whose wings have been clipped and voice strangled, is dominated by a country solicitor with ridiculous pretensions to literature, 'bullied by the old horror of Putney' as Gosse said, adding that Watts-Dunton had a 'rattlesnake fascination over him'. Gosse's friends T. J. Wise and Max Beerbohm assisted this with descriptions of Watts-Dunton's anxious and absurd paternalism, Wise's pedestrian but Beerbohm's unforgettably brilliant. When Gosse came to write the book which Watts-Dunton was too old or too lazy to write, his *Life of Swinburne*, he tried at first, through the mediation of Wise, to exchange for Watts-Dunton's knowledge the benefits to Watts-Dunton of a favourable interpretation of him, but failing in this produced a portrait, after Watts-Dunton's death, which shows only too plainly the depth of his hatred. He did not live to see the exposure of his friend and associate T. J. Wise as a forger and a fraud,••

• *The Life and Letters of Sir Edmund Gosse* by The Hon. Evan Charteris, K.C., 1931.

•• Gosse's long association and collaboration with Wise argues either that his literary judgment was blindly at fault or that he assisted in Wise's fraudulence. There is no other explanation.

or to read in Georges Lafourcade's *Swinburne: A Literary Biography* that author's understanding appreciation of Watts-Dunton's good qualities, so must have felt, as he spoke about Watts-Dunton's 'lies' to the end of his life, that the last word had been with him.

Both men, Gosse and Watts, deserve more study than they have received, for Watts-Dunton has been considered only as an elderly nursemaid to Swinburne and when Evan Charteris wrote his life of Gosse he seems to have been unaware of the salient fact emerging from a letter from Gosse to John Addington Symonds which is printed by Phyllis Grosskurth in her book about the last-named. For years Symonds had hoped Gosse would admit to fellow-feeling in the great problem of his life, set out in *A Problem in Modern Ethics* and *A Problem in Greek Ethics*, and at last, in 1890, Gosse wrote that he knew it all, the solitude, the rebellion, the despair. Years ago he had wanted to write to Symonds about this but withdrew through cowardice. He had had a fortunate life but there had been this obstinate twist in it. He had reached a quieter time—the wild beast is tamer but not dead. Now he understands him and the trick of his claws.

Charteris does not conceal Gosse's friendships with others with this 'obstinate twist', like Symonds himself, Robert Ross, E. F. Benson, Walt Whitman and the rest, but his long biography, written without apparent knowledge of, or reference to, this somewhat anomalous truth about his subject could not do him justice.

Lafourcade speaks of Watts-Dunton as a pathetic figure, yet pathos was more evident in Gosse. Son of a schoolteacher and preacher in Hackney, he lost his mother when he was six and lived with his studious puritannical father who became a scientist of some repute. Gosse feared and loved him and in the one book by which he may be remembered *Father and Son* he gives a full and moving account of their unusual relationship. At seventeen he came to London to work at the British Museum and from that time on became a resolute, an indefatigable literary aspirant, determined to meet men of letters, determined to write, determined to succeed. He published (in the way of most literary aspirants of that time and others) collections of poems at his own expense and sent them to eminent writers. He became a critic, a contributor to learned journals and translator to the Board of Trade. His earnings from writing increased yearly but he was 'hanging by my eyelids to the outer cliff of fame', consumed by unsureness of himself and his scholarship, aware that it lacked any sure academic foundation. He edited indefatigably, wrote *Gray* for the *English Men of Letters* Series, wrote *Seventeenth Century Studies* and lectured in America. What he lacked in scholarship he made up for in a pleasant and enthusiastic approach and was beginning to feel more self-confidence when he was suddenly confounded by an attack from a former friend.

To realize the force of this it must be remembered that in the 1880s literature was for only a small proportion of the population but that those who professed devotion to it did so with earnestness, even fanaticism. Every controversy in every quarterly, monthly or weekly review was followed eagerly and reputations were made by the almost omnipotent editors of these publications. 'Attacks', 'Replies', 'Commentaries' were studied with fierce prejudice and a minor reputation could be killed outright by a clever and hostile critic.

Gosse had published a book with the Cambridge University Press which had a grandiose title *From Shakespeare to Pope: An Inquiry into the Causes and Phenomena of the Rise of Classical Poetry in England.* Perhaps his appointment to the Clark Lectureship in English Literature at Cambridge had gone to his head, or perhaps he underrated other literary historians since he wrote to his step-mother that the subject had scarcely been touched. At all events his scholarship was not equal to it and the book contained a number of bloomers. These appear to have been unnoticed by reviewers but when the October number of the *Quarterly Review* came out it contained an article by John Churton Collins, a Balliol man and a scholar of considerable reputation who had been a guest at Gosse's home.

After some generalizations about 'the spurious wares of literary charlatans' he said of *From Shakespeare to Pope* that 'not the least mischievous characteristic of which is the skill with which its worthlessness is disguised'. After this he had to produce some pretty heavy ammunition but he had it ready. Gosse had apparently not known whether the *Arcadia* of Sidney and the *Oceana* of Harrington were in prose or verse. He had confused James Harrington the prose writer with Sir John Harrington the poet born half a century earlier. He had described Henry More's *Psychozoia* as an epic poem. He had dated Hobbes's translation of Homer twelve years earlier than Dryden's *Annus Mirabilis* though it began to be published seven years after it.

He had confused Shaftesbury of the *Cabal* with Shaftesbury of the *Characteristics* and George Savile Lord Halifax with Henry Savile, and been guilty of many more careless blunderings.

It was a reasoned and documented attack which no writer who depended on his scholarship could survive, and as such Gosse did not survive it. He wrote a confused reply trying to make the quarrel a personal one by saying that Collins had been his guest, but he never swam in such deep waters again and to the end of his life was touchy and opinionated with an over-bearing self-assurance which revealed his inner insecurity. He was made librarian to the House of Lords and expected that his tenure of office would be extended beyond the age prescribed for retirement but he had behaved with such familiarity among the Peers that some considered him to show effrontery and the Clerk of the Parliaments insisted on the enforcement of the Superannuation Rule. He became in his old age a panjandrum, a diner-out, a name-dropper, critic to a Sunday newspaper, aspiring to Grand Old Manhood as he had once aspired to recognition as a young poet.

That he defeated Watts-Dunton in the ghoulish fight over the corpse of Swinburne as Watts-Dunton had defeated him in the poet's lifetime is true, but it may well be that posterity will find it owes the greater debt to the dull little lawyer who saved Swinburne's life.

Dull? He must have seemed so, even to Swinburne in the first months of their acquaintance. For the conviction is irresistible that Watts-Dunton suffered from that most unhappy of all human disabilities, more isolating and cruel even than Swinburne's deafness, he was a man without charm. No one of the writers who have remembered him has ever said an affectionate thing about him, and, though many have paid tribute to his sterling qualities, his loyalty, his competence, his sincerity, his generosity with time and effort, no one has said he liked Watts-Dunton or found him good company, or was in any way attracted to him. Promoted by Gosse there has been plenty of ridicule thrown at him, his walrus moustache, his somewhat pompous manner, his awed consideration for Swinburne in front of others and his power over him in private, but never a hint of interest in the strange creature himself or in what made him write poetry, love gypsies, devote himself to writers at the expense of his own career or write that curious, so nearly splendid best-selling novel *Aylwin*.

The truth, perhaps, was that like many outwardly dull people he was an intense romantic. Brought up to follow his father in his legal practice in Huntingdonshire, he read Borrow and became his disciple in gypsy lore, met Rossetti and the Pre-Raphaelites and eagerly made himself useful to them as the man of affairs they so urgently needed and finally, at the age of forty, threw up his country practice and settled in London, drawn by idealistic cravings which perhaps none of them suspected. He loved mystery for its own sake and read and talked—and later wrote—of the gnostics. He was welcomed by the erratic brotherhood of Pre-Raphaelites not as a fellow writer but as a wise counsellor who undertook to straighten out their confused affairs. Watts the Wise they called him and doubtless laughed at him among themselves, but he was getting what he wanted, he was accepted among writers and artists and achieving a position as a critic. (He was writing regularly for the *Athenaeum* when he met Swinburne).

At first, so Gosse says, he failed to attract Swinburne's notice, for in Lafourcade's words he was provincial and middle-class while Swinburne was aristocratic and cosmopolitan. But he persisted and 'straightened out' Swinburne in his publishing affairs as he had done the rest of the group, and though Swinburne was cagey towards him and only after a year suggested 'we might begin mutually to drop the Mr in writing as friends' his gift for giving sound advice eventually triumphed. Swinburne fought hard for his independence and more than once snubbed Watts-Dunton for his efforts, but, when Swinburne's crisis came in June 1879, Watts-Dunton was ready to take over the pitiful remains of Swinburne who had not eaten for three days. A little conspiracy with the poet's mother over a legacy completed the plot and Watts-Dunton found himself in possession.

Many have wondered why Swinburne succumbed to that benevolent tutelage, but a more valid question concerns Watts-Dunton's part in it. What made a man, who had his private ambitions, his by no means negligible abilities, his natural passions and share of self-conceit, dedicate no less than thirty years of his life to the care of a precariously reformed alcoholic whose friends abused him for his pains and whose family regarded him, however necessary he was to their peace of mind, as a common interloper? It is true that towards the end of that time he married, but nobody can guess what sacrifices he made in the meantime for *Aylwin* is the book of a full-blooded man half in love with his heroine. He never expressed any pride in what he had done or any self-pity for himself; he seems to have acted under compulsion, but his motives can only have been altruistic. The man loved literature and believed that Swinburne was the supreme living poet so that no sacrifice was too great. The truth of this has been, I think, too simple and too grand to be recognized and it has been more comfortable for several generations to see in Watts-Dunton a literary snob rather than a diffident hero to whom we owe not only Swinburne's later work, such as it is, but the completion and revision of *Tristram* and *Mary Stuart*. Who is to say there would have been more great poetry in Swinburne if he had continued to live on a diet of alcoholism and de Sade? And then surely Swinburne's own health and happiness count for something, or are we to expect all poets to die young to save us from bemoaning mealy-mouthed the inferiority of their later work?

As we saw Swinburne with his blaze of red hair skipping about Oxford with the Pre-Raphaelites, we can see him, an active sexagenarian, taking his walk across the Common, slipping into the Rose and Crown for a quick one while Watts-Dunton was safely at home, an old deaf man to whom his friend had taught habits of punctuality and orderliness in dress. Photographs show that the beard was no longer the thin straggle of his youth and now hid the weak chin. He still walked vigorously and to some visitors, carefully selected by Watts-Dunton, he broke out in conversation with such fire that Watts-Dunton would sweat with alarm and indicate to their caller that Swinburne should be left to cool off.

All this has been depicted many times and the books and pictures at The Pines have been listed, while the exterior of the house with its little oblong garden has been described. But no one has been able to say much of the domestic life of these two old gentlemen and no one has even tried to imagine their conversation when alone. That they never used one another's Christian names is known and understandable—Algernon and Theodore made an intimidating combination—while nicknames, even after a quarter of a century of daily association would have been unthinkable to them. Swinburne in a letter to Watts-Dunton once facetiously called himself 'your minor', so it may be that Watts-Dunton sometimes indulged him in his schoolboy fantasies, but it is more likely that for the ten or eleven thousand days of their life together their greeting over the Victorian breakfast table was 'Good morning, Swinburne' and 'Good morning, Watts-Dunton'.

Were there stern headshakings when Swinburne wanted a second glass of claret when a guest came to lunch? We know that there were readings from Dickens—did Watts-Dunton confide passages from *Aylwin*? What servants did they employ—loyal, kindly women who understood their quirks, or greedy sluts who gave them the food they liked themselves? Were they comfortable, in fact? Were they interested in comfort?

Nothing in his letters suggests that Swinburne longed for his former dissolute freedom or resented Watts-Dunton's rules for his reform, and with time he was weaned from all his old associations. Wisely Watts-Dunton gave him his head in political thought and writing but was delighted to find that although his vigour of expression remained unimpaired his opinions grew milder. He had never been an agnostic but as a young man was savagely anti-God as he was anti-Royalty. He believed in Heaven but wanted it to be a Republic as he wanted European countries to be. In his last years he became reconciled even with the reign of Victoria. He still enjoyed his own eloquence in writing on a diversity of subjects. He may have become a disgruntled, irritable, lonely old man but he was not bored and he was not tragic.

PART TWO

John Addington Symonds and the Greek Ideal

CHAPTER FIVE

Symonds and Five Schoolmasters

PHYLLIS GROSSKURTH's *John Addington Symonds*• makes literary history for it is the first biography which discusses a homosexual without fuss, without puzzlement or affected horror, and without the smallest reserve. The only regret one can feel about it is that the author has such sympathy for the unhappy man whose life she relates that she does not appear to see him as sometimes unlikeable and often ludicrous.

At Harrow, for instance, he must have been a most odious boy. The son of a successful, intellectual and Nonconformist doctor he had been coached to a point in advance of boys older than himself. His cousins, also older boys, had amused themselves by letting him masturbate them in turn and this gave him erotic daydreams about a circle of brawny sailors whom he had to satisfy. Yet at Harrow the healthy bawdiness of childhood and the playful bullock-like love-making between boys inexpressibly shocked him.

He was thus doubly a prig. His intellectual precocity gave him immediate relief from fagging and made him view other pupils and most masters as boors. He was 'amused' at the ignorance of the Sixth

• *John Addington Symonds: A Biography* by Phyllis Grosskurth, 1964.

Form on historical subjects, he wrote home, and felt contempt for most of the masters, and considered that the school 'corrupted his moral sense'. Himself the victim of frequent boils and styes, with an acute stammer, he played no games and for a long time made no friends. He was evidently not a boy to attract much affection but later a pretty chattering boy called Alfred Pretor went about with him and competed with him for the Headmaster's Scholarship. Symonds won this, Pretor coming third, and it automatically made him Head of the School. It is not surprising that the previous Head of the School whose place he had usurped kicked him and Pretor down the stairs of the Great School, or that Symonds immediately ran to the headmaster to report this. He was afterwards ragged by juniors who imitated his voice when he called for a fag, all of which, from his high level of learning, he regarded as beneath contempt.

He felt much the same about the youthful lechery which was popular at Harrow just then. Reading the *Phaedrus* and *Symposium* of Plato he discovered that he had an ideal conception of love which had nothing to do with rollicking in the dormitories, a love between men different from the sordid unfeeling lust of his schoolmates. This caused him to steal and keep sentimentally the hymn-book of an attractive boy, but not to speak to him.

High-minded, artificially religious, emotional, Symonds had succeeded at the age of seventeen in repressing while at school the animal instincts he knew himself to possess, partly from natural squeamishness, partly out of fear and affection for his father. It was therefore unfortunate for the headmaster of Harrow, who was so much infatuated with Pretor that he wrote him love letters, that this clever but indiscreet boy should have confided in Symonds, revealing a state of things not to be reconciled with the 'ideal love' of Plato's *Symposium.*

Dr Charles John Vaughan was one of the most successful headmasters in Harrovian history. He had been a favourite pupil of the great Arnold of Rugby whose muscular Christianity he had introduced to Harrow together with a stronger version of the monitorial system. He had purged the school of the quite heavy drinking and gambling under his predecessor and increased its numbers from sixty to four hundred and sixty-nine. He had the gift—which made Symonds call him a hypocrite—of making any boy addressed feel that *his* affairs were all that concerned him; he had enormous influence over his senior boys, as

Arnold had, and he was a fine-looking man with frank eyes and a noble profile.

There is no reason to think he could be called vicious. His affair with the attractive young Pretor was a tickling, caressing, sentimental thing rather than a seduction. He was a patter, a stroker, a hugger, perhaps a kisser who might be charged with gross indecency but not with what the press call euphemistically 'serious offences'.

During the Christmas holidays of 1857–58 Pretor wrote to Symonds telling him, perhaps not without a touch of pride, of what Dr Vaughan felt about him. When Symonds expressed doubt Pretor showed him the headmaster's love-letters. Symonds thought over this and 'trembled with agitation' when he was alone with Dr Vaughan, but kept the secret for eighteen months till he was on a reading party from Oxford with a don and famous classical scholar named Conington. Of him Phyllis Grosskurth says that 'while scrupulously correct in his own conduct, he was sympathetic towards the infatuations of young men as long as any physical element was suppressed'. Perhaps Symonds overrated that sympathy for one evening, without having told Pretor of his intention, he gave Conington the story. Conington evidently felt that in this case his proviso about the physical element had been flouted and sent Symonds back to his home at Clifton to report the whole matter to his father.

This was just the job for Dr Symonds, a man of impregnable self-righteousness, rich, influential and sternly intolerant. He wrote at once to Vaughan demanding his resignation on pain of exposure, ignored Vaughan's immediate visit and that of his pleading wife—a Bishop's daughter—and insisted that he should leave Harrow at the end of the following term.

Young Symonds convinced himself with some tortuous rationalization that he had done the right thing. Falling back on his father's strength, he decided that Vaughan had encouraged vice at Harrow and he determined to suppress all such tendencies in himself. Pretor's contempt for his treachery expressed in letters to two school friends was icy and enduring—none of the three ever spoke to him again.

Vaughan left Harrow heartbroken but there was no public scandal. It is difficult not to find some animus in Dr Symonds's conduct, however, for he pursued the wretched Vaughan with threats of exposure to the end of his own life. He permitted him to become Vicar of Doncaster where he made his chief task preparing young men for

Ordination, but when Vaughan accepted Lord Palmerston's offer of the Bishopric of Rochester Dr Symonds rushed off a telegram and the unfortunate man had to resign. It was not until after Dr Symonds's death that he ventured to become Master of the Temple and Dean of Llandaff.

This episode during Symonds's schooldays does not seem to have had any lasting effect. By taking his father's side with a sense of virtue, he continued to persuade himself that Vaughan's influence was corrupt and he clung to this to defend his own conduct in betraying him, even after he himself had begun to have affairs with young boys.

The first of these was not long in coming for during his last holidays from Harrow he fell violently in love with a tailor's son of fourteen who sang in the choir of Bristol Cathedral. He found out where he lived, wrote anonymously for his photograph to be sent to a GPO address and finally met him secretly in the cloisters of the cathedral. In his last term at Harrow he thought perpetually of him and neglected his studies to read of passionate male friendships in Greek literature, his interest in Willie Dyer turning the boys of Harrow, hitherto oafs, into beautiful swimmers and graceful cricketers. But it was more than a year before he kissed the boy—in Leigh Woods.

Once again he broke confidence and told his father something of what he felt and Dr Symonds, who by now must have realized a little about his son's make-up, calmly exacted a promise from Symonds to break off the relationship which thereafter became clandestine, continuing for a total of three years and inspiring some sickly verses called *What Might Have Been*.

The love we might have known, if we
Had turned this way instead of that;
The lips we might have kissed, which he
For whom they parted, pouted at.

It might have continued longer if Symonds had not fallen for another Bristol chorister, a more knowing and realistic character named Alfred Brooke, a boy who understood Symonds's desires and was somewhat bored by the etherealized form they took. Symonds recognized this and it made his Greek ideals difficult to maintain, so that seeing the boy pass his window he wrote more verses—

Before the house with wondering wide blue eye
That said, 'O wait.' Why will you not reply?

It is hard to know whether Symonds was remembering Willie Dyer or Alfred Brooke when later he wrote (and included in his book of essays *In the Key of Blue* in 1892, the year before he died) a lyrical piece with insertions in verse called *Clifton and a Lad's Love*. The verses must surely have been written while still at Oxford and it was an obstinate perversity which made Symonds publish them without explanation among nostalgic prose descriptions of his native country.

He was all beautiful: as fair
As summer in the silent trees;
As bright as sunshine on the leas
As gentle as the evening air.

It is embarrassing stuff to read now and can have seemed little better in the Nineties.

It is not for the love of God
That I have done my soul this wrong;
'Tis not to make my reason strong
Or curb the currents of my blood.

But sloth, and fear of men, and shame
Impose their limit on my bliss:
Else I had laid my lips to his,
And called him by love's dearest name.

Willie or Alfred? Or a composite memory of both? There is worse to come.

I saw a vision of deep eyes
In morning sleep when dreams are true:
With humid eyes of lazy blue
Like seas that kiss the horizon skies.

Then as I gazed I felt the rain
Of soft warm curls around my cheek,
And heard a whisper low and meek
"I love, and canst thou love again?"

A gentle youth beside me bent
His cool moist lips to mine were pressed . . .

And so on. It is difficult not to remember that prickly beard.

Meanwhile he formed an erotic friendship with a fellow undergraduate named G. H. Shorter. Symonds had entered Balliol College as a Commoner in 1858 and in the following year Shorter came up from Rugby, a plump little queer with long yellow curls. The two made love and quarrelled and wrote one another poems and letters, but Shorter was frankly pederastic and tired of Symonds sending him verses addressed to the Shepherd Hymenaeus by Hesperus and all the exalted lyricism of Symonds's ideal love.

When Symonds obtained a Fellowship at Magdalen Shorter was delighted for he was hot in pursuit of a Magdalen choirboy and in coming to Symonds's rooms at Magdalen to be coached in philosophy he expected to find opportunities, so Symonds maintained, of obtaining what he wanted. This seems highly improbable on the face of it and it is likelier that their quarrel was over the choirboy himself. (Choirboys seem to have been natural prey for the pederasts of the 1860s as Boy Scouts have been in later decades.) Symonds in these earlier years played such tricks of self-justification and rationalization that his interpretations of his own conduct are not to be trusted. But he certainly told Shorter not to come to his rooms again and Shorter in fury took a mean and bitter revenge. He put together in a tell-tale sequence the letters and poems Symonds had written to him and sent off copies of them to six of the Magdalen Fellows.

There was, of course, a blazing row. Oxford, no less than Cambridge, was only too aware in these decades of the air of 'corrupt Greek ethics' which was discernible in the books and lives of several of their leading Classics men, of the exaggerated brotherliness among undergraduates which some saw as the fruit of Arnold's Rugbeian muscular Christianity and others attributed to the 'unhealthiness' of Ritualism. But for the moment Symonds rode the storm. He was exonerated by a general meeting at Magdalen and though he was censured for the 'bad taste' of some of his letters and poetry. But he decided to leave Oxford, had a nervous breakdown and from then onwards followed the life of a semi-invalid. But also he determined, he said in his journal, to become 'a natural man'.

This determination he took seriously and for six years seems to have renounced the urgings of his own nature, though he continued to read and talk of the subject which was to be an obsession for the rest of his life, while his most intimate friends throughout the period were a couple of queer schoolmasters, Arthur Sidgwick and Henry Dakyns in whom he confided the progress of his struggle.

This was a period in which the pederasty of schoolmasters, sometimes sublimated, sometimes expressed in clandestine caresses and indiscreet letters, and sometimes fully exploited, caused a number of scandals in the schools, two of which as we shall see became common knowledge while others, in less publicized foundations, were tactfully manipulated without open disgrace. The teaching profession before Arnold in the days of birch and bottle men, the indecent sadism of public thrashings for which boys were stripped or exposed, the convention that all events at school were shielded by the conditions of masonry and schoolboy honour and could in *no* circumstances be revealed to parents, produced a good deal of raw vice in boarding schools in which many of the ushers were involved. Following Dr Arnold, himself an upright man of unassailable character, there had entered the profession a new type of pedagogue, or a new form of behaviour, in which the brotherly love allowable to fellow Christians received an anomalous interpretation and righteous men, leading their pupils to God, formed intimacies with them or allowed themselves favourites with whom they dallied on the pilgrims' way.

Symonds was not a schoolmaster but his life till now had been passed in scholastic circles and with his memories of Dr Vaughan he saw the danger of this, both moral and practical. He believed that any scandal would kill his father and he knew how narrowly he had escaped a serious one in the Shorter affair. He had no illusions about his own nature but he believed that, whatever the cost to himself, he must repress it. He was to outlive his passionate interest in young boys and achieve less perilous and culpable relationships, but he had no idea of this at the time and considered that all his desires were, in the strictest sense of the word, pederastic. His resolution was not without nobility and, though it broke down even before his father's death, for a time he fought his own tendencies with manful singleness of purpose.

His father, conscious or not of what was going on in the mind of his brilliant son, helped him by sending him abroad. On one of these visits, when accompanied by an Oxford friend, he first met the girl he was later to marry, Catherine North. She had no sooner returned to England than he decided to pursue a picturesque fifteen-year-old in peasant costume, the niece of Swiss innkeepers at Mürren. He was as nearly attracted to her as he could be to a woman but was rejected as a cultured foreigner.

His efforts to be 'a natural man' and fall in love with a woman were aided by his oculist, Dr Spencer Wells, who told him that his eye trouble and other disorders were caused by repressed sexual instincts and advised either a hired mistress or a wife. His father was pathetically anxious that Symonds should marry and Symonds decided to seek out Catherine North, the English girl he had met at Mürren. With quiet calculation he made up his mind to marry her, followed her about in London and abroad, and eventually secured her agreement. He married her in his twenty-fifth year and during this period the first two of his daughters were born.

All this he confided in letters, which were often written daily, to Henry Dakyns and less frequently to Arthur Sidgwick. Dakyns with the inevitable beard of the period, with thick youthful hair parted at the side and an expression of interest and surprise, was a classics master at the then recently founded Clifton College. Arthur Sidgwick, the younger brother of a remarkable scholar of the time named Henry Sidgwick, was a master at Rugby and was always called good-looking. In return for Symonds's confidences about his own state of mind, his health, his changing view of God and himself, his struggle to be 'a natural man' and his marriage, these two told him of their difficulties with favourite pupils.

Dakyns's, at Clifton, was named Cecil Boyle and it caused Symonds much jealousy and self-pity when Dakyns took him to Mentone instead of passing some of his holiday with Symonds. 'It is very weary, this head of mine, and I want to lean it on your shoulder', Symonds complained, but devoted as Dakyns was to him a trip abroad with 'Cecy' was not to be resisted.

Arthur Sidgwick caused Symonds anxiety of another kind because his boy friend at Rugby seems to have been less reliable than 'Cecy' and Symonds was apprehensive lest the affair expose his friend to 'external danger'. The love between Arthur and his unnamed favourite was not, Symonds said, 'Greek' and if it had been it was not the sort of thing Plato would have allowed. It was not 'established in modern society' but would be called 'romantic, sentimental, effeminate, on the verge of vice'. It was not based on 'intellectural sympathy' or 'moral good' or 'consentaneity of tastes', but was chiefly 'aesthetical enjoyment and the pleasure of highly refined sensuousness'. And so on. Symonds, in his new virtue as a married man, wrote endless lectures to his friends.

He had temptations to resist himself. Another friend, Roden Noel, described by Phyllis Grosskurth as a 'practising invert', tried to persuade him to join him on forays to queer meeting-places, of which London in the 1860s was not devoid. Often Symonds would rise early to reach the Serpentine while naked swimmers could still be seen there or visit swimming baths later in the day. And on one occasion, as if to show that the personnel of male prostitution has not changed much in a century, Symonds was thrown into a tizzy by being accosted by a Grenadier Guardsman. Leaving the Century Club one midnight in the spring of 1865 he turned down a passage leading from Trafalgar Square to Leicester Square and was approached by the man wearing, Symonds noticed, his scarlet uniform. Symonds, in an opera cape, must have seemed obvious to the Guardsman for he made his proposals quite unreservedly. At first Symonds did not fully grasp these; when he did so he hurried away. He was drawn to the big fellow who followed him for some distance mentioning an address to which he could take him, but resisted the opportunity. The whole story was confided to Dakyns in a letter next day. It was not until twelve years later that Symonds deliberately sought such contacts as this; at twenty-five, a young married man and a father, he was horrified by them.

2

Two other 'Arcadian' schoolmasters (as the phrase was at the time), less fortunate than Dakyns and Sidgwick, had some part in Symonds's life, though one of them, William Johnson (Cory), he never met and the other, Oscar Browning, though a lifelong acquaintance never became a close friend. Both taught at Eton and both were dismissed summarily.

Round the memory of William Johnson, who changed his name to Cory when he left Eton, there hangs a faint fragrance of old gardens and the Thames, an echo of the *Eton Boating Song* which he wrote. He loved his pupils too well, but they in turn, and those who had been most intimate with him, revered his memory for the rest of their, mostly distinguished, lives. He was not a great poet but he achieved some of the most memorable lines of English verse. Who could forget his *Heraclitus* with its catch-in-the-throat quality of sunset colour and musical regret:

They told me, Heraclitus, they told me you were dead,
They brought me bitter news to hear and bitter tears to shed.
I wept, as I remembered, how often you and I
Had tired the sun with talking and sent him down the sky.

He was a soft-voiced, short-sighted man, clean-shaven at a time when that was an eccentricity, secretly shy until quite late in life, particularly of women, with a feminine adoration of his pupils whom he hero-worshipped throughout their lives.

The son of an indigo planter who had made money in India, he was sent to Eton from his Devon home and returned to Eton as a master soon after a brilliant Cambridge career while still only twenty-two years old. He was daunted by the disorderliness of the place, the large classes and the ragging he underwent but his modest obliging nature, with mild oddities of appearance and habit at first amused the boys, then slowly attracted affection and with time—he taught at Eton for twenty-seven years—he became a character, and a beloved one, and an inspired teacher of individual boys.

He was forever surrounded by boys, in term-time and vacation, and the 'court' he kept, a peculiarly Anglo-Saxon thing, was of a kind familiar to many men who have been through an English education, or examined parochial life, or seen the workings of youth clubs, Boy Scout organizations and such. Men who in a sometimes paradoxical phrase are 'good with boys', usually suffering from that kind of arrested development which gives them intense sympathy with the interests of teenagers, become unnaturally popular because of this, are even loved in a half derisory way, and give their energies, their enthusiasm and their time to the service of the boys who respond to them. Their instincts are often repressed and their influence, especially when they are intelligent schoolmasters, may be a valuable one, for no one else can so readily understand the urgent problems of pubescence. But all too often the thing becomes emotional, sentimental, silly and occasionally vicious.

These little circles, forming round a curate or a schoolmaster, at their worst become seraglios with particular favourites and jealousies, but are usually conducted with outward heartiness, jolly nicknames to recall the characteristics or achievements of particular boys, legends about what happened at camp last year, all with a great deal of laughter and cheerful ragging in which the man-boy at the centre is a ringleader.

Although it must have had its precedents in former times, perhaps among the pages of great mediaeval households or in the gymnasiums of ancient Greece, in its present form it goes back no more than a century to the reformed Public School of the Victorian age.

William Johnson was far too intelligent and fastidious a man to have been guilty of the worst of such sentimentalities but during his years as a master at Eton he built up an aristocratic version of it and his perpetually changing circle of devotees had many of its characteristics. A succession of pupils adored him and in those days of parental *hauteur*, when many fathers regarded their sons as beneath their outward notice, creatures to be brought up on the strictest principles and to be severely disciplined by schoolmasters as in their own youth they had been, this led to dangerously intense affection for a man temporarily in authority over them, who yet listened to their problems, received their most intimate confidences and loved them without concealing his love. One biographer of Johnson has suggested that the jealousy this roused in parents may have accounted for Johnson's downfall.

He was never tired of them. He organized river parties for them which sometimes brought them back to Eton as late as eleven o'clock at night. He took them abroad in the holidays or had them to stay with him at his Devonshire home. He worked indefatigably as their tutor and was proud of their scholarship. He saw great careers for them and expected to be consulted on these. He wrote poems for them and about them, and textbooks (in which schools were then deficient) to help their studies. Unable because of his weak sight to join their sports he watched these with an eager and unflagging interest and wrote poems about them like the *Eton Boating Song*, the mournful tune and dated words of which are shouted by Etonians to this day. He wanted gratitude from them and affection but had a shy detestation of flattery. Few of them ever forgot him and he lived in their affections to the end of his life. In their stove-pipe hats or loose flannels they surrounded him, a little mockingly and with more affection than formal respect. He stayed at their homes, many of which were great English houses, and was treated by their parents as one of the boys themselves rather than as a guest of mature years. He gave his life to them both at Eton and for some time after he had left.

He was not, it seems from the recollections of many about him, a man of the world. Except for some sightseeing abroad and for holidays in Devon he scarcely left Eton and, although he heard the conversation of statesmen and church dignitaries in his pupils' homes, his views were elementary, prejudiced and unreal on politics and religion. But this in itself endeared him to the immature minds of his pupils who preferred his boyish opinions to those of their eminent parents. No witticisms of his are remembered and nothing he is recorded to have said has much significance today, but he was an understanding student of the classics and passed on his own devotion to them.

The boys he specially loved were all handsome. One biographer says, with no intention to be humorous, that he 'was not so short-sighted as to be indifferent to the lure of good looks and graceful ways' and if his own accounts of his pupils are true he found plenty of these at Eton a hundred years ago. Many of their identities and future careers are still known. One of the first was Reginald Brett, afterwards (2nd) Viscount Esher, to whom Johnson wrote 'your life is more like what the books tell one of a Provençal Troubadour than anything I have seen . . . you showered blessings and comfort on my loneliness'. Another future peer, afterwards the Fifth Earl of Rosebery, was young Lord Dalmeny who would become, Johnson said, 'if not a poet a man poets will delight in'. Of Henry Scott Holland, later Canon of St Paul's, he recorded at his leaving 'I cannot bear to think that he is lost', and to Algernon Drummond, while a subaltern at Lahore, Johnson sent the first draft of the *Eton Boating Song*. The eight sons of the fourth Lord Lyttleton were all his pupils; from 1854 till he left Eton he was never without one or more of them and he kept their long row of photographs till he died. Of Francis Elliot, another favourite pupil, Johnson wrote: 'I have always relished and worshipped his mere mind, besides his character . . . and I am proud of having by perseverance overcome his singular shyness. . . . When he was little I remember old Vidal calling him a "delicious boy".' Jack Trefusis, a neighbour in Devonshire, had a path of Johnson's garden named after him, the Whistler's Walk, and to W. O. Burrows, later Bishop of Chichester, Johnson sent one of the few letters about his forced retirement 'to you, whom I love and trust and long to see again'. He also loved and trusted Jack Wallop, later 7th Earl of Portsmouth, 'ideally thoughtful and gentle', and the volatile charming wild younger son of Sir Thomas

Acland, a dazzling youth known as 'Gib' who went out to India as a subaltern and came home to die. Then, too, there was Cecil de Salis who had, Johnson said, all Elliot's merits 'but is attached to me in a way Elliot never was', and a Japanese pupil called Sanjo who stayed at his home for coaching.

This formidable list leaves out those closest of all to Johnson, the brothers 'Mouse' and Charles Wood and 'Chat' Williamson. Charles Wood was the older and would later be Viscount Halifax, and used to invite Johnson enthusiastically to stay with the family at Hickleton, where he was made much of by everyone, particularly 'Mouse', 'who has been my companion, the constant helpmate in my troubles; he was grave, pitying me, as he has always been truly compassionate in my illnesses and gloominesses'.

'Chat' Williamson was probably the most beloved of all Johnson's pupils. His nickname was short for Chatterbox, a gay good-looking boy. He and his friend Bickersteth went abroad with Johnson and at Baden Bickersteth died suddenly. Chat was overcome by the loss and became 'very thoughtful, tender and devout', but later, staying with Johnson after his departure from Eton, he was 'extremely sweet, gay, sage, cosy. Much more affectionate to me than he used to be, and not at all gloomy. He made me call him in the morning and often came to take his candle, and sitting by his bedside was perhaps my nearest approach to what I have lost and to what I have imagined.'

No detail of the crash, or exposure, or accusation which caused Johnson to leave Eton overnight has ever been revealed by Etonian archivists, though something must have been recorded. It is said that a parent wrote to the headmaster, Hornby, a letter of complaint such as that lazy and peace-loving man dared not ignore, but from which parent or parents it came is unknown—certainly not from the fathers of the favourites quoted above for these continued to visit his home. Whatever the complaint it cannot have been a trivial matter of indiscreetly worded letters or ambiguous intimacies. The dismissal was too peremptory to leave any grounds for defence and Johnson packed up a few belongings and departed instantly, leaving his friends to call later for his books and furniture. Moreover his name was at once removed from the textbooks he had written which were used anonymously for many years, and in the same year he resigned his Fellowship of King's College, Cambridge and changed his name to Cory. He never returned to Eton or made any complaint about the way he had been treated after twenty-seven years' service. He was certainly guilty of something more than one of Conington's infatuations in which 'the physical element was suppressed'.

Yet most of his young friends were loyal to him and continued to visit his family home at Halsdon in the Barnstable district, and he remained there for seven years in a post-Etonian dream. That he had regrets may be seen from the passage from his memoirs quoted above about 'Chat', but he does not seem to have complained with any bitterness or to have bored his friends with the rights and wrongs of the case.

It is Symonds's journal and correspondence, however, which at an earlier date enable one to draw a firm conclusion, even if other evidence were lacking. Conington gave him a copy of *Ionica* described by Phyllis Grosskurth not quite accurately as 'a series of romantic poems addressed by an Eton master to one of his charges, Charles Wood, later Viscount Halifax'. Symonds was so excited by the poems that he wrote to Johnson, admitting his own feelings and asking advice to be sent to one of his anonymous pen-names at the Oxford Union, used as an accommodation address. He received a 'long and passionate defence of pederasty' in which he detected a 'wistful yearning'. Johnson seems to have had few reserves.

At his home for the first few of those post-Etonian years Johnson had 'Chat' Williamson's company frequently but when the boy reached the age of twenty he became a Catholic. This disturbed Johnson who had violent prejudices against 'Popery' but at first he put a bold face on it. 'Now that he has gone over to the Pope he will be at ease; he will be merry, imaginative, not without sentimental sympathies', but all the same he became one of Johnson's most urgent preoccupations. Chat's father cut him off from money and Johnson helped him, but the boy gave up his original intention of going into the Guards and lived penuriously in London.

Johnson travelled up to see him and they sat on Greenwich Hill together on a stifling afternoon, Chat having none of his usual sparkle but with a drawn face. Chat had been described as 'the best looking boy in the school' but was not approved of by the masters because he was so often with the bigger boys. Now he seemed to cling to Johnson for advice and support and wanted to come down to Halsdon where his own boat *Lalage* awaited him. Johnson was afraid of priestly prohibitions, as he may well have had reason to be, and discouraged the boy but took him to the Royal Academy. No record is left of their parting but it must have been for the last time.

A year or two later Chat, having got his degree, decided to join the Congregation of the Oratory of St Philip Neri, of which Newman had introduced a branch into England thirty years earlier. This seemed to Johnson to widen the breach between them but when he was laid up with a cold that winter he was made happy by a letter from Chat, who had heard he was seriously ill, asking that if he ever felt himself near death he would send for him. Johnson's reply is unfortunately lost; it probably accounted for the sequel. He said he wrote 'with all possible tenderness and humbleness' but it seems likely that he recalled things in their relationship which the young convert and novice wanted at that time to forget and Chat answered with a 'formal dry note saying he was not a free agent' and asking Johnson to take this as his last communication.

Impossible to measure the effect of such a blow on a nature like Johnson's, but it may have been a heavier one, with greater effect on his spirit, than his dismissal from Eton. 'It trampled on the elementary principles of gratitude', Johnson said, and never forgave the Church for taking his lover from him. 'How glorious is imprudence, passion, romance compared with the confectionary sanctities of Rome!' he exclaimed bitterly. He disposed of all relics of Chat, photographs, pebbles picked up by him on the beach, bits of manuscript, a shirt and an old dressing-gown which had once belonged to Ernest Bickersteth, the friend whose sudden death had given Chatterbox his first serious thoughts. There was a locket, too, with Chat's and Ernest's hair entwined, but Johnson could not bring himself to part with this.

The loss of Chat made Halsdon unendurable and, taking advantage of a doctor's advice, Johnson set out for Madeira, and a few months later lent Halsdon to his favourite nephew John Vidal, who had just married. Frivolous even now though his letters often were, he was for the second time a broken man.

But not for long. Never profound, he was capable of swift re-orientations and now fifty-five years old he found himself followed to Madeira by the sprightly young daughter of a local vicar whom he married that summer. He lived with her for the remaining fourteen years of his life first in Madeira then in Hampstead and he gave her a son in 1879. She was twenty years old when they married but had always wanted to marry 'an old clever man, tender and true' and they seem to have been happy together. He brought out a collected edition of his *Ionica* in 1891 and produced a *Guide to Modern English History* but otherwise wrote no more. He will be remembered by *Heraclitus* but more revealing of himself and his life at Eton is *Academus* written at the height of his career as an Eton master.

Perhaps there's neither tear nor smile,
When once beyond the grave.
Woe's me: but let me live meanwhile
Among the bright and brave;

My summers lapse away beneath
Their cool Athenian shade:
And I a string for myrtle-wreath,
A whetsone unto blade;

I cheer the games I cannot play,
As stands a crippled squire
To watch his master through the fray,
Uplifted by desire.

I roam, where little pleasures fall,
As morn to morn succeeds,
To melt or ere the sweetness pall,
Like glittering manna-beads.

The wishes dawning in the eyes,
The softly murmured thanks;
The zeal of those that miss the prize
On clamorous river-banks,

The quenchless hope, the honest choice,
The self-reliant pride,
The music of the pleading voice
That will not be denied,

The wonder flushing in the cheek,
The questions many a score,
When I grow eloquent and speak
Of England, and of war—

Oh, better than the world of dress
And pompous dining out,
Better than simpering and finesse
Is all this stir and rout.

I'll borrow life, and not grow old;
And nightingales and trees
Shall keep me, though the veins be cold,
As young as Sophocles.
And when I may no longer live,
They'll say, who know the truth,
He gave whate'er he had to give
To freedom and to youth.

3

Three and a half years after Hornby the Eton headmaster had dismissed Johnson he was faced with another crisis caused by the intimacy with boys of another of his assistants, but this he found a more difficult case to handle. Oscar Browning, also an Old Etonian though a Colleger of obscure parents who had fought his way to a lucrative housemastership from poverty, did not make the gentlemanly resignation that Johnson had done but fought the headmaster every inch of the way.

He was an aggressive and conceited man and had been so from his youth when he was impatient for fame, success and intimacy with the great. Every slight in his early career was something to be avenged—he prayed to God for vengeance on two boys unpoetically named Hicks and Pinchard, 'Thou knowest what I say is true . . . I leave the vengeance to thee.'

William Johnson was his tutor and reproved him for unsociability but he had passionate attachments to other boys. Of one, F. T. E. Prothero, he wrote: 'For the last three weeks I have prayed to God that his heart might have changed and he might love, and my prayer has been answered. I told him it was my birthday and his lips wished me many happy returns of the day.' Of another, 'A half or two ago I saw a boy named Dunmore. . . . My wishes, my hopes and fears begin and terminate in him. I have found he is a lord but I loved him before'.

Ferociously ambitious, he finds he is going to hell fast, *but worse to obscurity*. This is a theme throughout the journal he kept as a boy. Distinction and above all fame were what he sought. 'How little I have done for fame. How much I might have. Alexander, J. Caesar, Byron all rise and reprove me.' 'Oh fame, I long for thee, long for thee.' When he came down from Cambridge and was offered an assistant mastership at Eton he saw this as leading to the fulfilment of his ambitions. He would teach the future rulers of the country and the hereditary aristocracy and be accepted by their fathers. He would make a name for himself and become rich—for an Eton housemaster at that time made an easy three or four thousand a year. He accepted at once.

Somewhat squat and fore-shortened in appearance he had a great head with sculptured features which were sometimes called noble, a long and hefty trunk and absurdly short legs which made his walk a roll and his whole figure almost dwarfish. His mouth and chin were clean-shaved but he wore curling and becoming side-whiskers. His colleagues found him from the first egotistical and opinionated.

He had not been long at Eton before he drew up an elaborate statement of his views for the reform of the school, but as time went on the reforms he advocated became more and more those which enabled him to live luxuriously with unbounded intimacy with chosen boys. As a housemaster and tutor he was making some three thousand pounds a year. He spent three hundred a year on his library, and extravagantly on his wine-cellar and food. He travelled in most vacations nearly always with one or another of his pupils, attended by his personal servant and a courier. Corresponding with Arthur Sidgwick at Rugby (that friend of Symonds's whose relations with his favourite pupil fell short of Platonism, Symonds thought), Browning asked why a man who became a schoolmaster 'be thought unfit for civilized society'.

He wanted to achieve distinction as a schoolmaster and gain the affection of his pupils without the application to scholarship shown by his old tutor William Johnson who, whatever else he may have done, coached his pupils conscientiously in the classics. Oscar Browning was not punctilious about hours or about the written work of his pupils. He fed the boys in his house well and opened it to boys in other houses. He would hold long conversations with them and looked on these as more important than the stern duties of coaching. He cut Chapel and rose late. He was reproved by the headmaster for interesting his Division in English poetry. ("The learning of English poetry I do not wish to encourage", wrote the headmaster, an incurable Classics man.) He unsettled the boys in their forthright Anglicanism, holding himself no particular religious views. He invited to his house in term-time well-known and sometimes notorious writers and painters and let them meet the boys, Walter Pater and Simeon Solomon among them.

He arranged the dining-room of his house so that it could provide a stage for theatricals and also held concerts in it for which he secured professional musicians. (These, too, were forbidden after a time by the headmaster.) He decorated his rooms with things considered modern at the time, Arundel prints and Morris curtains. He tried to persuade his pupils to regard games as second in importance to culture. He heard confidences and gave advice on sexual matters and did not regard too seriously cases of 'immorality' between boys, accepting the boys' word 'spooning' for this. ('Dangerous confidences', the headmaster said.) He issued free invitations to the boys in other houses to breakfast with him and his mother and sisters whenever they wished. Like his old tutor he gave river parties. Worst of all, in the eyes of his colleagues, he was reputed to have favourites and intimate friendships with many of the boys.

Dr Hornby, who had so recently avoided scandal in the school by the prompt resignation of Johnson, was deeply concerned about this. There was no proof, as there was in Johnson's case, of anything which in the phraseology of the time could be called 'immoral' but he suspected it and for some years it seems that he awaited a parental letter about Browning's relations with a boy such as had shocked him in the case of Johnson. Browning, an old pupil of Johnson, appeared to share his views and, unless the headmaster was mistaken, his habits. So Hornby watched him, listened to tittle-tattle about him, sympathetically heard other masters who were jealous of Browning's personal success and prosperity and waited his chance to intervene.

Once he believed he had found it. He received a complaint from another housemaster named Woolley-Dod that Browning was unduly friendly with one of his boarders, George Curzon, one day to be Viceroy of India. George was a good-looking boy, so much sought after by seniors that any older boy seen with him was suspected of 'spooning'. Two of Browning's own seniors wrote him rather hypocritical letters deploring this and Browning, who was already deeply interested in George, decided to take him up and make a friend of him.

George's housemaster was outraged at this. The boy had been prevented from playing games by a cricket accident and Browning, Woolley-Dod complained to the headmaster, took him for drives, wrote letters to him when he did not see him, and helped him with his iambics. The headmaster sent for Browning and greeted him with—

"So I hear Mr Woolley-Dod has a good-looking pupil." To this Browning replied with suitable indignation, but he allowed it to pass without demanding an apology or withdrawal. Woolley-Dod spoke of Browning's 'irrepressible attentions' to the boy and said he had grown 'querulous and spoilt' under Browning's influence. The headmaster demanded from Browning an undertaking that the intimacy with George Curzon should cease and that Browning should be more careful in encouraging boys' confidences. Browning asked for more exact terms and Hornby was ready with these: "What I mean is that *all* intercourse should now cease between you and Curzon", and added that boys speak of these matters in 'somewhat plainspoken and possibly coarse terms'. After consulting various friends and authorities Browning gave the assurance demanded of him but continued, with the father's permission, to see the boy in the holidays. Hornby openly spoke of Browning's 'sinister influence' and said he was 'unfit to be a master'.

The ostensible reason for which Hornby dismissed Browning from his post was a technicality concerned with the number of boys in his house over which through negligence he had transgressed regulations, but no one had any doubt, during the scandal which followed, of the real reason. There were accounts in what were known disdainfully in the academic world as 'the public prints', the *Times* supporting Hornby and the *Daily News* Browning. There were questions in the Commons. But Hornby's authority was upheld and Browning left Eton and took up his residence at King's College, Cambridge where he held a Fellowship.

In his *Memories of Sixty Years* published in 1903 Browning threw some of the blame for his dismissal on Johnson, who, he said, left Eton 'conscience-struck'. He suggests that Johnson's dismissal had been caused by the discovery of certain letters left by a boy who died (Bickersteth?) with instructions (which were ignored) that they should be burnt, and that Browning, unaware of this, had defended Johnson in a speech which Lord Selborne said was the best he had ever heard. From the moment he sat down (noticing Hornby with 'his head in his plate') he guessed that Hornby was determined to sack him as a 'continuation of the Johnson poison'. It could be true in principle though it would be foolish to suppose that Browning was sacked for making the best speech Lord Selborne had ever heard. He was sacked because he was a homosexual and the rest of his life proved it.

Browning was of a far more robust disposition than Johnson, with whom he must inevitably be compared because of their common experience at Eton. He was also less of a scholar and had little of Johnson's selfless devotion to his work. He neither idealized nor idolized the boys he taught and there was little of that contemporary nonsense about the worship of boyhood as a revival of the Greek ideal in his earthy attitude to young males.

With an income reduced, as he said, from £3,000 to £300 a year, he remained at Cambridge as a Fellow of King's for more than thirty years and became what can only be called a character there.

Cambridge allowed him to inflate his ego, as it was possible in Victorian times for very rich men, artists and university dons to do, each making himself the centre of a world of fantasy in which his smallest gestures were significant. An audience was necessary, too, the tenants of a great estate, hero-worshippers or gossip-collectors among artists and writers, or, most inflammable of all, undergraduates. With these to watch Browning's cultivated eccentricities, his sturdy tricycling, his shipboard walk, his gormandizing, his noisy musical parties when he played wind instruments, his addiction to the spookier kinds of spiritualism, his famous Sunday evening entertainments and his curiously stunted appearance he soon became a personality and acquired—sure mark of the fame he had long coveted—a universal nickname, 'the O.B.'.

Perhaps he was followed from Eton by his reputation as a homosexual—though that ridiculous Graeco-Roman word had not yet been invented. Certainly he was no more discreet at Cambridge than at Eton, indeed he seemed to scorn discretion for the rest of his life. His friendships were never intense or soulful but cheerful affairs chiefly with young roughs, sailors and the like, to whom he was kind and hospitable. If the age in which he lived was narrow it was also ignorant—at least until Havelock Ellis and Symonds informed it—about sexual phenomena and no one seemed to think it strange that the O.B. should fill his rooms with blue-jackets shouting nautical songs and drinking, or with rescued stable-boys, or 'several boys who are protégés of mine, a young blacksmith, a young printer and a young instrument-maker', or that he should always have a well-chosen manservant to sleep in his rooms at night 'in case he were seized by sudden illness', or that he might (as on one recorded occasion) have two youths in his rooms, one drying him after his bath, the other playing the violin, or that he sometimes employed three young secretaries and two young language teachers at the same time. Perhaps his friendships with Simeon Solomon and Oscar Wilde or Robbie Ross may have raised eyebrows when their public scandals came, but his addiction to boys of the working class was put down to his kind heart or his general oddity of character. Even his mother, a shrewd old lady, explained as enthusiasm in his profession the fact that he never came to stay with her without a young man in tow.

Yet in certain enquiring people, whose own repressions had made them less charitable than those who accepted O.B. as a bluff and entertaining old party incapable of corrupting anyone, certain questions remained unanswered, and by the authorities who held various kinds of promotion in their power he was not considered 'reliable' or 'suitable' or 'quite the man for the job'. Browning's efforts to make the world take him at his own estimate were indomitable and not without pathos. He wanted to convince his graver seniors that the unique scholarship and genius which he saw in himself deserved recognition and with it some adequate pecuniary award, for he was extravagant and always hard up. But when he found his potential patrons remained sceptical, his ebullient nature rose above his reverses and he soon saw them as after all the best things that could have happened.

Within a year of his arrival at King's the Vice-Provostship became vacant and he seriously thought he might be chosen, and even when he was passed over he believed he would be made Dean, though there was no such likelihood. When a tutor was sought for the Prince of Wales and the privilege was given to J. K. Stephen, Browning thought he lost the post only because the official arranging the matter had failed to find him in his rooms.

In 1889 the Vice-Provostship of King's again became available and Browning was again disappointed, for the post went to his one-time friend Whitting. Five years later he applied for the Professorship of History at Glasgow University but was turned down, as he was for other appointments, only some of which (it may be guessed) are recorded. He applied for the degree of Litt.D. but it was refused him on the grounds that he was at that time the author of no serious book, and he was no more successful in his attempt to become Whewell Professor of International Law at Cambridge. His last recorded application was to his friend Lord Latymer to obtain a knighthood for him as it 'would give great pleasure to many people all over the world'. This, too, was refused. Some of these attempts came from the merest wishful thinking, but it is obvious that no one was anxious to give Browning any official position. The most he obtained was the directorship of a teachers' training college at Cambridge and, three months before his death, that ambiguous decoration the O.B.E.

He had, in fact, to be eased out of what positions he held, though never as peremptorily as he had been dismissed from Eton. There had been murmurings and dissensions at King's for some years. In 1894 the Senior Tutor told him he had done a great deal of harm to the College and in 1904 when M. R. James had been appointed Provost he limited Browning's long-standing tenure of the History Tutorship to three instead of seven years and at the end of that time his work at King's was ended. Soon after he was asked to resign as Principal of the teachers' training college.

His last years were spent in Rome where he wrote a number of now almost unreadable history books including a *History of the Modern World* in 400,000 words. He became famous as a snob, his rather pitiful devotion to obscure Italian royalties and his talk of English ones entertaining a series of visitors to the capital. But he saw himself as a great historical writer and complained that his entry in the *Encyclopaedia Britannica* dwelt on him as a personality rather than as an historian. He was surrounded to the end by young men who rented him and stole from him. A macabre touch was given to his death-bed when his last words were an order that a young girl present should leave the room.

In the last five years of his life he wrote over a million words and made, he said, £840, but his history was unreliable and spoilt by personal prejudices and prejudgments. His *Memories of Sixty Years* was full of trivial gossip about the already publicized but it contains a few details about Simeon Solomon who had died before it appeared. Browning lays some stress on his pride in having been Solomon's friend and it is difficult to know whether this was contrariness and indiscretion, inserted to contrast with the respectful familiarity he claims with the great men of his time, or whether he kept after all those years a sentimental soft spot for the handsome young Jewish painter he had known.

He first met him, he said, at Fryston Hall, Lord Houghton's great house, though in fact he was introduced by Walter Pater, and Solomon became a frequent visitor at Eton. It may be that the headmaster did not know this, or hear of Simeon Solomon's conviction and imprisonment in 1873, but the possibility cannot be ruled out that one of the 'facts' which Hornby had against Browning, 'facts' that were never revealed, was that he had invited the painter to his house in term-time and introduced him to the boys. The Solomon scandal was kept out of the newspapers but where his two recalcitrant masters were concerned Hornby's ear was to the ground.

At all events during Browning's time at Eton he saw much of Solomon and assisted him with money. Solomon wanted to visit Rome to 'escape the temptations of London' which were 'ruining' him, and Browning offered to take him at his own expense. They had a delightful journey, travelling from Florence to Rome in a hired carriage and staying at Siena and Orvieto. Browning remembered that Solomon's favourite picture was Titian's *Sacred and Profane Love*. but 'all he brought back with him was a sketch of an Italian boy whose acquaintance he made at Rome'.

Solomon afterwards designed a bookplate for Browning, 'Labor and Theoria'. After Browning left Eton he lost touch with Solomon but when he saw him from a hansom cab in Fleet Street—presumably during Solomon's evil days—they embraced like Virgil and Sordello, but never met again.

Solomon did a portrait of Browning as a youngish man in which he is already bald. It makes him look painfully effeminate and sensual with curling pretty lips, delicate features and soft eyes under curling lashes, not at all the robust old Roman seen in later portraits.

Browning's second volume of reminiscences *Memories of Later Years* is written with the same monotonous attention to great names. There is nothing in all his work, in fact, likely to interest a future generation but he created a legend for himself which may win him a small place in the academic history of his time. That, at least, is more than was achieved by the many who were jealous and disapproving of him, for whatever his faults and failures he triumphantly escaped nonentity.

CHAPTER SIX

Symonds, Roden Noel, Walt Whitman and Edward Fitzgerald

WHEN Symonds with his young family had returned to Clifton to be near his ailing father, Graham Dakyns gave a dinner party for some of the Sixth Formers he taught and in one evening all Symonds's resolutions and his six-year attempt to be 'a natural man' were swept away by his falling precipitately and desperately for a seventeen-year-old boy named Norman Moor who has been considered by some the love of his life.

The story of this relationship which Phyllis Grosskurth has reconstructed from Symonds's Journal and his letters to Dakyns is of particular interest because no homosexual has left so detailed, so analytical and so merciless an account of his love for a young male. Some will think it repugnant or morbid, others will find pathos in it, but it is impossible to doubt Symonds's sincerity in laying bare his tortured emotions.

After his first meeting with the boy in Dakyns's rooms he deliberately set out to win his affection. He first persuaded the headmaster of Clifton College to let him lecture the Sixth Form on Greek literature in order to have opportunities of seeing Norman, but when his offer was accepted he took his task seriously and from it came his *Studies of the Greek Poets.* He would send daily bundles of books and invitations to Norman and confided in Dakyns, just two months after meeting Norman, "If I had any strength I would in one way or another make him mine and be good to him." He sent a love-letter to the boy who seems to have accepted his advances with remarkable calmness then set out to 'enlarge and stimulate his mind' and incidentally help with his essays. Norman came to his home on most evenings and became 'incalculably sweet' to Symonds when he leant against his shoulder, but there were evenings when he failed to turn up or seemed bored and indifferent, and these threw Symonds into agonies. Nor did he fail to notice that Norman was attracted to younger boys which made Symonds suffer all the miseries of a jealous lover.

At the end of March Arthur Sidgwick came for a visit and it was now his turn to counsel caution. Symonds showed him a poem called *Eudiades* about a Greek boy and his older lover, but Arthur pronounced it degrading and asked Symonds to destroy it, which annoyed Symonds but made him think. When Arthur had gone back to Rugby he decided to change his relationship with Norman, scorning its sentimentality and putting it on a less dangerous level. Norman, an obliging boy, agreed to this as he agreed to almost everything else proposed by Symonds during their hectic relationship. Another lecture, this time from Arthur's elder brother Henry, further unsettled Symonds but he had already asked Norman to stay with him in London, where after some days of sight-seeing and theatre-going, they eventually slept together, just four months after they had first met. "I am satisfied. I think my poems were not all untrue to life", wrote Symonds.

But such an ardently followed affair could scarcely remain unnoticed and one woman, Norman's aunt, had suspicions, while another, Symonds's wife, was very well aware of his obsession.

Symonds was not much worried about Norman's aunt whom he believed he could 'conquer', whatever that might be, but he was deeply concerned with Catherine who since the birth of her third baby was depressed. She was forever meeting Norman about the house and called him, most unfairly, 'the ugly boy'. (A contemporary photograph shows him as beautiful but inane like a bad rococo carving of a young pink-faced saint.) But Symonds had it out with her and to his delight she agreed that his breakdowns had been due to frustration and that he had better go his own way. She was not above a violent scene some months later when she found letters to Norman more passionate than Symonds had ever written to her, but on the whole she showed, then and thereafter, a miraculous understanding of the hybrid creature she had married.

During a summer term of fine weather Norman became infatuated by a younger boy and this, with cricket and the river, absorbed much of his time. "He has not come tonight which was to have been one of our sacred nights", wrote Symonds miserably as many an older man had written before him, hopelessly loving a healthy boy with youthful enthusiasms to keep him from gloomy love-making and introspective quarrels. 'I have offered him all and he may still take all or part. But I must let him put forth or hold back his hand according to his good will".

Norman never committed himself. He may have been a little vain, he certainly enjoyed Symonds's attentions and does not seem to have minded his sexual approaches, in spite of Symonds's age, beard and dreary habit of analysing all they did. But Symonds wanted the impossible. Norman could not be man and woman too.

In July he took Norman to France and Switzerland, and they hiked together in the sunlight, lying together at night in the bedrooms of country inns. One's sympathy goes to Norman during that long holiday for Symonds tormented them both as he sought desperately for what he thought their friendship had once promised. Norman can only have been bored, whatever he felt about the scenery. Interrogation, regret, brief self-assurance and dismal hours of despair must have been almost unendurable to the boy and he showed a saintly patience. "Norman has not in him the tracts of undiscovered country I imagined," was Symonds's disillusioned comment at the end of the holiday.

That November Norman heard that he had been elected a scholar at Balliol and in January spent two nights with Symonds before going up to Oxford. They slept together and Symonds noted in his journal that after the boy had left 'he smothered his pillow with kisses'.

They met at intervals while Norman was at Oxford and Symonds took him about London and to the theatre, but found his hours with him full of the old torments. "Would God that he really loved me. I do not think he does." But he decided to try another continental holiday and in 1872 invited Norman to Switzerland and Northern

Italy. Now twenty years old Norman may have felt that he knew how to treat Symonds and his psychoses. But no one knew that, certainly not Symonds himself who wrote to Dakyns that he was shackled with 'a living corpse of a dead damned doleful passion'. Norman had lost his *naïveté*. The actuality was second-rate.

That was pretty well the end. Norman was appointed a classics master at Clifton, married six years later and became the father of a family. Whether he and Symonds saw anything of one another in Clifton after that holiday seems unimportant. Before the end of the year Symonds had started on his long series of affairs with grown men, sturdy peasants, soldiers, Swiss villagers and gondoliers. His interest in boys turned to a new aspect of his own brand of Greek Ideology, the athlete, the warrior, the discus thrower, the magnificent male.

2

There had been symptoms of this in his character since childhood when he had dreamed of satisfying a circle of rough sailors, but the romantic pederasty of his early twenties, shared in conversation with so many of his scholastic friends, had absorbed him, and only now that he was disillusioned with Norman Moor and all he stood for did he take the course which was more natural to his invert's nature. He put choristers and public schoolboys for ever behind him and we find him in 1872 (still only thirty-two years old) writing to Dakyns of a cable-layer he has observed with 'huge haunches' who was 'strong and sweet and magnetic, so full of the charm of animals'.

He began to hire male models, pretending to draw them while he stared entranced at their nakedness. A friend took him to a male brothel near the barracks in Regents Park and he arranged to take a trooper he met there to a private room and had relations with him, trying to find in their talk afterwards a Whitmanesque comradeship.

Phyllis Grosskurth suggests that the friend who acted as Virgil in this subterranean excursion was Roden Noel and speaks confidently of this man as a 'practising invert'. This makes one wonder whether journals such as Symonds's are being kept today and whether posterity will be beguiled by catalogues of twentieth-century addictions, for nowhere else, to my knowledge, is there any account of Roden Noel which suggests this interesting fact. He is the subject of three short memoirs, all printed as introductions to collections of his poetry, and from these it would appear that he was the dutiful father of a family, as he may indeed have been, devoted to men of the working-classes, as he was, though perhaps not altogether in the sense that his sister Victoria Buxton who wrote one of the memoirs intended, and a poet of high achievement, which he certainly was not.

The first collected edition of his verse, which was published in 1902, seven years after Noel's death, had as introduction an adulatory essay by Symonds which had appeared in the *Academy* as a review of an earlier volume during the lifetime of both of them. It is difficult to understand how Symonds, whose impartiality in judgment was his pride, could have lent himself to this sort of log-rolling. The book in which it was reprinted consists of five hundred double-column pages of excessively bad verse with a Tom Hood socialist slant, little better than the parish hall 'recitations' of the last century. "It is possible," wrote Symonds, "that his poems will not receive due recognition until a Noel Society has been founded. By this I mean again to place him in the same rank as Mr Browning."

There is a portrait frontispiece and it shows a face which might have been that of a blond negro with large protruding lips and crinkly hair. Another collection has a more flattering portrait from a painting by Richmond in which it is possible to see how Noel believed himself to resemble Byron and cultivated the likeness in his outward appearance, for he was painfully vain.

Born in 1834, the son of the first Earl of Gainsborough, Roden Berkeley Wriothesley Noel was educated at Harrow and Trinity College, Cambridge. As a young man travelling in the Near East he fell dangerously ill in Beirut and was nursed by a certain Madame de Broë whose daughter Alice he married. There were three children, Frances, Conrad and Eric and on the death of the last at the age of five he wrote a brief sincere poem which is distinguished from the rest of his verse by its simple effectiveness, *A Little Child's Monument.*

Noel became Groom of the Privy Chamber to Queen Victoria in 1873 but found that protocol and convention interfered with the habits he had already formed of association with service men and good-looking manual workers, associations which in that kindly undiscerning age gave him no worse than a reputation for socialism, in spite of his effeminate appearance.

He tried to persuade Symonds to abandon both his enforced heterosexuality during his 'natural man' period and his morose and delicate relations with pretty boys, his own approach to such things being robust and unsentimental. Symonds called him 'the Centaur' and was both shocked and envious when he saw the uncomplicated way in which Noel would hire male lovers as other men hired prostitutes. Trying vainly to emulate Noel's *sang froid* he went into the park with a soldier and, greatly daring, 'touched him intimately', only to be overcome by remorse which he expressed in a penitent poem *The Valley of Vain Desires*.

From the little recorded of Noel he seems to have been amiable, rather shallow, but of considerable charm. Symonds almost revered his off-handed sensuality and even towards the end of his life, when he was no longer haunted by the need to repent after casual contacts, he lived in some awe of such uninhibited men as Roden Noel and Lord Ronald Gower. His admiration of Noel's verse may have been sincere for even Tennyson, a notoriously erratic critic, thought Noel's *Vision of the Desert* 'one of the finest things I have ever read'. ("Agglutinative use of epithets," said a newspaper critic less partially.) Symonds dedicated his book *Many Moods* to Noel.

Noel died suddenly in 1894 leaving behind him his vast collections of bad verse and more usefully a cabmen's shelter at Penge and a branch of the R.S.P.C.A. at San Remo. His last memoir-writer, another odd character worth a glance of retrospection named Percy Addleshaw, said without conscious *arrière pensée* that his interest in 'the toiling masses' was one of the chief concerns of his life, and that 'he had long laboured among the children of the lower classes and bidden successfully for their love'. Relaxed himself, Noel seems to have had a stirring influence on Symonds's early life, for Symonds was fascinated by a man who dared so much in such weird enchanted places and his name for Noel, 'the Centaur', was apposite.

3

But what helped most to bring about that salutary change in Symonds from a morbidly sensitive verse-writing pursuer of young boys to a man of fulfilled loves was a matter of circumstance. His tubercular condition was well recognized and during the spring, while riding alone on the downs, he had a serious haemorrhage and after months of weakness he was ordered not to spend another winter in England. He intended to go to Egypt but arrangements were baulked and he spent the winter at Davos Platz, afterwards settling there for the rest of his life.

Within a few months of arriving in the Swiss mountains he met and made friends with a young Swiss named Christian Buol who for some years satisfied all his longings.

The Graubünden peasants were fine independent people, mostly smallholders and farmers who followed a democratic life of their own with no distinctions of wealth or caste. They lived simply but without extreme poverty, a race fitted by centuries of hard conditions to withstand the rigours of the climate and the harsh circumstances of their life, given to merry-making and primitive music, enjoying Valtelline, a wine of their own countryside, marrying into neighbouring communities, bringing up their sturdy children, bearded, benevolent, courageous, hospitable. The men with their rough and hairy appearance and their superb if clumsy physique at once attracted Symonds, and Christian Buol, a magnificent young giant of nineteen who worked as a sledge-driver and reminded Symonds of a 'Greek charioteer', became his lover.

There will be nothing surprising in this to those who have seen the humorous generosity, the unquestioning ease with which the unsophisticated young male in any country can respond to the aching introspective need of the intellectual. Never wavering in his ultimate desire for women, with nothing in the least extraneous in his nature, unspoilt by doubt, having no need to rationalize or probe into motive, or to look for explanation or defence, he can give himself with grace and cheerfulness, even with enthusiasm, and this is enchanting to a more tried and experienced partner. He finds no mystique in this and has no wordy hesitations or self-conscious constraints. There may be an element of sexuality in what he does, or one of gainfulness, but generally it is a bountiful careless instinct which leads often to happy and enduring relationships.

Symonds was very ready to appreciate it in his young friend. With a boldness that came from his tortured encounters with immature characters in England, Symonds accosted Christian as he stood in a barn doorway. That was during the first December in Davos and by

Christmas Symonds knew him well enough to present him with a pipe and ask him to his hotel. In the spring he lent the family a thousand pounds to save their hotel—it was afterwards repaid—and this he thought 'cemented' his friendship with Christian. There was, he believed, a healthy physical relationship between them, free of vice or squalid passion such as he had found in London on excursions with Roden Noel.

Before the spring was out Symonds had taken Christian to Italy with him and wrote to Dakyns that it was a splendid sight to see him asleep with folded arms and 'the vast chest of a young Hercules, innocent of clothing'.

Christian wanted to marry and naively told Symonds so. Symonds had so far outgrown the aching possessiveness with which he had treated his younger friends that he agreed to assist the project and on later journeys to Italy took Christian's younger cousin, also named Christian, in his place. Both must have known, probably with innocent amusement, what the journey entailed. Through them Symonds came to know their neighbours and grew to be an accepted friend to the whole community.

To those who see Symonds as an imaginative and graphic historian, Christian's influence on his life, the influence of a semi-illiterate man who gave Symonds a new happiness and a new ideal, was valuable. From the half-disguised eroticism of his yearning verses, from his fussy essays and the not very profound or accurate scholarship of his literary criticism, he progressed to the confident satisfying work by which he is remembered. It is not easy to pick this or that among his writings and predict for it that kind of immortality to which the Victorians aspired, but he gave generously to the development of his time and if no specific achievement of his will be remembered his contribution to nineteenth-century letters was a considerable one.

Released from the most enervating of his mental torments by a fulfilled passion, strengthened in body by the mountain air and prevented from wasting his time and energies in the diversions he found in cities, he settled down to work and wrote vigorously, sometimes feverishly, to the end of his life. The first three volumes of *The Renaissance in Italy* were already completed before he came to Davos, but although he had enjoyed the use of reference books and the appurtenances of research for these it is not fancy which has made critics rather than historians find in the last four volumes something more than pedantic scholarship. "As he warms to his theme," wrote Disraeli, "he even evinces some spark of the divine gift of imagination, in which he appeared to me at first deficient."

His translation, the first in English, of Michelangelo's sonnets was sensitive and sure, and his own collection of poetry *Vagabundi Libellus* (though much of it came from the past) deserved more consideration than the alternating outpour and repression of his early verse. His short book on Shelley was perceptive and sympathetic and may still be read with enjoyment, and he did a tremendous amount of critical and biographical work in the eighties which made Gosse write gushingly that his mark was made, he was a leader in living literature. There was not a single man in England born since 1840 who held such a place in literature as he did, Gosse continued, and added that in ten years' time Symonds's status would be enormous.

A friendship with Robert Louis Stevenson who came to Davos for the sake of his health further stimulated Symonds, though the two were antipathetic in many ways. Symonds still had moods of depression but he was happier than he had ever been. His wife had accepted his homosexuality whatever her own feelings about it, and his daughters while not understanding it were amused at his devotion to handsome young peasants, one of them writing a skit about their life at Davos showing Symonds, his face 'transfigured and full of joy' on the appearance of a sledge-driver whom he tries to persuade to enter his home and begs to come very soon to see him. ' "I'll maybe come in this evening," said the youth, in a sort of condescending manner.' What his womenfolk thought privately about Symonds is unguessable; though his wife grew dour and obsessed with her garden the household was for the most part a cheerful one.

4

Symonds's disillusion with Norman Moor and with the adventures he shared with Roden Noel certainly led him to find in the 'Greek charioteer' Christian Buol an idealized fulfilment of his longings, but it was a literary influence which prepared him for this, perhaps the dominant one of his life. It was F. W. H. Myers who first introduced him to Whitman's poetry and *Leaves of Grass* at once became, and remained to the end of his life, a primer.

> And when I thought how my dear friend my lover was on his way coming, O then I was happy . . .
>
> For the one I love most lay sleeping by me under the same cover in the cool night,
>
> In the stillness in the Autumn moonbeams his face was inclined toward me,
>
> And his arm lay lightly around my breast—and that night I was happy.

This was nothing less than inflammatory to Symonds who had only dared make such revelations in verses circulated privately among his friends. He was so sure of his own interpretation of Whitman's sentiments—and who could mistake them after reading the *Calamus* section?—that he wrote sending him a poem called *Love and Death* and revealing himself as far as he dared. Whitman accepted his discipleship gladly and the correspondence thrived. Whitman is reported to have said, "About every three months he (Symonds) writes me, O the most beautiful, splendid letters: I dare not show them to anyone hardly, they are so like those *tête-à-tête* interviews with your chum, your mate, your comrade who throws off everything." Yet Whitman seemed cagey to Symonds in his replies for he would never make an open admission of just what he meant and felt about his chum, his mate, his comrade.

It is possible that by the psychological standards of today Whitman did not know. He was at that time in the first years of his long and passionate love affair with a horse-bus conductor named Peter Doyle, but he was a law to himself in his life as he was in his poetry and believed himself a normal or perhaps a super-normal man.

The Victorians had many defences against criticism or interference with their secret lives. Swinburne's, as we have seen, was to treat his masochistic aberrations as a private joke; others concealed their activities under cover of Christian love for their fellows, or philanthropy, or artistic curiosity. Whitman's was either a huge bluff, which by its immensity might be reconciled with his nature but not by the subtlety it sometimes showed, or else, a more interesting and probable explanation, he simply did not know what he was in relation to the rest of the world. Gosse who had met him wrote: "I don't believe in those 'children'! [Whitman claimed to have six illegitimate children.] For reasons, of course, precisely opposite to those put forward by the servers of pillows to all armholes. The real psychology of W. W. would be enormously interesting. I think the keynote to it would be found in a staggering ignorance, a perhaps wilful non-perception, of the real physical conditions of his nature. But the truth about him (the innermost truth) escapes from almost every page for those who can read."

Symonds *could* read and not admitting for a moment that his idol might be guilty of 'staggering ignorance' even about himself pressed him again and again to come out in the open.

Gosse may well have been right. Whitman's letters to his mother about the young men he nursed in hospital and others could scarcely have been written by one who had the least sense of guilt or who thought he belonged in some special physiological category. 'Cleanness' was a word often on his lips; he seems to have found some special kind of cleanness in his love for young men as opposed to other men's —presumably messy—relations with women. After his death his lover Peter Doyle giving an account of Whitman said ingenuously: "I never knew a case of Walt's being bothered by a woman . . . His disposition was different. Women in that sense never came into his head. Walt was too clean, he hated anything that was not clean. No trace of any kind of dissipation in him. I ought to know about him in those years—we were awful close together."

There can be no doubt about that closeness or about Whitman's relations with young men known before 1869 when he met Doyle, or friends of Doyle's who worked on horse-cars and freight trains. The way in which he and Doyle met, as related by the Irish-American after Whitman's death would be enough for an examining magistrate today.

> You ask where I first met him? It is a curious story. We felt to each other at once. I was a conductor. The night was very stormy,—he had been over to see Burroughs before he came down to take the car—the storm was awful. Walt had his blanket—it was thrown round his shoulders—he seemed like an old sea-captain. He was the only passenger, it was a lonely night, so I thought I would go in and talk with him. Something in me made me do it and something in him drew me that way. He used to say there was something in

> me had the same effect on him. Anyway, I went into the car. We were familiar at once—I put my hand on his knee—we understood. He did not get out at the end of the trip—in fact went all the way back with me.

If more were needed there are Whitman's letters to Doyle published two years after his death under the title *Calamus: A Series of Letters Written During the Years 1868–1880 by Walt Whitman to a Young Friend, Peter Doyle* (New York, 1897). Two extracts from these will suffice to show how Whitman felt about Doyle, the first sent when the young man was ill and had said something about life not being worth living.

> My darling, if you are not well when I come back I will get a good room or two in some quiet place, and we will live together and devote ourselves altogether to the job of curing you, and making you stronger and healthier than ever. I have had this in my mind before but never broached it to you. I could go on with my work in the Attorney General's office just the same—and we would see that your mother should have a small sum every week to keep the pot a-boiling at home. Dear comrade, I think of you very often. My love for you is indestructible, and since that night and morning has returned more than before. Dear Pete, dear son, my darling boy, my young and loving brother, don't let the devil put such thoughts in your mind again—wickedness unspeakable—death and disgrace here, and hell's agonies hereafter—Then what would it be afterward to the mother? What to *me*?—Pete, I send you some money by Adams' Express—you use it, dearest son, and when it is gone you shall have some more, for I have plenty. I will write again before long—give my love to Johnny Lee, my dear darling boy. I love him truly—(let him read these three last lines)—Dear Pete, *remember*—Walt.

Or, on another occasion when Whitman was writing to cheer Doyle in a mood of depression,

> But I want you to try and put a brave face against everything that happens—for it is not so much the little misfortunes of life themselves, as the way we take them and brood over them, that causes the trouble. About the "tiresome" all I have to say is—to say nothing—only a good smacking kiss and many of them—and taking in return many, many, many, from my dear son—good loving ones too—which will do more credit to his lips than growling and complaining at his father. Walt.

Algernon Charles Swinburne

Simeon Solomon (*Ch. II*)

Charles Augustus Howell (*Ch. III*)

Swinburne and Adah Menken (*Ch. IV*)

Theodore Watts-Dunton (*Ch. IV*)

Edmund Gosse (*Ch. IV*)

John Addington Symonds
(at Oxford)

Symonds
(with father and sister)

Norman Moor (*Ch. VI*)

William Johnson (Cory) (*Ch. V*)

Oscar Browning, from a portrait by Simeon Solomon (*Ch. V*)

Roden Noel (*Ch. VI*)

Peter Doyle with
Walt Whitman (*Ch. VI*)

Edward Fitzgerald (*Ch. VI*)

W. Kenworthy Browne (*Ch. VI*)

"Posh" Fletcher (*Ch. VI*)

Angelo Fusato (*Ch. VII*)

Symonds (in Venice)

Edward Cracroft Lefroy (*Ch. VII*)

Oscar Wilde

Edward Lear with
Chichester Fortescue, later
Lord Carlingford (*Ch. VII*

C. L. Dodgson (Lewis Carroll)
(*Ch. VII*)

Rev. C. L. Dodgson with some young friends (*Ch. VII*)

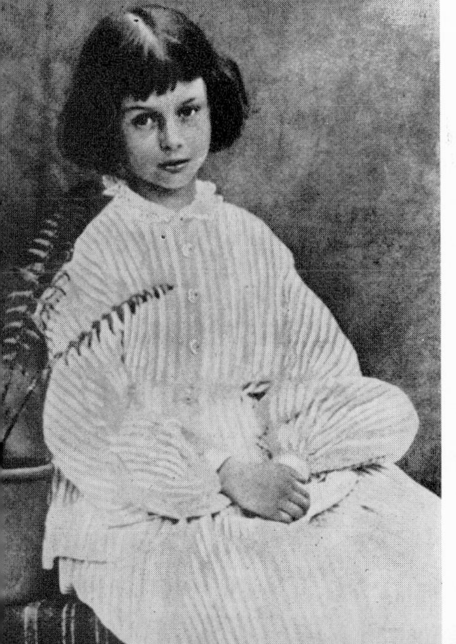

Alice Liddell (*Ch. VII*)

Young girl.
A photograph by C. L. Dodgson (*Ch. VII*)

Walter Blackburn Harte (*Ch. VIII*)

Walter Pater (*Ch. VIII*)

Richard Jackson (*Ch. VIII*)

Reginald Harding (*Ch. IX*)

William Ward (*Ch. IX*)

H. Sherard (*Ch. IX*)

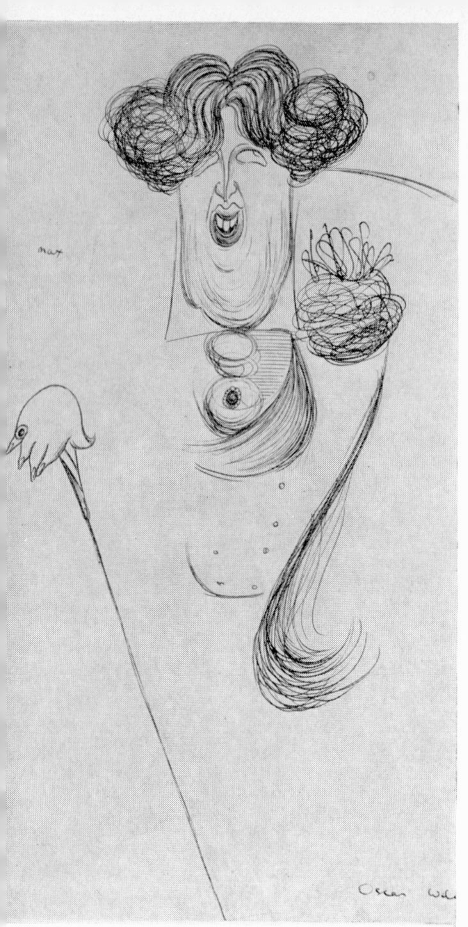

Caricature of Oscar Wilde
by Max Beerbohm

Richard Le Gallienne (*Ch. VIII*)

Ernest Dowson, from a drawing by Charles Conder (*Ch. X*)

John Gray (*Ch. IX*)

Lionel Johnson (*Ch. X*)

Lord Alfred Douglas and his brother Francis (Lord Drumlanrig) (*Ch. VIII*)

During the years when Symonds was trying to draw Whitman into admissions which would enable him to write more freely about himself so that they might exchange cosy confidences about their 'comrades' he knew nothing of Doyle, but Whitman's poetry was enough. When in 1890 he received a copy of the complete poems from Whitman and found that a particularly 'comradely' poem which had been in the early editions had been omitted (disingenuously, he thought) he wrote once again to Whitman, this time pulling no punches, and asking flatly if 'adhesiveness', a word Whitman had used, included sexual relations between men.

What did he expect? For twenty years the old poet had been dodging that question and now he lost his temper. His reply still does not tell us whether Whitman was deceiving himself or deceiving others, but it answered Symonds. "That the Calamus part has ever allowed the possibility of such construction as mentioned is terrible. I am fain to hope that the pages themselves are not to be even mentioned for such gratuitous and quite at the time undreamed and unwished possibility of morbid inferences—which are disavowed by me and seem damnable."

Symonds was convinced that Whitman was stalling and in reply, though he accepted the basis of Whitman's denial, he wrote that the language of *Calamus* is closer to that of the Greeks in their extollings of comradeship than anything else in modern literature. Before he wrote his *Walt Whitman, A Study* which was published a year after the poet's death, he had somehow come to see the old man's letters to Peter Doyle and wrote rather slyly about them.

> I have been privileged to read a series of letters addressed by Whitman to a young man, whom I will call P., and who was tenderly beloved by him. They throw a flood of light upon "Calamus," and are superior to any commentary. It is greatly to be hoped that they may be published. Whitman, it seems, met P. at Washington not long before the year 1869 when the lad was about eighteen years of age. They soon became attached, Whitman's friendship being returned with at least equal warmth by P. The letters breathe a purity and simplicity of affection, a naïveté and reasonableness, which are very remarkable considering the unmistakable intensity of the emotion. Throughout them, Whitman shows the tenderest and wisest care for his young friend's welfare, helps him in material ways, and bestows upon him the best advice, the heartiest encouragement, without betraying any sign of patronage or preaching.

> Illness soon attacked Walt. He retired to Camden, and P., who was employed as "baggage-master on the freight trains" of a railway, was for long unable to visit him. There is something very wistful in the words addressed from a distance by the aging poet to this "son of responding kisses". I regret that we do not possess P.'s answers. Yet, probably, to most readers, they would not appear highly interesting; for it is clear he was only an artless and uncultured workman.•

His sulkiness was understandable. He had not been able to tell Whitman, whom he had long idolized, all about Christian Buol (and later Angelo Fusato) in return for Whitman's rhapsodies about Doyle.

5

Unknown to both Symonds and Whitman, unknown to all but a very few of his cultured friends, another man was pursuing the same illusory ideal, though he had too much sense of humour to call it 'Greek'. Edward Fitzgerald was in love with a Norfolk fisherman.

No man's life makes the mumbo-jumbo of psychologists and Freudians more trivial or absurd. Fitzgerald loved men, particularly two men, and knew no sexual attraction to women. Whether or not he could be called homosexual in medico-legal parlance, whether or not anything he did could have laid him open (after 1885 when the Criminal Law Amendment Act was passed) to a charge of gross indecency, is of little consequence. He loved Posh, his big Viking-like fisherman, as Symonds loved Christian Buol and Whitman loved Peter Doyle. Who cares whether or not they went to bed together? It would not add to the glory of *Omar Khayyam* or detract from it to know the truth of what happened in darkness aboard the little ship they shared, the *Meum and Tuum*, or to believe that they were satisfied with a fond 'goodnight'. But of Fitzgerald's aesthetic appreciation of, and devotion to, his young giant there can be no question for to his intimate friends he proclaimed it. Of Symonds and Whitman we happen to know the truth because Symonds left a journal and Doyle kept Whitman's letters. Of Fitzgerald's adoration of Posh a legend persisted in Norfolk until well into this century, tales of Fitzgerald putting to sea in a top hat and feather boa to be near his friend, of their appearance together, which roused friendly laughter at the time, Fitzgerald with

• *Walt Whitman—A Study* by John Addington Symonds, 1896.

his high-stepping walk and the blond giant lumbering along beside him, of Fitzgerald's losses on their fishing ventures and attempts to keep Posh off the liquor. But we need to enquire in no more detail.

Fitzgerald had known one passionate friendship before this. No young man loved by any of the artists given to the worship of youth stands out as more freshly attractive and virile than W. Kenworthy Browne. Even William Hickey did not make the irresistible Potts as delightful as this hard-riding, elegant, good-natured young fellow, so full of spirit and yet so gently understanding of his difficult older friend.

They met on a steam-packet bound for Tenby when Browne was sixteen years old and Fitzgerald twenty-three. Browne is described by Fitzgerald's biographer Thomas Wright• as 'a handsome, merry-eyed wildish lad of sixteen . . . with longish auburn hair'. "Between this youth and Fitzgerald commenced a friendship which was severed only by death."

Wright, who examined their correspondence, seems to have been puzzled by their devotion and records that Fitzgerald went to stay at Browne's home in Bedford every year till the young man's death. "They spent many a happy hour together talking, reading and smoking" while—a cheerful touch—"Browne's top boots polished like a mirror, stood on a chair, with his scarlet coat hung over the back—all ready against the hunting season. Browne's handsome, dapper little figure made a striking contrast to the larger, shambling, carelessly dressed form of Fitzgerald."

Fitzgerald wrote a book called *Euphranos*, a dialogue on youth which, says Wright, is 'simply and solely a glorification of W. K. Browne'. He adds: "Fitzgerald's intense admiration for Browne would be incredible to any one who was not minutely acquainted with the facts. To him Browne was at once Jonathan, Gamaliel, Apollo—the friend, the master, the god—there was scarcely a limit to his devotion and admiration; and literary history offers no parallel to the conjuncture." Literary history offers a great deal, from its beginnings to Wright's time, as he might have remembered. But in his mind the over-statement was an honest one.

Browne received this adulation as a sensible young man would. "He devotedly loved his friend and gave him such welcomes at

• *The Life of Edward Fitzgerald* by Thomas Wright, 2 volumes, 1904.

Bedford as satisfied even Fitzgerald; attributed all the virtues that he was accredited with to a friend's partiality and quietly assumed that in every matter Fitzgerald was a more competent authority than himself." He also put up with Fitzgerald's occasional acrimony.

Four portraits were made of Browne, including a sketch by Thackeray and an unfinished painting by Lawrence. Thackeray used to call him 'Little Browne' for when he was full-grown he was five foot seven in height, and Fitzgerald's own name for him was Stubby.

Browne married in 1844 and Fitzgerald lamented it in a letter to a friend. "Browne is married and I shall see but little of him for the future. I have laid by my rod and line by the willows of the Ouse for ever. 'He is married and cannot come!' " But when twelve years later Fitzgerald conceived it his duty to marry Lucy Barton, Browne did everything he could to dissuade him. (The marriage was a failure and ended in a few months.) "Give her whatever you like," said Browne, "except your hand. Make her an allowance." But Fitzgerald persisted and his friend was proved right.

Browne died in 1859 after lying for six weeks expecting death after being thrown from his horse. Fitzgerald was with him at the end and Browne wrote in painful child's handwriting—"I love *you* very—wherever W. K. B."

Five years later, being now fifty years old, Fitzgerald met Posh.

He was already familiar with many Norfolk sailors and fishermen, particularly with a Pakefield man named Lew Colby and his young son 'Dickymilk', and other longshoremen from Lowestoft. It is amusing to find that in those less democratic days nothing was thought strange in a well-to-do educated man spending his time with rough fishermen while today his conduct would at once attract the attention of the police. He was accustomed to cruise about the Deben and down to Harwich on a yacht of his own, described as a smart fifteen-ton schooner called the *Scandal*, and it was through his skipper Tom Newson and his son Jack that he met Joseph Fletcher whose nickname from boyhood had been Posh.

Posh was then twenty-four years old and already wore a beard, and it can only have been facetiously that Fitzgerald called him, in a letter to Posh's father, 'your little boy Posh'. Fitzgerald was dazzled immediately by the personal beauty of the man, his strength and gentleness, and by qualities which in the manner of a lover he could see in him though others might have found his assessments partial. Some of the things he said about him in letters during the next years show his infatuation. He might be Symonds writing of Christian Buol.

He found first in spite of the difference in build something reminiscent of W. Kenworthy Browne.

> When I got acquainted with this captain three years ago I asked him why he had never come down to see me at the time I speak of. Well, he had often seen me, he said, among the boats, but never thought it becoming in him to accost me first, or even to come near me. Yet he was the very man I wanted, with, strangely enough, some resemblance in feature to a portrait of you may guess whom, and much in character also, so that I seem to have jumped back to a regard of near forty years ago, and while I am with him feel young again, and when he goes shall feel old again.

He was a man, Fitzgerald wrote, 'of the finest Saxon type with a complexion *vif, mâle et flamboyant*, blue eyes, a nose less than Roman, more than Greek, and strictly auburn hair which any woman might sigh to possess'. A man of simplicity of soul, justice of thought, tenderness of nature, a gentleman of nature's grandest type, the greatest man Fitzgerald (who knew Tennyson, Thackeray and Carlyle) had ever met.

He was, said Fitzgerald in another letter, 'a man of royal nature' and in yet another 'broader and taller than all the rest, fit to be a leader of men, body and soul, looking Ulysses-like'. Posh 'looked every inch a king' and 'was like one of the Elgin marbles in a guernsey, which is a fine dress for a fine figure'. When Fitzgerald read Carlyle's *Heroes and Hero-Worship* some years after it was published he sent Carlyle a photograph of Posh.

> Your 'Heroes' put me up to sending you one of mine—neither Prince, Poet or Man of Letters, but Captain of a Lowestoft Lugger, and endowed with all the Qualities of Soul and Body to make him Leader of many more men than he has under him. Being unused to sitting for his portrait, he looks a little sheepish—and the Man is a Lamb with Wife, Children, and dumber Animals. But when the proper time comes—abroad—at sea or on shore—then it is quite another matter. And I know no one of sounder sense, and grander Manners, in whatever Company.

Fitzgerald also wrote of Posh that he was much more the gentleman than the gentlefolks of the place 'and very much more ladylike than the ladies'. Later, when he was anxious about Posh's occasional drinking bouts, he wrote to a man named Spalding whose letters from Fitzgerald are reproduced in *Two Suffolk Friends* by Francis Hindes Groome.

> I declare that it makes me feel ashamed very much to play the judge on one who stands immeasurably above me in the scale, whose faults are better than so many virtues. Was not this very outbreak that of a great genial Boy among his old Fellows? True, a Promise was broken. Yes, but if the Whole Man be of the Royal Blood of Humanity, and do Justice in the Main, what are *the people* to say?

Posh lived until some time after 1908, an old Lowestoft beachcomber with a frill of white beard from ear to ear who got what he could for the long affectionate sermonizing letters which Fitzgerald wrote him and would give questionable reminiscences of his old Guv'nor in return for pints in the local pubs to those credulous enough to listen to him. One of these, James Blyth, made a whole book• of Posh's stories and Fitzgerald's letters, and others competed with him for both. Posh was clearly a handsome fellow in youth in the markedly North European way of so many Norfolk men who still keep traces of their Scandinavian and Saxon ancestry. He was an ordinary enough chap, ignorant of all things ashore, imaginative only in his calling, roughly kind but without perception of where sympathy should be given, spendthrift but having a peasant's natural thirst for money, no more of a drunk than his fellows, as good as the next man but no better. Yet in Fitzgerald's eyes from the first he was a god.

In the early days of their incongruous friendship they went about together, sat talking over their beer in fishermen's pubs, and went for long walks along the sands which cannot have given great pleasure to Posh who had a sailor's dislike of walking on land. Wright describes his visits to Fitzgerald's home.

> When Posh was at Woodbridge no food or drink was good enough for him. On one occasion, after an imperial feast, Alfred Smith being present, Posh felt inclined for a rest and laid himself full length on the sofa. 'Poor fellow,' said Fitzgerald, in sincere tones, 'look how tired he is!' 'It seems to me,' said Mr. Smith, 'that you have made him half-drunk with your old Scotch ale.' Fitzgerald, however, was quite sure that Mr. Smith did not understand the hardships of a seaman's life.••

• *Edward Fitzgerald and Posh* by James Blyth, 1908.

•• Thomas Wright, *op. cit.*

A favourite haunt of the two friends was the bowling-green of the Old Suffolk where in one of a series of alcoves they smoked and drank beer. Another story told by Alfred Smith who knew them both recalled how in the early days of their friendship Fitzgerald would take Posh for cruises on the *Scandal*, and on one up the Suffolk estuaries Fitzgerald saw

> some old women going to a farmhouse with pitchers for milk, and that made him and Newson and Posh feel thirsty; so, he added, 'We also got some milk.'
> 'I suppose Posh or Newson fetched it for you?' said Mr. Smith.
> 'Oh, no,' replied Fitzgerald; 'I took the pitcher myself and went to the back-door along with the other old women.' To include himself among 'old women,' 'elderly ladies,' and 'dowagers,' was a favourite pleasantry.•

Wright also said,

> In the company of Posh, Fitzgerald could generally contrive to get rid of the gloomy thoughts which recollection of his unfortunate marriage so often produced, but not always. One day at Lowestoft he came upon him just as he was preparing to drive to Yarmouth 'in a new smart cart with a rug mare between the shafts.' Fitzgerald suddenly made up his mind to go too. On arriving at their destination they dined at an hotel, sauntered about the town, and visited St. Nicholas' church. On their way back, passing through Gorleston, Fitzgerald said to Posh, 'I want you to turn down here,' pointing to a street. 'I want to go and see the house where I lived with my wife.' When they reached the spot, he cried 'Stop!' and then sorrowfully, 'Ah! ah! Posh, had you but come to me at Lowestoft *then*! If I had only known you at the time I used to wander on those hills—unhappy!' and he pointed to the uplands to the west of Gorleston. 'Her ways were not my ways, and we parted. Drive on, there's a good fellow!••

Fitzgerald could be jealous, too. Once another man, who may have had his share of admiration for Posh's 'Ulysses-like' appearance, got into conversation with him on the South Pier at Lowestoft while Fitzgerald's back was turned. Fitzgerald was furious, and pulling Posh away by the guernsey he wore, said to the stranger, "This is *my* guest!" So peculiar and possessive was Fitzgerald's behaviour with the easy-going Posh that people who did not know them are said to have thought him a mild lunatic and Posh his keeper.

• *Ibid.* •• *Ibid.*

Posh had the gift, not unusual among seamen of the eastern counties, of hitting on a picturesque phrase and Fitzgerald reported some of his remarks to Tennyson. Speaking of a gale on a day of sunshine Posh said, 'the spoondrift flew so thick over the vessel that it cut the sun into little stars,' and of a lion seen at a travelling zoo that it looked 'a grand fellow for'ard but very lean aft.' Fitzgerald treasured his remarks and used some of them in his *Sea Words and Phrases along the Suffolk Coast*, but he learned many of these from his other friends, for he kept in touch with these during his years with Posh and took Dickymilk down to Woodbridge for a week.

His friendship with Posh might have gone on without the rancour which eventually separated them if Fitzgerald had not decided to build a herring-lugger for Posh. When they had first met Posh had a longshore punt or 'beach lugger' and made a modest living from inshore fishing. Fitzgerald stayed in Lowestoft to be near his friend and went to sea with him in the decaying *Little Wonder*. But this was not good enough for Fitzgerald who wanted to see Posh in command of a ship, and after an experiment with an old lugger named the *William Tell* to equip which he lent Posh some money, he decided to build him a herring-lugger for £360.

His first idea was to give this to Posh, but the influence of friends, or his own wish to be identified with Posh in the venture caused him to make it a partnership and the boat was called the *Meum and Tuum* (known locally as the 'Mum and Tum').

At first their hopes were high for this and we hear of Fitzgerald in the *Scandal* following her six miles to sea to take leave of Posh, and insisting on his carrying lifebelts, unheard-of among the fishermen. But soon a long series of misadventures, misunderstandings and quarrels came to the partners. Accounts of these are complicated and we have only Posh's muddled recollections of them as an old man, and some of Fitzgerald's letters to Posh and others from which to reconstruct them. Fitzgerald certainly expected too much of poor Posh, a high degree of honour, exactitude in business dealings and well-kept accounts, a sense of responsibility foreign to his easy-going nature, assiduity and strict sobriety. Posh who came from generations who took their chance from the providence of the sea and thought little of the future was baffled by his older friend's attention to detail and business methods, and exasperated by Fitzgerald's 'lecturing' every time he had a few drinks with his friends. The partnership was eventually broken up and the ship sold, but Fitzgerald's misery during the long period of the friendship's disintegration was drawn-out and painful. In one of Fitzgerald's sermonizing letters he wrote to Posh: "Do not let a poor, old solitary, and sad Man (as I really am, in spite of my Jokes), do not, I say, let me waste my Anxiety in vain. I thought I had done with new Likings: and I had a more easy Life perhaps on that account: *now* I shall often think of you with uneasiness, for the very reason that I had so much Liking and Interest for you."

There were no more friendships in Fitzgerald's life and during his last years of misanthropy and failing sight he could only give his old man's affections to the young boys who came to read to him in his solitude. "I am an idle fellow," he once wrote to a friend, "of a very ladylike disposition, and my friendships are more like loves, I think." John Addington Symonds himself could not have spoken more frankly.

CHAPTER SEVEN

Symonds, Edward Cracroft Lefroy, Edward Lear and Lewis Carroll

HELLENIC love may be a splendid ideal for the homosexual but under modern conditions, with a police force trained to spot it, even provoke manifestations of it and prosecute it, it soon loses its glamour and refinement and, driven underground, it becomes mere promiscuity. Most of the ruttish inverts of today, following an obsessed existence in queer meeting-places all over the world, started with the hope of some ethical purpose in their lives, dreamed of male relationships as honourable as marriage, tried to create something from their friendships to compensate for the sterility of them, but with time and persecution fell into facile lechery. So it was with John Addington Symonds, and in the period between 1878 and 1890, says Phyllis Grosskurth, he made advances to scores of men.

Edmund Gosse, having once made his admission to Symonds that he shared his tastes, entered with gusto into correspondence on the subject. "I am just above a bridge," wrote Symonds from Venice a few months after Gosse had opened the way to this sort of confidence, "up and down which go divine beings: sailors of the marine, soldiers, blue-vested and trousered fishermen, swaggering gondoliers. I can almost see their faces as they top the bridge. By rising from the chair a little—I do so at once, and get some smiles from passing strangers." The matter of such correspondence has not changed in all the years since then. Nor have the enclosures. Symonds, among his friends, used to exchange bundles of photographs of young male nudes, some of them no doubt the masterpieces of Baron Gloeden who lived at Taormina for many years and photographed naked shepherd boys. He could produce pictures of three generations all photographed in their teens. Gosse was so excited by one of these that he took peeps at it during Robert Browning's funeral service.

Whatever sympathy we may have for Symonds, his frequent illnesses and the physical disabilities against which he fought, his attempts to defeat the self-pity which plagued him, his habits of tormented introspection and his struggle with his Victorian conscience, it must always be remembered that he was throughout his life a well-to-do man and able, in the blackest moments, to give himself a change of surroundings. He satisfied all his whims. Even with Christian Buol his friendship could be 'cemented' by the loan of a thousand pounds.

He worked hard because he loved his work but he was never constricted by the economical need to stay in one place. He could buy lovers as he wished and luxuriate in remorse afterwards. If he had been a poor man with similar impulses it is probable that he would have been in trouble with the law on more than one occasion. He could afford to live well and had an expensive taste in wines. Though in much that he wrote he made of his life a long hard luck story, there was a good deal in it that was enviable.

In the years after he had settled at Davos he spent the spring and sometimes the summer in Venice, finally taking a flat there, very near the house of his most devoted disciple Horatio Brown.

Brown had been one of the boys in the Sixth Form at Clifton whom Symonds had lectured in order to see more of Norman. Unlike the picturesque favourite, Brown was a stocky Scot with deepset eyes and an honest, grimly attractive face. He hero-worshipped Symonds from the first and never failed in his devotion right up to Symonds's death and after. (He was Symonds's literary executor and biographer.) He visited Symonds regularly at Davos Platz and when Symonds began to spend some months each year in Venice he went with his mother to live there. In his quiet way he loved Symonds and devoted much of his life to him, but dour and unexciting as he appeared he was given to discreet affairs with young gondoliers, and wrote poetry full of veiled pederasty. A photograph of him in early middle age shows a serious but pleasant face with what one suspects to be a sensual mouth concealed by a heavy moustache.

In Venice Symonds freed himself from all restraints and with Brown sailed through the lagoons in a *sandolo*, the orange sails of which were ornamented with fleur-de-lis, or played games with Brown's gondolier Antonio. Symonds appeared at Brown's Monday at-homes at which a rare miscellany of the foreign colony gathered, but more of his time was spent in pursuit of uninhibited Venetian males.

Among these was a certain Angelo Fusato, a gondolier in whom Symonds noted 'an electric quality'. A photograph of Angelo shows him a bottle-shouldered young man with a good profile, very Italian, having a studio expression so unnaturally Napoleonic that it might have been assumed to hide his volatility and gaiety. Symonds made a date with him but, finding Angelo accustomed to hire himself out to wealthy homosexuals, fled in disillusion, and went to Monte Generoso where he wrote verses about his dilemma. Four months later he returned to Venice, persuaded Angelo to leave his present employment and at considerable cost attached him to himself as a personal servant and gondolier while Angelo's wife was employed as housekeeper. It suited everyone and with time Angelo began to feel some attachment to Symonds and was with him when he died. Angelo may have pimped for him, for Symonds had many other adventures in Venice.

Intellectually as well as physically Symonds became, in the last years of his life, obsessed with what he called variously '*l'amour de l'impossible*', 'unisexual love', 'adhesiveness', 'comradeship' or 'U . . . threm', a term derived from the substantive used by Ulrich's 'urning'. At first when he had read *Phaedrus* and the *Symposium* it had seemed to him a poetic ideal, but with time and experience he began to defend homosexuality —not too openly at first but with growing courage—and ended by proclaiming himself in favour of changes in the law which would make life tolerable for homosexuals. In all these attitudes he was sincere, but with the heightened sexuality of the phthisic opposed to inherited constraint and puritanism, he lived on a battleground. Even with Christian Buol and Angelo he had to believe his relationships were enduring and above commonplace vice, and with Angelo at least he tried to inculcate principles of loyalty, fidelity, monogamous comradeship which must have puzzled the gondolier who had thought him a straightforward prospect such as he had often served. Yet while he was trying to create these comradeships he could never resist casual and tempting encounters.

In all he wrote he was conscious of his own bias, and only too often made his readers conscious of it, while in all he read and saw he was looking for what he called 'the aura', in paintings, sculpture and books. He had taken on an ill-paid task in translating Benvenuto Cellini's autobiography but became reconciled to it as he realized with what frank enthusiasm Cellini had recalled his raffish life. Symonds found Carlo Gozzi's memoirs dull by comparison.

He probably hastened his end by his feverish application to a task which he could not resist—a Life of Michelangelo in two volumes which was published in the year of his death. At one time he worked nine hours a day on this and he made an original discovery after his own heart which provoked a letter to Gosse saying that his book would be 'revolutionary', though as he admitted in a phrase all too apt 'the pace was killing'.

The discovery was made among the archives of the Casa Buonarroti in Florence to which he had been given access by the Italian government. Symonds found that certain of Michelangelo's letters had been suppressed by previous biographers and that others written to a young man had been made to appear as though they were addressed to a woman. The letters of the young man, Tommaso Cavalieri of a noble Roman family, were also in the archives and Symonds thought there was something 'inexpressibly pathetic' in this exchange of love-letters between the aged genius and the beautiful youth which he could read after they had been undisturbed for more than four centuries.

But he dealt circumspectly with the matter in his book. Michelangelo's emotions were 'ideal, imaginative and chaste'. A reviewer afterwards saw that Symonds was faced by the same problems as a writer dealing with Languet's letters to Sir Philip Sidney or Shakespeare's sonnets to Mr W. H. It is surprising that although Symonds circulated privately his *Problem in Modern Ethics* while he was working on his Life of Michelangelo he found ways to evade the issue in his biography, and only in the work he did with Havelock Ellis for a semi-scientific textbook in an effort—on Symonds's part—to change the law could he be absolutely frank.

2

Symonds had a sixth sense by which he perceived 'the aura' in unexpected places, but he needed none when he read in *The Artist*, then edited by a well-known invert named Charles Kains Jackson, some verses from a book called *Echoes from Theocritus and Other Sonnets* by Edward Cracroft Lefroy. Three specimens of the 'other sonnets' were enough for Symonds, as they will be for a modern reader, but to do justice to them and the man who was moved to write them they should be quoted in full. The first is called *Bill: A Portrait*:

I know a lad with sun-illumined eyes,
Whose constant heaven is fleckless of a cloud;
He treads the earth with heavy steps and proud,
As if the gods had given him for a prize
Its beauty and its strength. What money buys
Is his; and his the reverence unavowed
Of toiling men for men who never bowed
Their backs to any burden anywise.
And if you talk of pain, of doubt, of ill,
He smiles and shakes his head, as who should say,
'The thing is black, or white, or what you will:
Let Folly rule, or Wisdom: any way
I am the dog for whom this merry day
Was made, and I enjoy it.' That is Bill.

The second, *A Football Player*, is in much the same spirit.

If I could paint you, friend, as you stand there,
Guard of the goal, defensive, open-eyed,
Watching the tortured bladder slide and glide
Under the twinkling feet; arms bare, head bare,
The breeze a-tremble through crow-tufts of hair;
Red-brown in face, and ruddier having spied
A wily foeman breaking from the side;
Aware of him—of all else unaware:
If I could limn you as you leap and fling
Your weight against his passage, like a wall;
Clutch him, and collar him, and rudely cling
For one brief moment till he falls—you fall:

My sketch would have what Art can never give—
Sinew and breath and body; it would live.

The third, naturally enough *The Cricket Bowler*, completes the trio.

Two minutes' rest till the next man goes in!
The tired arms lie with every sinew slack
On the mown grass. Unbent the supple back,
And elbows apt to make the leather spin
Up the slow bat and round the unwary shin—
In knavish hands a most unkindly knack;
But no guile shelters under this boy's black
Crisp hair, frank eyes, and honest English skin.
Two minutes only. Conscious of a name,
The new man plants his weapon with profound
Long-practised skill that no mere trick may scare.
Not loth, the rested lad resumes the game:
The flung ball takes one madding tortuous bound,
And the mid-stump three somersaults in air.

Now it happened that Symonds, who never forgot an attack on himself, particularly when it was based on his Hellenism, had seen this not easily forgettable name before. It was in 1877 when Symonds had hoped to be elected to the Professorship of Poetry at Oxford. For a time his chances seemed good but Richard St John Tyrwhitt had attacked him and all he stood for in an article called *The Greek Spirit in Modern Literature* published in the *Contemporary Review* which had been followed by a similar attack called *Muscular Christianity* in *The Oxford and Cambridge Undergraduate's Journal*. The last was signed by Edward Cracroft Lefroy.

It was fifteen years later when he read Lefroy's poems in *The Artist* and his curiosity was roused in a man who at one period in his life could attack him and Walter Pater for the doctrine—which neither had ever openly proclaimed—that a man should live by the promptings of his own nature,• and at another publish these lively sonnets dedicated to the charms of young athletes. He made enquiries of Charles Kains Jackson and learned that Lefroy had been a clergyman who had recently died at the age of thirty-six.

Symonds, once on the scent of something that appealed to him as having 'the aura' went further and discovered that Lefroy's lifelong

• 'The promptings of human nature are not always so entirely beautiful,' Lefroy had written sarcastically.

friend was a man named Wilfred Austin Gill who was now his literary executor. Gill was delighted at having caught Symonds's interest in his dead friend, for Lefroy's verses had all been published at his own expense by a Blackheath printer and had been pretty well ignored. He readily agreed that Symonds should see all the papers, including certain quite unambiguous letters, and sent him a photograph of Lefroy. This showed a young man clean-shaven but for side-whiskers, with a thin mouth turned down at the corners and that wistful, distrustful look in the eyes common to so many homosexuals. He wore the white bow-tie of the evangelical clergyman, a lapelled waistcoat and a frock-coat, and looked every inch what he had been, a junior Chaplain at Lambeth Palace.

Stirred by these Symonds wrote an article about the poet which was published in the *New Review* and afterwards in his book of essays *In the Key of Blue*. It was, unfortunately, a piece of disingenuousness in which he sought to prove that Lefroy's 'temperament assimilated from the Christian and Greek ideals only what is really admirable in both: discarding the asceticism of the one and the sensuousness of the other'. This, in view of his having read the letters (why did the Victorians leave packets of tell-tale letters behind them?) was sheer casuistry.

Though Symonds's whole essay was plain enough to be understood by those who were familiar with his devious rationalizations, it funked the main issue. This may not have been surprising so soon after the man's death, but why did Symonds become involved at all if all he could do was to proclaim that Lefroy, through some special privilege of temperament, hit by instinct upon the right solution of different problems which many less well-balanced natures seek after in vain because they are too coarsely fibred, too revolutionary or peradventure too intemperate? Did he really envy the ailing clergyman for his emasculated passions and yearning after athletes?

He goes on to say of Lefroy:

> Thus he felt able to write candidly to a friend upon a topic which is not often discussed among men (1883): "I have an inborn admiration for beauty of form and figure. It amounts almost to a passion. And in most football teams I can find one Antinous, sometimes two or three. And surely it is very beautiful to see the rapid movement of a perfect animal, &c. Some folk would say it was a mark of sickly

> or diseased sentimentalism to admire any but feminine flesh. But that only proves how base is the carnality, which is now reckoned the only legitimate form. The other is far nobler, unless it be vilely prostituted: and were I painter, sculptor or poet, I would teach the world so. Platonic passion in any relationship is better than the animalism which will go to all extremes."•

What animalism? What extremes? Was he in the morbid condition of Symonds during his first approaches to Willie Dyer and Alfred Brooke? And what did he mean when he said in another letter that he intended to diminish the frequency of his 'lapses into Hellenism'?

Symonds's essay was repetitive and not very honest, dwelling again and again on Lefroy's success in reconciling Christianity and the Greek ideal. But it delighted Wilfred Austin Gill who proposed that they should collaborate on a book to perpetuate the memory of Lefroy. Symonds seems to have made at least a partial agreement, stipulating that Gill, who knew Lefroy, should write of the man, while he, who understood the poems, should discuss these. The scheme never got off the ground and Gill's biography, which was published by John Lane in 1897, was a wearily pedestrian thing saying little more of the essential Lefroy than that he was educated at Blackheath Proprietary School and Keble College, Oxford and was ordained in 1878, and passed through various kinds of religious convictions. There is, however, one pregnant sentence—Lefroy was never in love because 'he preferred idealism to experience'.

3

In 1888, while Symonds was moving into the flat he had taken in Venice, an old friend of his, Edward Lear, died in San Remo, which Symonds called 'this most despicable dreary watering-place'. Lear was seventy-six years old and it was twenty years since he had met Symonds at Cannes and written *The Owl and the Pussycat* to amuse the youngest of Symonds's daughters, Janet, to whom he was devoted.

Lear and Symonds spent much time together walking and talking but if they ever touched on 'the problem' it is not reported by Phyllis Grosskurth from Symonds's Journal. This seems a pity for both men would have been happier for a frank discussion. It is quite likely that

• *In the Key of Blue and Other Prose Essays* by John Addington Symonds, 1893.

in all his long life Lear never discovered that he was not as other men were and explained, even to himself, his passionate friendships with men and his sexual indifference to women by his own grotesque appearance which he thought put women off, or by his own ill-health and poverty which, he believed, were his reasons for not wanting to marry.

Once again the question arises of whether he had any sexual experience at all and it can only be said that if he did so it was with men for he was by nature what Symonds called homogenic. His most percipient biographer* Angus Davidson while not minimizing the importance of Lear's friendships says nothing, and perhaps discovered nothing, which suggests they were more than those devoted relationships between men which were common before the emancipation of women made them companions who could be taken on rough and sometimes hazardous excursions abroad such as writers, particularly, loved; before they had any part in political or academic life. Lear's biographer certainly shows that on Lear's side such friendships were emotional and sensitive in an unusual degree and that his young friends responded to his enthusiasm and humour, but that is all.

Born of prosperous parents, Lear's boyhood was disturbed by his father's sudden imprisonment for debt which scattered his large family. But before this happened the son had developed physical disabilities which made his life as much a struggle for survival as that of Symonds, though of a different kind. The sight of his small eyes was pitifully weak and he peered from behind large spectacles, he suffered from recurrent bronchitis and asthma, and worst of all from the age of seven for the rest of his life he was a victim of epilepsy, having at some periods as many as eighteen epileptic fits in a month.

He was brought up by his eldest sister Ann who was twenty-one when the crash came. He was an ugly little boy with a large unshapely nose and he slouched about paying little attention, then or thereafter, to his clothes or appearance. He laughed about this and ridiculed himself in writing but he laughed about most things, particularly those which hurt him.

He showed an early talent for draughtmanship, drawing birds and butterflies with such accuracy that before he was twenty-one he was commissioned by the Zoological Society to illustrate a book about

* *Edward Lear, Landscape Painter and Nonsense Poet* by Angus Davidson, 1938.

parrots and by Dr Gray of the British Museum to do the drawings for his *Tortoises, Terrapins and Turtles.* Through this and other work he was invited by the 13th Earl of Derby to illustrate a book he planned on his private zoo and he spent the next four years at Knowsley Hall.

He was at first treated as a governess or tutor might have been but soon Lord Derby and his children and grandchildren adopted him and he actually ate with the family, a tribute to his charm and good manners as well as to the good sense of Lord Derby, if one remembers the times. For the rest of his life he had countless friends and patrons among the peerage. There is no evidence that he was a snob or a lickspittle. At first he may have been impressed, as any middle-class Victorian youth would have been, by the great world in which he so ambiguously moved, but with time he took titles for granted. It was while at Knowsley, to amuse the Earl's grandchildren, that he wrote the first of his nonsense rhymes.

After Knowsley he went, like many another Englishman looking for a warm climate, to Italy and remained there four years, publishing a book, *Views in Rome and its Environs* with twenty-four of his own water-colours as illustrations.

In Rome he met the first of his great friends, a man twelve years younger than Lear who was making the 'grand tour' and had the imposing name of Chichester Fortescue. An instantaneous and deep friendship was formed between them which lasted to Lear's death. For weeks after they met they spent the best part of every day together, went for long walks and for a three-day excursion to Tivoli and Palestrina. Nor was the sudden affection all on Lear's side. "I don't know when I have met anyone I like so much", wrote Chichester in his diary, and "He is one of those men of real feeling it is so delightful to meet in this cold-hearted world". Lear, conscious of his own ugliness, admired the brilliant, good-looking Irishman with his straight finely cut nose and large clear eyes.

Their correspondence over the forty years of their friendship was published and was full of absurdity, intimacy and affection. Lear used to stay with Fortescue in Ireland and always relaxed in his company, while Fortescue occasionally lent him money which he always repaid. When Fortescue married a famous hostess Lear noted 'every marriage of people I care about rather seems to leave one on the bleak shore alone'. In his last words he sent an affectionate message to Fortescue, by then Lord Carlingford, and to his two other life-long friends Franklin Lushington, now a judge, and Thomas George Baring, Lord Northbrook.

He met these two in much the same manner as he had met Fortescue, when they were young men travelling abroad and he an indigent painter some years older than they were. Perhaps of the three he loved Franklin Lushington most, though Lushington, a lawyer and in later years a dour and dry man had little outward reciprocation to show him. One feels that it was Lear who created and maintained the friendship for although Lushington was sincerely fond of him he was not the kind of man who could show his feelings. With Fortescue, Lear had little reserve; with Lushington, though he was more emotionally involved, he was forced by the other's taciturnity to conceal his tense sensitive devotion.

They met in Malta four years after Lear had met Fortescue in Rome and their friendship was as quickly formed. Within a week they set off together for a tour of Greece which lasted two months and in spite of discomforts inconceivable today (even in Greece) they were the happiest months of Lear's whole life.

The friendship which was born of those weeks was not always a happy one for Lear was—no other words will do—in love with Franklin Lushington and the other, a sincere, kind, unemotional man, could never give him the response for which he craved or even understand that he was the centre of Lear's life. When Lushington was appointed to a legal position in Corfu Lear accompanied him there, having nursed Lushington's dying brother for some time in England. Their journey out was delightful for he had Frank Lushington to himself and 'nothing can be so kind and thoughtful as my dear friend all the way . . . he is wonderfully good and even-tempered as he is learned and wise'. But in Corfu Lushington became remote; he was one of the two British judges there and so busy that Lear could rarely see him. 'The greatest sadness is that I hardly see anything of my friend . . . I hardly know what to do for sheer melancholy sometimes'.

He went off on his perpetual travels, this time to Jerusalem and Petra where he was nearly murdered but returned to Corfu to be near Lushington. But Lushington was sent home and soon after was married. Their friendship continued and, says Angus Davidson, 'probably Lushington never noticed any essential difference in its quality', but for Lear it was the end of a long struggle to establish the unreserved intimacy with another man he so ardently craved.

The third of his greatest friends, Thomas George Baring, later the first Earl of Northbrook, was fourteen years younger than Lear and a friend of Fortescue's when they met in Rome. 'He is an extremely luminous and amiable brick and I like him very much and suppose he likes me or he wouldn't take the trouble of knocking me up as he does, considering the lot of people he might take to instead'. Twenty-five years later when he had become Viceroy of India Northbrook invited Lear to come and spend a year or two in the country at his expense.

Lear received another kind of devotion, and one which Symonds would have understood and perhaps envied more. When he was staying in Corfu to be near Lushington, and seeing so little of his friend, he engaged a young servant named Giorgio Kokali, a native of Albania, who remained his faithful companion for twenty-seven years and died five years before Lear. Lear taught him to read and write, took him with him on his travels to his great comfort and solace in difficult times, quoted his naive remarks in his diaries and referred to him as his 'faithful Suliot', 'my good old servant', 'dear good servant and friend' and in the last years 'dear old Giorgio'. He quarrelled with him; even, in the heat of an Indian summer, dismissed him but afterwards took all the blame on himself and reinstated him. He nursed him through illnesses and shared his anxieties about his sons, one of whom was consumptive and the other a bad hat. When Giorgio died he raised a tablet to his memory at San Remo. What Giorgio did for Lear is less easily chronicled but it seems to have been been illimitable from cooking for him, finding comfort for him in their rough travels, acting as a punctilious servant on occasions of ceremony and tending him through his constant illnesses.

Lushington, Fortescue and Baring may have been the three younger men who most stirred Lear's imagination and made him write in his diaries strings of adulatory epithets. But there were many more with whom he shared excursions and afterwards corresponded—Evelyn Baring, cousin of Thomas George, who was a young ADC when they met and afterwards became Lord Cromer of Egypt, Charles Church, later a Canon of Wells Cathedral, who made a disastrous journey with him in Greece, Herbert Congreve whom he taught to draw as a boy and who afterwards accompanied him on a different mission when both Lear and Giorgio were ill, John Cross with whom he went on an expedition to Mount Sinai. All these became his friends, regular correspondents and often his patrons.

That leads to the most interesting question about Lear to which his biographer can give no satisfying answer. How did this man, with every disadvantage, succeed in being one of the most loved and sought after personalities of his time? With a bankrupt stockbroker for a father and a background at first suburban then of harassed poverty he had no conventional or expensive education and no boyhood friends of any significance in his later life. He had no social graces and his ugly, almost grotesque appearance showed his chronic ill-health. A poor man all his life he was not above borrowing from his distinguished friends or persuading them with naive persistence to attend his exhibitions and buy his pictures. He was scarcely considered in his lifetime as a serious painter and what fame he achieved rested on his nonsense rhymes which brought him only that amused patronage the Victorians gave to those who could make them laugh. He was abroad for most of his adult life, rarely at hand when an extra man was needed for a dinner-party. He was shabby and untidy in appearance to a point that embarrassed his friends and his more conventional hostesses. His ill-health rarely left him any peace of mind, he was often depressed and sometimes desperate.

Yet Queen Victoria never forgot him after the twelve drawing-lessons he gave her, spoke of landscapes as reminding her of Mr Lear and threatened to visit him at San Remo. Her son when Prince of Wales spent an hour looking at his drawings during a visit to Rome and seventeen years later recognized him at a reception and spoke to him for some time 'most amiably'. He could spend his summers in England going under pressing invitations from one great house to another and as a diner-out could choose the occasions on which he wanted to accept. In financial crises he was offered loans or commissions to do work invented for his convenience, being sent to places considered 'good' for him, to paint pictures his patrons did not want. He was one of the few men whom Tennyson could stand near him during periods of bearishness and misanthropy and he was a friend not only of peers and royalty but of great men like Browning, Millais, Holman Hunt, the Stracheys, the son of Shelley and Symonds himself.

Moreover, by children and by his more intimate friends, he was deeply loved.

What was it about him? Charm? Humour? He had both in plenty. His gift for laughing at himself rather than at others? His passionate sincerity hidden behind his façade of fun, punning and whimsicality? No one has quite explained it and it may be that the answer is a simple one—he was a good and a lovable man.

4

His rival first, then as many think his master in writing nonsense verse, The Reverend C. L. Dodgson (Lewis Carroll) was less lovable and not so unquestionably good. In fact if he behaved today as he did in the last century people, more knowledgeable about the attractions of very small girls to certain natures, might in our earthy modern way call him a dirty old man.

Derek Hudson• takes a more charitable view. For Dodgson, he writes, 'children were an escape from sex rather than any sort of conscious satisfaction of it, but they gave him the affection he needed and helped him to fulfil the Platonic and protective love which was characteristic of his nature'.

Florence Becker Lennon•• is more realistic, perhaps. "He had an odd, and of course frustrated, love for little girls—in part identifying himself with them, in part substituting child friends for more difficult adult relationships." The 'of course' loses a little of its point when she goes on to quote Isa Bowman, one of his infantile harem, as saying that Dodgson used to kiss her 'passionately' when she was no more than ten or eleven years old.

Whether or not he was 'frustrated' by the standards of his time, there is plenty of evidence that he became obsessed with very small girls and behaved in a highly ambiguous way with them. Frustrated in the last analysis he probably was but what would be said today of a man who persuaded an ex-child-friend when a widow to obtain child models for him to draw and later to photograph naked?

It was not easy for the English, or the people of any country where the Alice books have been loved for more than a century, to recognize

• *Lewis Carroll* by Derek Hudson, N.D.
•• *Lewis Carroll* by Florence Becker Lennon, 1947.

that they may have been inspired by a sexually aberrant clergyman's passionate interest in little girls. The contemporary defence, among those who knew Dodgson, was that he was an artist, a minister of religion, a man of saintly life, that not an impure thought ever crossed his mind and that anyone who could think evil of the author of *Alice in Wonderland* and *Alice Through the Looking-Glass* must himself be full of obscene thoughts. Only here and there were parental prohibitions to disturb this comfortable supposition.

A clergyman's son brought up with six younger sisters, Dodgson turned naturally to young children. Shy, even hostile towards adults, he followed his academic career in solitude and with considerable success—Rugby, Oxford and a lectureship in mathematics at his own university. Stuttering badly and considered something of an old lady he made few friends and throughout his life had a morbid distaste for the young of his own sex, seeing something ugly and even cruel in masculinity. 'I confess I do *not* admire naked boys in pictures', he wrote to Harry Furniss in later life. "They always seem to me to need clothes—whereas one hardly sees why the lovely forms of girls should ever be distorted."

His letters to the many little girls who were for a time his friends are full of kissing, and the memoirs of several of them who claimed to be the original of Alice talk of sitting on his knee beside the fire and other intimacies which, before he began to take photographs, stopped short of impropriety. Many of the letters, edited or not, have been published, but Mrs Liddell, the professor's wife for whose little girl *Alice* was certainly written, made her daughter burn all her pre-*Alice* letters from Dodgson for reasons that were never stated.

Perhaps the most ominous aspect of this was his quite ruthless dismissal of his little favourites when they reached the age of fourteen or so and ceased to interest him. He refused to go walking with one of them when she put her hair up and claimed he had 'lost' his friends as soon as they ceased to be children. Each was then succeeded by a new favourite and, kind and indulgent as he was to little girls, he was adamant and unscrupulous in cutting them out of his life when they passed beyond the age limit of his affections. When it was time to take off his hat to one, he said, it was time the friendship ceased. "Nobody knows how many girl friends he had," laments Florence Lennon, "but at any time there was a reigning favourite who was superannuated at about fifteen." "She has a beautiful figure I think," he wrote to Miss Thomson, "but she is turned fourteen and I like to draw a child best."

That Dodgson wrote the Alice books to catch the attention of the Liddell children, to please them, to ingratiate himself with them or with one of them, takes away nothing of their merit, of course; it is only a pity that with time his cravings became promiscuous and none of the so many later favourites was able to inspire him again. He grew with the years less discreet, perhaps one may say less sane. His voracity for models for his photographic studio seems to have been unbounded and Florence Lennon says hundreds, perhaps thousands, of these portraits still exist. He photographed little girls singly, in pairs, in groups and in many costumes—Chinese, Cinderella, parlour maids, beggar maids, Dolly Varden. Helmut Gernsheim• who devoted a study to Dodgson as a photographer said that he considered children's simple night-gowns most becoming and quite a number of little girls were posed in them. One child, Ella Morice Williams, was photographed sitting up in bed in a fright, another, May Marshall who was pictured in beach costume, recalled afterwards that she was so young at the time that she had trouble putting on her street clothes, tying her hair and buttoning her boots. Dodgson showed great proficiency in buttoning her boots and making a great bow on her head.

There were many others whose names were not recorded and one or two who remembered Dodgson when they grew up, like Ethel Arnold, the Bowman sisters and Gertrude Chataway. Maud Stephen was picked up with another little girl in the public gardens at Reading and Nellie Knight on a train in 1888. As an elderly gentleman Dodgson walked about with puzzles and toys in his pockets with which to attract the attention of little girls and a pair of scissors he used for snipping off locks of their hair, which he kept. He also when walking on the beach carried safety-pins for those who wanted to paddle.

Of his nudes Helmut Gernsheim says that they were sentimental and void of artistry. But he adds that Dodgson ordered them to be returned to his sitters or their parents after his death so that as far as is known none have survived. How then does Mr Gernsheim know what they were like? One thing has been recorded. That the rests between poses were unduly long and during them Dodgson supplied cake.

• *Lewis Carroll, Photographer* by Helmut Gernsheim, 1949.

There is reason to think that as he became an old man more obsessed with his hobby Dodgson knew what risks he ran, and he grew more secretive and more attentive to the least sign of disapproval from parents. His references to Mrs Grundy may have been the innocent expressions of any Victorian railing at her stupidity and her habit of misconstruing motives but they do not always sound like that. In 1889 he wrote, "I go down every summer to Eastbourne and I still make friends with children on the beach, and sometimes even (being now an old man who can venture on things that 'Mrs Grundy' would never permit to a younger man) have some little friend to stay with me as a guest".

What, one cannot help wondering vulgarly, would the Eastbourne police say about this today? Dodgson's clergyman's habit would no longer protect him from suspicion, rather the contrary. One can almost see the headlines—Famous Author Charged with Soliciting. Child Invited to Stay in Lodgings. Search Reveals Indecent Photographs. Mother says Daphne aged eight was playing with her friend Doreen when this man . . . and so on. The question is not so facetious as it sounds. Were the Victorians cleaner-minded, or more gullible, than we are? Has common knowledge of elementary psychology made us nastily suspicious or more able to protect young children? Dodgson died in the odour of sanctity the honoured author of an immortal classic. Today, 'frustrated in the last analysis' or not he would find himself in Wormwood Scrubs. Are we right or were the Victorians?

5

In Symonds's last years what had been a secret obsession became a public cause. "I am eager about the subject for its social and juristic aspects", he wrote to Dakyns. "You know how vitally it has in the past interested me as a man, and how I am therefore in duty bound to work for the elucidation of the legal problem."

This was sheer altruism for by the very circumstances of his life he no longer felt himself restricted by English law, although the Labouchère amendment had been added to the Criminal Law Amendment Act in 1885. ('A disgrace to legislation', Symonds called it, 'by its vagueness of diction and the obvious incitement to false accusation.') He believed he should use what authority and knowledge he had for the benefit of others and spoke of 'my brethren the Urnings'. He was, and remains down to the present, one of the very few homosexuals who has dared to take any part in the long struggle against monstrous legislation; most of them, even those in public positions, have discreetly kept out of it, while repressed or secret, or unnaturally restricted homosexuals have often been those to speak most loudly, sometimes hysterically, against any change in the law. If any significant change comes it will be through the courage and decent-mindedness of men who have a public conscience but no personal interest in the subject.

Symonds read a great number of textbooks which had recently appeared, chiefly from German sources, Krafft-Ebbing's *Psychopathia Sexualis* and works by Albert Moll, Westphal, Liman and particularly Carl Heinrich Ulrichs with whom he corresponded. He decided to write his own textbook on the subject which he called *A Problem in Modern Ethics*. It was printed privately and sent to his friends for comment. He believed—unlike Freud when he came to discuss the matter—that homosexuality was congenital. He believed too that the greater tolerance of the working classes towards sexual deviation to be in healthy contrast to middle-class inhibition and hypocrisy. He discovered 'the aura' in a great many books published at this time and wrote to Gosse, "What a number of Urnings are being portrayed in novels now! *Un Raté*, *Monsieur Venus*, *Footsteps of Fate*. I stumble on them casually and find the same note." But he did not approve of Wilde's *Picture of Dorian Gray* which he thought would 'confirm the worst suspicions of the uninformed'.

Then he decided that his own story should be written although it might 'never be fit to publish'. 'The study of this evolution, written with the candour and precision I feel capable of using, would I am sure be interesting to psychologists and not without its utility'. So he wrote the lengthy journals, dedicating nearly two years to them though he knew that in his lifetime they could bring him no benefit of any kind. Horatio Brown, his literary executor, put them in the hands of the London Library after his death with a proviso that they should not be published for fifty years after his (Brown's) death which occurred in 1926. Phyllis Grosskurth, however, before writing her life of Symonds was allowed to examine (though not to quote Symonds's own words from) these journals and reports it to be in essence the history of Symonds's sexual life, 'the anguished record of a man whose energy had been drained by his struggle to reconcile his instincts with mores of society'.

Meanwhile *A Problem in Modern Ethics* had found its mark and Symonds told Dakyns that he was 'surprised to see how frankly and ardently and sympathetically a large number of respectable persons felt towards a subject which in society they would only mention as unmentionable'. He wanted to see the law changed and he thought of a public edition of his book with certain other papers. It was at this time that he got in touch with Havelock Ellis and the two planned to collaborate in a historical and scientific study of the question which finally, after Symonds's death, was issued under the title *Sexual Inversion* as the first of Ellis's series of *Studies in the Psychology of Sex*.

But Symonds's extraordinary energy as a writer was failing. In 1892 he went to England for the last time, as usual taking Angelo and enjoying his delight in the theatre as he had enjoyed Norman Moor's a quarter of a century earlier. He met Lord Alfred Douglas, just then in the first years of his friendship with Wilde, and seems to have viewed this with some jealousy. "You can't always be pampered in the Savoy. It was very pleasant for Oscar pampering you, I doubt not. I wish you would come and see how I can make you comfortable" —here he seems to have fallen into the phoney aesthetic jargon which those around Wilde must really have used to one another—"and feed your soul on honey of sweet-bitter thoughts—in Italy—in Switzerland —it is all the same." This was an unexpected interest for Symonds to show, since Bosie was the very antithesis of the peasants he loved. Three months after writing it he died and one of the kindest obituary notices appeared in Bosie's magazine *The Spirit Lamp*.

Perhaps in all Symonds's troubled life no one was quite in love with him. His wife was quick to realize that their relationship could only be a lame and crooked one. The dream which returned to him again and again was of a young man who stretched out loving arms to him but in life he had only vain shadows of this. He had the good-natured response of Christian Buol and the bought caresses of many others but not their love. Yet his story is not all tragedy. He achieved and was happy in achievement. He loved others and they endured his unceasing revelations about himself with patience. His wife and daughters were loyal and one of them at least, his beloved Madge, loved him faithfully to the end. And although he made many claims that he was frustrated, his life shows that this was less than half-true. He never found complete fulfilment, but who does?

PART THREE

Oscar Wilde and The Iron Lilies

CHAPTER EIGHT

Wilde and Walter Pater

ONE of the most misleading and superstitious phrases which have dazzled the senses of historians is *fin-de-siècle*. It suggests that our invented decimal calculations of time really have some influence on human life. It distorts our vision of the past. It is a supposition for which people, once they have accepted it consciously or not, will rationalize and lie, forcing the wildest fancies to fit their polemics.

The last decade of the nineteenth century was, as it happens, a particularly lively and adventurous time. In it was broken up at last the ugly gothic type in which life had been set since Queen Victoria was crowned. The development of the internal combustion engine enabling the earliest motor-cars to take the road, the popularity of the bicycle which meant that for the first time in history people—even quite poor people—could move about at will, the advance in sea transport which made crossing the Atlantic no longer a far-flung adventure, the first real consciousness of the forces of socialism and feminism, all these and many minor changes came, or came to fruition, in the Nineties, and the reign of Edward VII which followed was a period of consolidation and steady advance rather than experiment.

There is a parallel, if not a close one, with the literature of the time and it may be noted that one of the first writers who considered the Nineties as a literary epoch, W. G. Blaikie Murdoch, called his book *The Renaissance of the Nineties*• and said 'the superb virility which marked our art of fifteen years ago seems to be largely gone'.

The Decadence of the Nineties was not so much a literary movement as a publishing stunt. It was promoted by John Lane and Richard Le Gallienne, his friend and adviser. Instead of high artistic purposes this precious pair discovered practical and rewarding principles—that poetry just then was a paying proposition, that any old book put out with a cover designed by Ricketts or a frontispiece by Beardsley was at once considered 'aesthetic', 'in the movement', 'Frenchified' or improper. That by giving books published by John Lane (at first with Elkin Mathews) a distinctive appearance they gave them, in the public mind, a distinctive 'tone'. That they had somehow managed to let off a stink of the eternal bonfire in their premises and it was better than patchouli, the favourite perfume of poor honest whores.

It was exactly these principles which they applied when they issued the *Yellow Book*. Yellow was the colour of naughty French novels; with this and Beardsley's world-weary drawings they could publish anything, however dull, under whatever name, however much respected, and give it an air of *fin-de-siècle*. And they did. A look at the list of contributors makes one wonder today how it could ever have been considered decadent. (Le Gallienne could make anything look decadent, even himself.) As it was, Lane was lucky to get even such examples of the critical abuse on which he throve as 'English rowdyism and French lubricity'.

It would have been difficult to fill such a thick quarterly except by the most catholic standards. Such writers as were trying to follow Swinburne's lead of thirty years earlier and learn from the French the real meaning of the word Decadence were doing so only in order to irritate the philistines. They were in a tiny and laughable minority struggling against 'the ordinary type with a stick and a pipe and a half-bred black-and-tan', against three men in a boat, against that overwhelming majority in town or country who still attended Eleven O'Clock Service, against purchasers of oak-framed prints of *The Monarch of the Glen*, occupants of the stalls at the Savoy operas, against

• Written in 1911.

Kipps and Sentimental Tommy. Any of these people might buy the *Yellow Book* if they thought there was a bit of hot stuff in it, but for the poor Decadents for whom it was supposed to speak they had no use at all. So these, driven to defiance, imbued with Wilde's grand idea of the artist being free from the obligations of society, paraded their aestheticism and obligingly died young of tuberculosis or drink or both. But the most they did towards being Decadents was to gather the fragments that remained from Swinburne's verbal orgies.

Graham Hough• has shown in just what way Swinburne was indebted to the French. "Swinburne's general conception of pagan antiquity as something nude and splendid, joyous and cruel . . . was certainly not picked up from Jowett at Balliol but at the feet of Gautier. In particular *L'acre Venus de gouffre amer*, a Venus who is also a goddess of pain and cruelty is one of the personages Swinburne takes over from his master." Again, "Swinburne's algolagnia would have been the same if no other literature existed; but without Gautier and Baudelaire he would have had considerable difficulty in finding means to express his abnormalities." But what was left of this after Swinburne had retired to Putney? It was a force in English intellectual life for a time after *Poems and Ballads* was published to bring Gautier and Baudelaire, scarred by Swinburne's personal underlinings, to the English consciousness, but as a force it was spent, leaving behind parody and imitation. It lived on as something derisorily called aestheticism or art for art's sake, something recognizable in *Punch* and popular humour but nowhere else. It had gone out into the streets and lost whatever virtue or inspiration it might have had. One can imagine a suburban dinner-party being sent into fits of laughter by paterfamilias saying of his hearty son who had forgotten to have his hair cut, "Oh, he's an aesthete!"

Swinburne's debt to French *Decadence* survived in the vulgar superstition that French things were naughty, French art, novels, dress, habits, were all alike immoral. A famous divorce case which ruined the career of a potential Prime Minister was lost by Counsel's sotto voce references to 'French practices'. Oscar Browning was almost sacked from his mastership at Eton when he was suspected (wrongly as it happened) of lending a French novel, *Mademoiselle de Maupin*, to a boy. Henry Vizetelly, a harmless old bore (whose work the present

• *The Last Romantics* by Graham Hough, 1961.

writer first discovered as an almost continuous series of clichés on wine) was sent to prison for publishing an English version of a Zola novel. French food was suspect, French music was discarded in favour of Wagner, French culture was scarcely mentionable, French women were called *cocottes* and French men believed to be either barbers or waiters, or aristocrats of dandified manners, dangerous good looks and no morals. Preventatives were called French letters and kisses that were more than a chaste touch of the lips were French kisses. Oscar Wilde, as we shall see, might never have gone to prison if he had not taken one of his boys to Paris and had his hair curled by a French barber.

Even French phrases carried sinister meanings and when people called the literary pseudo-movement of the Nineties *fin-de-siècle* it added an ominous purple hue to the earlier writings of Wilde and of those, like Richard Gallienne (who called himself Le Gallienne), who imitated them.

A great deal of effort has been spent on trying to make of it a 'period' in which poets were persecuted and died young, wrote with wistful or defiant eroticism, owed their culture to continental models, lived recklessly vicious lives and influenced their time. Most of the valid poetry of the Nineties could have been written and published ten years earlier or later and only some of the pre-comedy writings of Wilde, Beardsley's *Under the Hill*, some minor poetry and a number of passages in the critical work of Arthur Symons who tried to speak for the period, have distinct if superficial characteristics. The adjective 'Ninetyish' as applied to literature means nothing in retrospect but the productions of John Lane before 1895. Lane not only issued anything—even poetry—with what he hoped was the scent of dying lilies about it, but a novel satirizing his own authors, *The Autobiography of a Boy* by G. S. Street.

The two figure-heads of this faked revival of Decadence were unquestionably Wilde and Beardsley. Beardsley remained loyal to the phallus at least until his last days when, it has been said, he begged that all bawdy drawings should be destroyed, but Wilde even before the Nineties had discovered that aestheticism in costume and subsidized poetry did not pay, and before the decade had advanced far was dressed in a frock-coat writing plays. All that the men of the Nineties had in common, from Wilde with his insolent pose as 'the artist' to the penurious poets arguing boozily in the Crown, was their determination to infuriate the middle-classes, and in this they were successful. Wilde was a past-master at it and the younger men, not by his methods but by professing diabolism or Catholicism, by drug-taking or absinthe drinking, by being French, by looking unkempt, by finding their mistresses on the streets or in the music-halls, were almost as successful.

Another name given to the young men of the Nineties is 'the Tragic Generation'. This is melodramatic terminology and does not bear examination. The two poets of the time whose lives are used as justification for it, Lionel Johnson and Ernest Dowson, both died young, both in penurious and ugly circumstances and both, partly at least, from alcoholism. But there was nothing in the work of these two that belonged especially to the period, for Johnson was a Roman poet and Dowson a Romantic. Other examples used to make out a case are those of Aubrey Beardsley and Hubert Crackanthorpe. Beardsley died of tuberculosis of which disease relatively little was known at that time and if he had never drawn a line or written *Under the Hill* his expectation of life would have been no more—perhaps less. Crackanthorpe threw himself into the Seine when his wife went off with another man, a not unprecedented tragedy. John Davidson was fifty-two when he committed suicide because he had cancer. But other poets of the generation, A. E. Housman, W. B. Yeats, Arthur Symons, John Gray, Alice Meynell, Alfred Douglas, Olive Custance, Laurence Housman, Richard Le Gallienne, Victor Plarr lived to rather more than average age while other figures associated with the Nineties had far from tragic lives. There is no justification for working up a sentimental picture, based on the last days of Johnson and Dowson, of a generation of tragic young men. There are too many precedents to quote from other periods, from Chatterton to Dylan Thomas.

So far from the Nineties having a decaying quality, noisome and poisonous, it was a time of considerable revival in literature as it was in life, and time may show it primarily as the decade in which an astonishing array of new talent was first seen, Rudyard Kipling, H. G. Wells and Joseph Conrad among story-tellers and Hilaire Belloc, A. E. Housman and Francis Thompson among poets to name only an incongruous trio of each. It was a time of hope for young artists, for the first time having a chance to earn a living by art which was not stereotyped, and for young poets, for the first time having a chance to earn a living at all. During the first five years of the decade the writers' pubs and cafés crackled with new names, new opportunities, new periodicals.

In this Wilde and his anti-mediocrity was, however indolently, a leader. He had been rousing the wrath of the philistines for nearly twenty years. His *Dorian Gray* was a war cry against Philistia, and voiced some kind of philosophy, derived from obscure French sources, Gautier, Baudelaire, Huysmans, from the noisy eroticism of Swinburne, from Pater's passionate but timid aestheticism, which all added up to Wilde's own delight in 'strange sins' and wonderful experiences. Wilde had a vocabulary and an imagery of his own, bizarre and precious, which he had at first used seriously and then repeated with delightful frivolity and self-ridicule, calling his receipts from a play 'the gold the Gryphon guards in rude Armenia'. What had been 'sins of the flesh' to theologians and moralists became deliciously awe-inspiring and mysterious, and what had been virtues became boring and vulgar. There was much play on the word 'beauty' as the ultimate ideal, though Wilde's own sense of beauty was narrow and his taste in music, art, domestic decor, costume and jewelry was disastrously opulent and sometimes comic. Wilde was defiant of the ethical values of his time, anti-bourgeois and at the same time anti-progressive. He himself showed no curiosity about the stirring changes in life which were becoming evident. He left no epigram about motor-cars but if he had done so one can imagine the form it would have taken and his Socialism was more literary and unreal than William Morris's. By romanticizing his defiance of the social values of the age he pandered to them, considering his passion for stable-boys and such to be daring and romantic and his love for the son of a Marquess the highlight of his life.

Above all, Wilde stood for the apotheosis of 'the artist' who according to the creed Wilde proclaimed was a being privileged to ignore all rules of human conduct, all ethical values, all conventions and even all legislation in his search for experience to be perfectly expressed in exquisite terms. This was a frivolous doctrine which no one but Wilde had the insolence to proclaim, but the man who had dared go about London in drag of his own invention to advertise his devotion to a system of aesthetics which never existed except in his mind, did not stop at calling himself a lord of language beyond interference.

For to Wilde 'the artist' was Wilde, though he demanded the artist's privileges for others.

On his own shoulders he took the whole responsibility for 'the artist's' position in the world. In his own words he affirmed it to be inviolable and in doing so brought on his own head all the invidiousness, animosity and contempt not only of the philistines but of his fellow-writers who sought for no exalted prerogatives but preferred the common lot of man. When at last he stood in the dock he was not seen as a good-natured playwright whom nobody had personal cause to hate but as 'the artist', the creature who had defied the fate which set men to rub along through life this way or that, the insolent fellow who had claimed the unheard-of freedom to live as he pleased.

2

If ever there was a case in which Freud's principle of sex as the mainspring of all human behaviour• is triumphantly justified it is that of Wilde, yet no one has given more than a hurried and blushing glance at his sex life or even collected what facts are known about it.

There is more than one reason for this. Wilde's most able biographers —and in spite of the fact that for fifty years he has been the most written-about writer in English, the definitive biography has yet to appear—have not been men with any particular knowledge of the subject. They may not have been the kind of morons, cads or repressed perverts who have opposed the implementation of the Wolfenden Report, but they have not had the special sympathy or experience which would give them insight into Wilde's motives, nor have they been acquainted with the sub-world of metropolitan vice and crime, so little changed since then, in which he moved.

Until recently, until perhaps the publication of Rupert Hart-Davis's edition of Wilde's letters,•• it has only been possible to write of Wilde as though he was a clinical case almost unique in England, or as a great writer with a tragic and irrelevant weakness which brought him to ruin, or as a fine man misled by evil associates, anything but as a promiscuous homosexual who enjoyed slumming and male prostitutes.

• Monstrously over-simplified, of course, but acceptable as a rough working hypothesis.

•• *The Letters of Oscar Wilde* edited by Rupert Hart-Davis, 1962.

While that kind of embargo persisted the chance to investigate was lost. It would have been possible in the Twenties and Thirties to have traced some at least of those who gave evidence against Wilde and to have persuaded them to talk, and one wonders why this never occurred to A. J. A. Symons, for instance. But now it is too late. The youngest of them, Charles Parker, if he is alive would be a year or two short of ninety and Alfred Taylor would be a centenarian.

Neither Robert Ross nor Reginald Turner left any written account of this side of Wilde's life, being anxious, naturally enough, to minimize its importance. There were other men who were his friends in a particular or general sense who survived until recent years, but most of them kept silence. Wilde himself left no testament of his follies before the trials except some passages in *De Profundis*, and though his letters were frank enough in his last years they almost never reverted to his pre-Parisian life.

There are two main sources of information on this, the *Letters* which even in the early years of discreet correspondence reveal more than is generally realized, and the accounts of the trials, both Christopher Millard's and H. Montgomery Hyde's. There are also, to be used with the greatest circumspection, certain details which Frank Harris claimed to have heard from Wilde. Harris was such a flagrant liar that in dealing with these each reader can only trust his instinct and common sense to choose what may be true. Indeed that is all he can do with much other material for the truth about Wilde is encrusted with barnacles of phoney anecdote, almost every contemporary of his wishing to produce in his memoirs at least one remark (always made at some respectable dinner-party), and scarcely a book of name-dropping reminiscences, published in hundreds between, say, 1910 (when it became permissible, even chic, to remember Wilde in his dining-out period) down to, say, 1950 when it became a mark of senility, is without at least one entry under Wilde, Oscar, in its index.

Hesketh Pearson, in the best biography so far published, sifted all this with skill and understood Wilde in many of his aspects but not in the essential one, and neither he nor anyone else has trusted his instincts sufficiently to produce an unveiled portrait. He was inhibited by the conviction that to call a man homosexual, or to suggest that at a certain time in his life a man had some emotional relationship with his own sex, was to disparage him.

The present writer is conscious of no such inhibition and moreover has had the advantage of discussing with Lord Alfred Douglas (his, the writer's, friend during the last twenty-five years of his life) Wilde's earlier acquaintances and activities. These discussions fortunately took place during Douglas's later years of life when his bitterness was forgotten and when he spoke amiably, but never scandalously, about Wilde. A few other men who knew Wilde with brief intimacy have been willing to talk frankly about him, like B. G. Horniman and Tom Kennion. Robert Ross gave Hesketh Pearson some information and Reggie Turner was always ready to gossip amusingly with his friends about him, but most of the scandalous stories exchanged by bar-room anecdotists have been the merest hearsay.

One of the most persistent myths repeated by almost every biographer has been that Wilde was accepted in Victorian society, was frequently invited to join 'the highest circles' and spent his week-ends in great country houses. This misconception probably came from Sherard, Ross and other Bohemian friends of Wilde who were so remote from the haughtily defended strongholds of that society that Wilde's precarious status on its outer fringes impressed them unduly, and when, for instance, he would arrive late at the Crown wearing evening dress to say he had dined with Lord Ronald Gower, the notorious sculptor friend of Roden Noel, or with Lady Mount-Temple whose house at Babbacombe the Wildes rented, or with Lady Dorothy Nevill who was a contributor to *Woman's World* when Wilde edited it, they would suppose he was a lion among Duchesses. Yet which were these ducal houses and who were Wilde's friends among the 'highest nobility'? If they existed they would certainly have burned Wilde's letters when the crash came but they could not have escaped being mentioned in his letters to others and it would be easy to identify them now. He was known to be an entertaining talker and for some time, till his conduct grew too flagrantly indiscreet, he was popular as a guest in certain wealthy households where rights of entry were not too closely examined, but the fact that he accepted invitations without his wife would have excluded him from those where protocol was respected.• Even in the society which received him it was for his

• That he did so is evident from his wife's Tite Street Visitors' Book. In it appear the names of many famous men and women, Swinburne, Browning and Sarah Bernhardt among them, but not one name of those prominent in contemporary 'Society'.

conversation and he occupied rather the position of a conjuror or musician who was expected to entertain the guests. A man whose name appeared in the popular press, who had once gone about in a kind of fancy dress, and who even now wore ostentatious clothes and jewelry, whose father had been the centre of an ugly scandal in Dublin and whose mother was an eccentric poetess devoted to Irish nationalism, a man who in later years was seen about in public with the most extraordinary youths, could never have been accepted in those boring and exclusive circles known as The Best Society in the last century. Nor would his friendship with Lord Alfred Douglas have helped him. Bosie's father had disgraced himself in the House of Lords, adopted atheism, insulted the Queen and finally forced his wife to divorce him. 'Society' was not so ignorant, even then, that Wilde's sensational friendship with Bosie escaped all criticism and those who saw him, for instance, returning to his home in Chelsea late at night and during his wife's absence accompanied by a teen-aged boy were not quite so unworldly, even in 1890, that they would pass it over without remark. If he had ever been socially acceptable he would long have been considered *déclassé*. He was not 'abandoned by his society friends when his fall came', as it has been unkindly said, for the reason that he had no society friends to abandon him.

Another myth is that Wilde was introduced to homosexuality by Robert Ross when he met him in 1886. Even leaving aside Harris's stories, this is out of character and is contradicted by Wilde's letters at Oxford and afterwards. Nor did 'prosperity lead him into evil habits', nor an unhappy marriage send him into the streets. (His marriage was in many respects an unusually happy one.) Bernard Shaw's theory that Wilde's behaviour was due to a pathological disease called giantism which he inherited from his mother is a particularly Shavian and ingenious piece of nonsense and Sherard's that Wilde passed through a period of lunacy is not even ingenious.

He was a queer like others, like millions of others in the world then and today, and, after discovering the promiscuous, unstable, somewhat lecherous life of conscious homosexuals in London (it might have been in any great city), he abandoned himself to it, morbidly captivated by the facility with which sexual curiosity could be perpetually excited and satisfied. There was none of Symonds's earnest search for ideals in the contacts he made. He was not in the least possessive or in search of constancy, fidelity, monogamy, or anything more than *pleasure*, a word whose labial and sibilant would come often and unctuously from his sensual lips. He had none of that ambition, which many a lecher, however facile his conquests, never loses, to reform, or at least to keep to himself, every whore he meets. He regarded his forays into the queer underworld as adventures and the young men he met there as strange and handsome beasts of some alien species while to his intelligent homosexual friends he described his experiences with that ironical mixture of humour and pride which made him talk of feasting with panthers. He wanted only the male part in the drama of sex and he came to regard himself as something of an animal-tamer.

For the rest, like others who followed this kind of existence under the gas-lamps of the London streets, the iron lilies as Le Gallienne called them, and in those bars and cafés where they became known to one another, he relied on alcohol to excite the nerves, the curiosity, the desire, and give him the courage and stimulus for pursuit. Many of the crassly indiscreet things he did and risks he ran were said at the time to be the actions of a madman; they were nothing of the sort, but came from the false daring of tipsiness. He may have been encouraged initially by the effrontery of those whom he met in that limbo beyond class, age, race and calling, he must have wondered as other neophytes have done how such a cabalistic society could flourish within a populace unaware of it. He became as bare-faced as the rest but he never ceased to believe that he was a pioneer from another class adventuring in dangerous places and from prison wrote melodramatically that two blackmailers from whom he had suffered, Clibborn and Atkins, were 'wonderful in their infamous war against life'.

It was this histrionic belief in himself as a man discovering 'strange sins' which sustained him through the sheer fatuity of such a life. He entered into it all, the antics of transvestists, the queer parties, the exaggerated anecdotes of what had happened to So-and-so last night, the sometimes comic always expressive idiom, the use of feminine pronouns for men, the hysterical quarrels and reconciliations, the ready tears and the shrill inconsequent laughter. He, a man of intellect and a scholar, apart from his distinction as a writer, listened to the shrill flippancy of queer conversation, laughed at the crude buffoonery of male prostitutes and displayed his conversational wares to young men almost, or perhaps quite, illiterate. That he found it interesting and delightful to cross the social bridge, to enjoy something of the confidence of a class mysterious to him (as to most upper- and middle-class people at that time) is not remarkable. It was part of the adventure. But that he could join in the chit-chat about 'drag' and 'cottages' among these skittish effeminates still seems remarkable and shows how far he was prepared to go in his search for experience.

With them, and with the male prostitutes he entertained and presented with inscribed silver cigarette cases, he found not only excitement, but release from many inhibitions. John Addington Symonds discovered and proclaimed more than once that the uneducated classes were nearly always more tolerant of sexual eccentricity than the bourgeoisie and among them a distinguished man in search of young male companionship might be a subject for exploitation but seldom for wonder or disapproval. Wilde knew this, too, and rejoiced in it; the restraints of boyhood, the stifled longings, the insistence by pedagogic moralists on a sense of shame and his own awareness of isolation fell away in their presence. He was not a creature apart, secretly conscious of his sexual incompatibility, but one who had found others of his own colour. He was still one apart in another sense for he was a giant intellectually, socially and financially among them, but the entourage he dominated had the same desires as he, or at least aped them.

With time he went deeper in. The demands of such society as he had known became intolerable to him, the responsibilities of family life, the rigours of his profession, all were neglected as he luxuriated in his squalid Lotusland. More and more he enjoyed the society of other friends with whom he could both share his exploits and discuss them, like Bosie Douglas, Robert Ross, Reggie Turner, Maurice Schwabe and the rest. It became as obsessive as drug-taking till in the last years before his fall he had to leave London if he wanted to work at all.

But what was most dangerous about this obsession was that Wilde, though in a less crude and abandoned manner, shared the fearless exhibitionism of so many of his fellow-homosexuals. They were urged by their flamboyant natures to show off their flashy clothes and jewelry or to dress as women, to gesticulate, ape or exaggerate the feminine motions and to use the sort of make-up then the sole prerogative of prostitutes. Wilde had worn his aesthetic costume before he knew what this would indicate to students of homosexual life, and still dressed ornately. But he indulged in another kind of exhibitionism, common enough among ageing inverts but to a man of his fame and notoriety fatal—he wanted to show off the young men he attached to himself. Certain as always of his taste he believed them to be remarkable specimens and liked others to see him surrounded by them. It was a minor but a most unfortunate demonstration of his belief in 'the artist' as a privileged human being, able to flout the good opinion of less exalted beings. It was a piece of bravado, but at the same time it was ill-bred and demoralizing and quite unworthy of a man of his intelligence and achievement.

The highest manifestation of it was his deliberately conspicuous association with Lord Alfred Douglas. Bosie was notably handsome with a teen-aged girl's complexion, brooding eyes, loose blond hair and the figure of an adolescent athlete. He was also the son of a Marquess and had a courtesy title 'like the name of a flower' as Wilde said. With an Oxford reputation as a cross-country runner, a poet, the editor of the *Spirit Lamp*, a rebel and an aristocratic *flaneur*, he attracted attention wherever he went. This, added to Wilde's, made the pair when they were seen together in the most public places, in the smartest restaurants, at first nights, a gift to gossip-writers and an attraction to that large usually harmless body of people who note the presence of publicized figures wherever they go. Small wonder that it grew into a scandal and that Bosie's parents—who were divorced—were alarmed and disgusted at it for different reasons, Lady Queensberry because she loved her son, and her husband because his friends were a disreputable mob of racing touts and horsy types who pulled his leg about it.

But Wilde was not satisfied with this. He was seen at his own first nights surrounded by queer young men like Robert Ross, John Gray, Pierre Louÿs and his publisher's office-boy Edward Shelley, while he would sit in a theatre box on other occasions with Charles Parker, one of two brothers (a groom and a valet who later gave evidence against him), or he would appear in the domino room of the Café Royal with a party of young footmen and stable-boys, just as in any queer club or bar today may be seen some well-to-do middle-aged queer clucking like a hen over a personable youngster he has found in the suburbs or during his summer holiday abroad, anxious to be congratulated on his acquisition yet fearful of losing it to someone richer. Wilde, in other words, instead of comporting himself like a gentleman, a successful playwright, the father of a family and a man with responsibilities to others, took the easy way of cheap adulation from mercenary sycophants and persuaded himself (not too seriously perhaps) that it was a bold and individualistic way, that he was a lover of beauty and an inspired dabbler in fabulous debaucheries resurrected from Imperial Rome.

Even in this there was nothing very remarkable. Erotic illusions and the phantasmagoria of vice occur in the most commonplace minds and Wilde was only giving rein to his personal fancies as many others did. What was unusual was the position he occupied and the circumstances in which his exposure came. These were unique. At no other time, in relation to no other person, could a sordid prosecution for 'gross indecency' make its victim the most famous pederast in the world's history.

3

A good deal is known of Wilde's parentage but virtually nothing of his boyhood since he never wrote of it and rarely recalled it in conversation. The only man with the impudence to set down confidences about early life he is supposed to have received from Wilde was Frank Harris in a book full of mischievous lies called *The Life and Confessions of Oscar Wilde*.

Though a history of Harris as a blackmailer and perjurer forms no part of the present book—it has been done effectively by several writers—some examination is necessary of his biographical fantasy about Wilde since there have been intelligent if gullible readers who have accepted parts of it.

Harris knew Wilde during the years when Wilde was successful as a playwright and Harris as an editor, but there was no intimacy between them, Harris disapproving of Wilde taking cockney boys to the Café Royal and Wilde saying that he did not know what a Rugby football scrimmage was but he imagined it to be like a conversation with Frank Harris. At the time of the trials he met Wilde and advised him to leave England, developing this later into a story of how he had kept a steam yacht in the Thames 'with steam up' to take Wilde to safety. Unforgivably during Wilde's imprisonment he went to see him, told him that he had just made £23,000 in South Africa and would pay him £500 before his release only to send a verbal message a few days later to say this was impossible. When Wilde was released Harris gave him some clothes and a little money but was 'so offensive to me and about me', Wilde said, that negotiations were impossible.

Harris acknowledged a copy of *The Ballad of Reading Gaol* when Wilde sent it to him and his letter 'touched' Oscar who promptly asked by post for £5 and got it, but complained after further requests that Harris had sent him nothing. At last, more than a year after Wilde came out of prison Harris went to Paris and took Wilde and Bosie to Maxim's for dinner ("The bill was terrific.") but some months later, after Bosie had inherited some of his patrimony, swindled him out of £2,000 on a confidence trick concerning a hotel in Monaco. He arranged to take Wilde to Napoule for 'three months on the Riviera' but failed to turn up and when Wilde went alone left him in anxiety for some time before sending him £30 to pay for his past eight weeks at a small hotel where he was being dunned. And so on. For Wilde's last three years they haggled interminably about money promised for a scenario of Wilde's which Harris turned into a play, and the last words Wilde wrote ten days before he died were to Harris, not an affectionate *vale* but "I rely on receiving the £150 you owe me".

When, then, did the long, minutely remembered 'Confessions' take place? Certainly not in London before the trials, and if in Paris afterwards they must have been alcoholic chats after a good dinner. In Wilde's letters in his last years he gave flippant and shameless and quite unselfconscious accounts of his casual affairs, with a nickname of his own invention for each boy; he lets one gather that he is drinking a good deal (or 'having vine-leaves in his hair', as he put it, quoting Ibsen), scrounging amusingly from anyone who had any money and giving value in his conversation for every meal he ate. It is impossible to imagine him sitting down to solemn confessions and banal philosophical reflections whispered to a sympathetic and presumably shorthand-writing 'Frank'.

As they appear in Harris's book they consist of three kinds of material. There are well-known facts about Wilde, his family, his trials and so on which were familiar to anyone, but particularly to any journalist like Harris, at the time. There are pieces from letters to Ross and others which Harris had seen and cunningly turned into passages of dialogue addressed to himself. And there is a mass of invention by Harris supposed to be in Wilde's words. This can be distinguished by trite aphorisms which Wilde at his most maudlin would never have uttered, continual interjections of 'Oh Frank . . . You see, Frank', and asides like 'he laughed charmingly', 'he laughed mischievously', 'he cried reprovingly, laughing at the same time delightfully'.•

Harris long intended that when the scandal would have died down and Wilde as a figure could arouse general and open curiosity he would cash in on his acquaintance with him to produce such a book and when during the war he found himself expelled from France, in flight from England where he had failed to assist Lady Warwick in blackmailing the Royal Family over Edward VII's letters, and stranded in New York, he settled down to it. He had tried to cut a figure in New York journalism as a pro-German Englishman, but as usual had gone too far and been dismissed from several newspapers. He wrote this book for a legitimate reason, to earn himself enough to live on, but he wrote it without the smallest respect for the truth. It would not matter if he had merely wished to give himself importance and exaggerate his intimacy with Wilde and his efforts on his behalf. It

• In *Bosie: The Story of Lord Alfred Douglas* (1963) the present writer gave another account of this book. "*Oscar Wilde: His Life and Confessions* is one of the curiosities of literature. No one but Harris would have had the impudence to put into a dead man's mouth a complete apologia for his life which is a shoddy and ill-contrived invention of the author's own. In the few years during which Wilde knew Harris he was scarcely ever alone with him for Wilde, like Wells, was unenchanted by Harris's bombast. Yet Harris produced two volumes of Wilde's supposed confessions to himself, including long passages of controversy in which Wilde is made to defend homosexuality with arguments that would not convince a moron and in words which would have shamed Amanda Ros. 'What you call vice, Frank, is not vice: it is as good to me as it was to Caesar, Alexander, Michelangelo and Shakespeare' and so on, pages of feeble remonstrance and lurid humourless confessions of an affair with a French soldier, utterly unlike the gay and shameless details Wilde gives in his letters of his promiscuities with Boulevard boys. Moreover Harris takes phrases of Wilde's used in letters to others, in court, even in his published writings, and giving them a twist or a small change of emphasis prints them as spoken by Wilde to him in one of the interminable conversations between a manly, understanding 'Frank' and a maudlin 'Oscar'. Most pitiable are his attempts to make Wilde profound or epigrammatic. 'And so the great romantic passion comes to this tame conclusion?' suggests Harris at the end of a long admission by Wilde of his failure with 'a soldier boy'. 'What would you, Frank?' replied Oscar. '*Whatever begins must also end.*' The italics are mine but the platitude, it is scarcely necessary to say, is Harris's."

would not have mattered if he had been content to adapt things Wilde had said or written elsewhere to the purpose of a conversation with himself. It would not have mattered if he had invented a few melodramatic touches like 'troops of the lowest women in the town dancing together and kicking up their legs in hideous abandonment' outside the Old Bailey after Wilde had been found guilty, or the monstrous hyperbole in his description of the exodus on the night of Wilde's arrest. "Every train to Dover was crowded; every steamer to Calais thronged with members of the aristocratic and leisured classes, who seemed to prefer Paris, or even Nice out of the season, to a city like London, where the police might act with such unexpected vigour." What mattered was that he gave information which if true would be of the greatest interest, that he made potentially valuable statements about Wilde and other people in which one cannot have the slightest trust.

This is particularly unfortunate when he is writing of Wilde's boyhood for (as seen) he is the only biographer who has attempted to do so at any length. He has a flashy little story about a boy at Wilde's school, for instance, which though it could happen between any two boys at any school would, if one could believe it, demonstrate that Wilde was utterly unconscious of the devotion of a younger boy when he was seventeen. It is told with much improbable dialogue in answer to Harris's question of whether he had not some younger boy to whom he told his 'dreams and hopes'. The climax comes in Wilde's words when Wilde, all unconscious of the other's dog-like adoration, is being seen off by him in the train for Dublin.

> "You must go now," I said to him.
>
> "Yes," he replied, in a queer muffled voice, while standing with his hand on the door of the carriage. Suddenly he turned to me and cried:
>
> "Oh, Oscar," and before I knew what he was doing he had caught my face in his hot hands, and kissed me on the lips. The next moment he had slipped out of the door and was gone. . . .
>
> I sat there all shaken. Suddenly I became aware of cold, sticky drops trickling down my face—his tears. They affected me strangely. As I wiped them off I said to myself in amaze:
>
> "This is love: this is what he meant—love." . . .
>
> I was trembling all over. For a long while I sat, unable to think, all shaken with wonder and remorse.

What is one to make of that? Sheer Harris? But the question becomes even more embarrassing when Wilde is pictured as describing to an attentive Harris a scene with Walter Pater when Wilde was an undergraduate:

> Pater was a very great man. Dear Pater! I remember once talking to him when we were seated together on a bench under some trees in Oxford. I had been watching the students bathing in the river: the beautiful white figures all grace and ease and virile strength. I had been pointing out how Christianity had flowered into romance, and how the crude Hebraic materialism and all the later formalities of an established creed had fallen away from the tree of life and left us the exquisite ideals of the new paganism. . . .
>
> The pale Christ had been outlived: his renunciations and his sympathies were mere weaknesses: we were moving to a synthesis of art where the enchanting perfume of romance should be wedded to the severe beauty of classic form. I really talked as if inspired, and when I paused, Pater—the stiff, quiet, silent Pater—suddenly slipped from his seat and knelt down by me and kissed my hand. I cried:
>
> "You must not, you really must not. What would people think if they saw you?"
>
> He got up with a white strained face.
>
> "I had to," he muttered, glancing about him fearfully, "I had to—once. . . ."

This is a more obvious fake, not because it is impossible in relation to Pater but as coming from Wilde. If the story were true and Wilde had told it at all—and he certainly would not have done so to such an unsympathetic a person as Harris during Pater's lifetime, that is until a year before his imprisonment—he could only have made it something grotesquely funny without being unkind to Pater for whom he had a lifelong respect. He might have recalled it to Ross or Bosie with good-natured burlesque, but never with all that hu-ha and mixed metaphor about the enchanting perfume of romance wedded to the severe beauty of classic form, and he would never, Oscar Wilde would *never* have said seriously that he himself 'talked as if inspired'. No, Harris was a liar, and his whole book on Wilde, and all his *Contemporary Portraits* and two-thirds of *My Life and Loves* remain to prove it.

4

Pater, on the other hand, apart from his work which more than most prose divides critics into advocates and detractors, was a highly interesting figure, secretive and paradoxical. If like John Addington Symonds he had left an introspective and self-revealing journal it would be one of the books most worth reading of its time. Only a man of intense feeling, of emotions that writhed out of sight, could have written *Marius the Epicurean*, yet even those who knew him best thought Pater, particularly in his later years, a dull stick, a shifty-eyed reticent scholar who had no words to waste on mere conversation. They proposed facile explanations for his dreary isolation—his ugliness, his parsimony, his self-dedication to scholarship. Scarcely a word he spoke has been recorded and such anecdotes as there are stress nothing but his reserve. He was not even a misanthrope with a spirited hatred for mankind who shut himself away—on the contrary he seems to have been willing to receive those who wanted to see him, though without much graciousness. He lectured conscientiously, but, when his students sought in private to provoke or persuade him to reveal at least some spark from the embers they suspected to exist, they were repulsed and his admirers received courteous chilly answers to their enquiries. Yet this was the man who had taught them to burn always with a hard gem-like flame.

Born in 1839, two years after Swinburne and a year before John Addington Symonds, he was the son of a doctor who died when he was five. He was brought up with strict economy by his mother. He was slightly hunchbacked and like Edward Lear pitifully conscious from childhood of his own ugliness which was in contrast to the beauty of his brother William.

The family was selfconsciously of the professional classes and looked down on tradesmen. Whether or not Pater himself was a snob must be like so much else about him a matter of guesswork but in *Emerald Uthwart* and *The Child in the House* he gave socially idealized pictures of his upbringing at Enfield with distinguished ancestors in the background.

He seemed to be cut out for a clergyman and as a small boy played at being one with a nightgown for a surplice. He was sent to King's School, Canterbury and like other famous men was unhappy there.

He was teased as a milksop, and on one occasion was ill for a time after being badly kicked by some boys near the Norman Staircase.

He made friends with two other boys as selfconscious as himself, Henry Dombrain known as 'Archdeacon Dombrain' and René McQueen. They were a solemn trio, Pater already whiskered, and there is pathos in their attempts to play and enjoy themselves in the Kentish woods or, when they were staying with McQueen at his home in Sussex, trying to be spontaneous and gay in dramas they wrote and produced in a barn.

Pater went through a phase of such extreme ritualism that his friends, who would both take Orders, feared that he might leave them for Rome. But after he had won a scholarship at Queen's College, Oxford and been there a year while McQueen was at Balliol he began to give them a different (but perhaps at that time no greater) anxiety by professing to have lost *all* belief, though he was determined to continue training for the church. This was too much for McQueen who said that Pater was 'nothing but a sad remembrance'. They were reconciled on condition that Pater would not attack or scoff at Christianity, but a year or two later they quarrelled again because of Pater's atheism and this time McQueen and Dombrain told him with sorrow that their friendship must cease and 'spoke to him for the last time in this world'. When he persisted in offering himself for the ministry McQueen wrote to the Bishop of London and prevented him from being ordained.

Why did he persist? It was not unheard-of for indigent scholars of no particular conviction to see in the church a means of livelihood, but surely this could not be so in the case of Pater to whom religion had meant so much. Had he secretly kept his faith but bored with the religiosity of his friends pretended to be an agnostic? The question is not without interest for he remained close to the church while professing scepticism for the rest of his life.

After this curious old-man boyhood and adolescence he became a Fellow of Brasenose and continued in residence there—though for eight years he had a London home for the vacations—till he died at the age of fifty-five. Surprisingly McQueen had a very different future. He hated Oxford and it is said• that he became a Scholar-Gypsy, 'shunning the city's din, and delighting in remote and sequestered

• *The Life of Walter Pater* by Thomas Wright, 1907.

country villages and the company of husbandmen and sailors'. There is no record of his having met Pater again.

The same writer says that Pater was 'the Caliban of Letters', though all his friends were good-looking. This remark is amplified by William Rothenstein• in both its particulars. Rothenstein was making portraits of Oxford personalities and had a letter to Pater. He found him with a thick moustache hiding rather heavy lips, grey eyes a shade too close together restless and evasive under dark eyebrows. He was, said Rothenstein, morbidly selfconscious about his appearance and, when the print of his portrait had been made, refused to allow it to be published. He studied it long and regretfully then asked his oldest associate at Oxford, Frederick Bussell, whether he really looked like a Barbary ape.

Yet as Wright said nearly all his friends, from Simeon Solomon onwards through a long series of young men, were good-looking and Rothenstein should not have been surprised when he found that Pater 'ignored the young *precieux*' and filled his rooms with football and cricket playing undergraduates. He gave regular luncheon parties on Wednesdays and Rothenstein met 'simple good-looking youths of the sporting fraternity'.

Bussell, he adds, was always there. The Reverend Frederick William Bussell was a well-known figure at Oxford at the time, M.A., B.D., B.Mus. and D.D. and a Fellow of Brasenose who became successively Chaplain, Tutor and Vice-Principal. He had almost every academic distinction and no other. He shared Pater's interest in handsome and athletic undergraduates but although the two were intimate friends and took a walk together every day Bussell did not always encourage Pater to participate in the excitement of new discoveries and when he began a somewhat passionate pursuit of Bosie Douglas, then an undergraduate in his first year, offering him Handel and Bach as a choirmaster might have offered tea and cakes, he did not introduce Pater and it was a year later when Wilde visited Bosie at Oxford that Bosie and Pater met.

Though at his Wednesday luncheon parties Pater entertained what were even then known as the hearties, his friends outside the university were of a very different kind. Simeon Solomon as a handsome young man used to stay with him at Brasenose and made a portrait

• *Men and Memories*, Recollections of William Rothenstein 1872–1900, 1931.

of him. Solomon, an extrovert trying to find profundity in himself and others, must have been fascinated by the strangeness of Pater's mask, and is said to have painted him, doubtless without revealing his purpose, as Judas Iscariot. Pater rarely laughed; it was as if he knew that laughter gave his face an almost diabolic look. Whether or not the painting existed or exists, Pater's nickname among undergraduates in later years was 'Judas'. An undergraduate explained this by saying that Pater was always in a dream and slouched by under a wall without looking anyone fairly in the face, yet it may have dated from those visits of Solomon in Pater's first years as a Fellow.

He met Solomon a good deal in London afterwards and was closely in touch with him when Solomon was arrested. When this was reported to Swinburne he was at first greatly concerned, insisting that Solomon, of whose character he was perfectly aware, must have been out of his mind. "Do you—I do not—", he wrote to Powell, "know any detail of the matter at first hand? *Pater I imagine did.*" The italics are mine for the words seem significant when it is remembered that Solomon was prosecuted for an offence in a public lavatory.

Pater seems to have been one of the few of Solomon's associates who concerned himself for the unfortunate man at this time. He went to see Solomon's sister Rebecca, also an artist, and meeting Swinburne in Oxford gave him hope of Solomon's 'ultimate recovery and rehabilitation'.

Another friend of Pater who fell from public estimation, as we have seen, was Oscar Browning. Pater had frequently stayed with him at Eton during term-time at that hospitable boys' boarding house where the seniors met so many interesting people. Pater had taken Simeon Solomon for instance; the painter and housemaster had become the most intimate friends and Browning had invited Solomon for trips abroad. Anything seems to have been possible in the last century under the guise of Christianity or Hellenism, more discreetly called a devotion to the Classics, but what is still surprising is the leisure and affluence of these academic old queers who had large comfortable homes in which to entertain one another, moved about often attended by servants, took their pupils or young friends abroad, invited their favourites to the theatre or to concerts, yet found time to write their stylish books on Greece, Rome or the Renaissance. Even when one of them came to trouble, as Johnson (Cory) and Oscar Browning did, there were always plenty, like the *cuadrilla* of a matador, to surround and protect the fallen warrior and Pater wrote to Browning, without a glint of humour: "All I can say is, that you know how much I admired your work at Eton when I was with you in the summer, and I was very glad to hear, not for your own sake only but on public grounds, that you had decided not to leave Eton without a struggle." Shortly afterwards he asked Browning to stay with him at Brasenose.

It would be interesting to know how Pater would have behaved in a far more public crisis, but he died a year before Wilde's arrest. Seventeen years earlier when Wilde was an undergraduate he had sent Pater a copy of the *Dublin University Magazine* in which he had an article on the Grosvenor Gallery. (Wilde sent copies of his published articles and later of his early books almost indiscriminately to people of importance.) Pater's reply suggests that Wilde's undergraduate reputation had already reached him and that he was distinctly interested, for the article itself was an undistinguished piece of writing.

> Dear Mr. Wilde, Accept my best thanks for the magazine and your letter. Your excellent article on the Grosvenor Gallery I read with very great pleasure: it makes me much wish to make your acquaintance, and I hope you will give me an early call on your return to Oxford.
>
> I should much like to talk over some of the points with you, though on the whole I think your criticisms very just, and they are certainly very pleasantly expressed. The article shows that you possess some beautiful, and, for your age, quite exceptionally cultivated tastes; and a considerable knowledge too of many beautiful things. I hope you will write a great deal in time to come. Very truly yours, Walter Pater.•

How much friendship resulted from this is another of Pater's secrets. Harris's inventions may be left out of reckoning, but we know that after he had come down from Oxford Wilde used to visit Pater and we know that he praised Wilde's writings with an extravagance that is difficult to understand in a critic usually so exacting. When Wilde sent him *The Happy Prince* he wrote:

> My dear Wilde, I am confined to my room with gout, but have been consoling myself with *The Happy Prince*, and feel it would be ungrateful not to send a line to tell you how delightful I have found him and his companions. I hardly know whether to admire

• *The Letters of Oscar Wilde* edited by Rupert Hart-Davis, 1962.

more the wise wit of 'The Wonderful [Remarkable] Rocket,' or the beauty and tenderness of 'The Selfish Giant': the latter certainly is perfect in its kind. Your genuine 'little poems in prose,' those at the top of pages 10 and 14, for instance, are gems, and the whole, too brief, book abounds with delicate touches and pure English. I hope to get away in a day or two, and meantime am a debtor in the matter of letters. Ever, very sincerely yours, Walter Pater.

After that they reviewed one another's books so that any personal significance in their log-rolling must be discounted.

It has been said that Pater could not forgive Wilde for vulgarizing his philosophy. This is a piece of loose literary chit-chat which has been passed down from the last century. For Pater had no philosophy and what passes for it among those who have (understandably) read nothing of his but the famous Conclusion of *Studies in the History of the Renaissance* was a series of remarks, almost afterthoughts, which are unsupported elsewhere in his work. The nearest he came to any such thing was in his tendency, it was no more, to judge works of art unimpeded by the religious bias of the Victorians. He was not original in this and he voiced it timorously and I think that Lord David Cecil• somewhat overstates the case: "Moreover though Pater is interested in the relation of art to morals and right conduct his approach is very different from that of most thinkers who have considered the subject. These nearly always start with a moral system, as it were, and then judge art by how far it conforms to it. Pater starts with aesthetic taste, and goes on to judge moral precepts by how far they satisfy that taste. He approves of goodness because it is beautiful, not beauty because it is good".•• Pater's early religiosity and the painful break with this which lost him his friends made him sometimes reach out fearfully towards the flamboyant paganism of Swinburne, but this did not amount to a philosophy or anything like one.

He was, in fact, horrified when any suggestion arose that he had something to say which might be applicable to human life, and withdrew the famous Conclusion to the *Renaissance* from later editions. When he wrote about the eighteenth-century German philosopher Winckelmann whose friendships with young men were notorious, he shied like a frightened mare at his Hellenism which he called a state 'in which man is at unity with himself, with his physical nature, with the

• *Walter Pater* by Lord David Cecil, 1955. •• *Ibid.*

outward world'. He had pockets full of fig-leaves to distribute, as when he spoke of Winckelmann's friendships which brought him 'into contact with this pride of human form, and stirring the thoughts with its bloom, perfected in reconciliation to this spirit of Greek sculpture'.

What Pater unquestionably had was a style, mellifluous, rich, expressive, of its kind superb and though he held that style and matter were indivisible he had nothing to use it for but integrally flaccid art criticism and that magnificently windy piece of fine writing *Marius the Epicurean*. He of all men should have recognized that style and matter can be separated as the soul can quit the body leaving, perhaps, a beautiful form and an exquisite texture which will soon be dust.

In all those gorgeously written books what did he say? Has any student of Pater discovered—not a 'message', for that need not be sought—but a theme, a point of view, something which enlarges or minimizes the genius of others, something that adds to human experience, thought, taste, stature? For years Pater's books were considered a part of a young man's academic education, for years they stood unread on the shelves of aesthetic undergraduates who would argue about them, profess to be guided by them, anything but read them. The words in them are manipulated with a cunning almost unprecedented in English prose, but they have no guts. If Pater had anything to say he never dared say it.

In any case what little philosophy there was in Wilde's art-for-art's sake reiterations was learned far more from Ruskin than from Pater, or second-hand from the Pre-Raphaelites, or even from Whistler who so expressively showed him that the artist is the supreme being and that purchasers of pictures, readers and such small-fry should be brightly insulted from time to time to keep them interested. Pater may have been a 'great man' to Wilde as Tennyson, Gladstone, Browning and others, to whom Wilde also sent his early writings, were great men. But as an influence, unless in some personal way of which we know nothing, he was negligible.

No one has told us those small human things about Pater the man which can reveal so much. We know he was parsimonious and we guess it was the result of his early upbringing. We know that entertaining—though he did his calculated share of it—was difficult for him and that he fussed lugubriously over his luncheon table and seating arrangements before his guests came. We know from Thomas Wright

—a surprising detail—that after 1869 for a time he suddenly began to become less restricted in his taste in clothes appearing in neckties of brilliant apple-green and peacock blue. We know he was a late riser and—discreditable as it was among Victorians—breakfasted daily in bed. This may have been redeemed somewhat by his reading of the *Dictionary of National Biography* while he had his coffee but was still by those who knew him considered a lazy habit. We know he liked, and discreetly sought, the company of handsome young men. Beyond that we know almost nothing indicative of his private thoughts, of his attitude towards mankind. Perhaps his contemporaries knew no more, for not one of them has left a personal record, and we can only suppose that it was Pater's intention that none of them should.

Yet no man can live entirely behind a screen and the story of one of Pater's few friendships removes it a little.

In 1877, when Pater was a year or two short of forty, that dangerous age at which Wilde met Alfred Douglas, Pater met a man twelve years younger than he named Richard Jackson. Jackson believed himself a poet; he was also rich. He became devoted to Pater in a sentimental if not a passionate way and this devotion lasted for many years. Wright believed that he was the original of Marius and in old age Jackson seems to have claimed this quite seriously. If it is true it is shocking to know what the writings of Marius would have been like, for this is a quatrain which Jackson wrote at Pater's request as a song for his birthday—

> Your darling soul I say is inflamed with love for me;
> Your very eyes do move I cry with sympathy:
> Your darling feet and hands are blessings ruled by love,
> As forth was sent from out the Ark a turtle dove.

"I am glad to write about you," he added, "for owing to you my life has been enriched, its minstrelsy swelled."

Pictures show Jackson as a soulful-looking rather serious man, bearded with the rest, an emotional young saint in a Victorian stained-glass window. He was, in fact, an ardent Anglo-Catholic immersed in the fierce controversies of the time. When a certain High Church parson named Tooth was sent to prison for 'ritualistic practices', or some such transgression, Jackson bought the *Church Echo* in order to attack the Bishops and champion his cause. (Few people alive today can realize the high passions, the genuine martyrdoms, the violence and bitterness that came from these controversies in the Seventies and Eighties of the last century, though Sir Compton Mackenzie saw them in their later stages and has graphically described them.)

Jackson's time was divided between his comfortable home Grosvenor Park, Camberwell, and a kind of High Church monastery founded by an equally rich Anglo-Catholic, the Rev. Father Nugée. This was in Walworth and was called St Austin's and was heavily endowed by Nugée and Jackson, aiming, as such movements often do, at the youth of the district. Jackson became a Lay Brother here and called himself Brother à Becket, writing sentimental hymns and painting murals for the chapel. He was an enterprising missioner and used to go down to the Embankment at night to pull in down-and-outs.

To both Grosvenor Park and St Austin's Pater became a frequent visitor, sharing Jackson's interest in certain of his young converts whom he asked down to Brasenose to stay. He would arrive in London exhausted saying, "Oxford pains me, slays me. It is impossible there to escape the ruts of convention". But the ruts of convention could be escaped at St Austin's where it was a Christian duty to befriend young hooligans or paupers, and Pater, in spite of his scepticism in religious matters, took a keen interest in the work. He did not, it is true, attend Mass at St Austin's but then, as Jackson recalled many years later, he was a late riser and would still be in bed when Jackson returned from church at eleven o'clock. They would later take a walk together, for Camberwell was then a semi-rural area with gorse growing on the Common.

Jackson introduced his young friends to Pater, and one of these, Veargett William Maughan, became a particular favourite of Pater's when he came up to Oxford as an undergraduate. Pater called him 'the Bishop' and 'admiration deepened into affection'. But after two years Maughan died at Oxford.

He was soon replaced in the affections of both Jackson and Pater by another youth of brilliant promise. This was Walter Blackburn Harte whom Pater first saw as an acolyte wearing a scarlet cassock in the chapel of St Austin's. He seems to have been irresistible to all who met him, having literary ambitions and a cockney sense of humour. Pater said he had 'a darling personality' and asked him down to Oxford, but most of Harte's time was spent at Jackson's Camberwell home, for he found Pater's dull dreary rooms at Oxford 'a great disappointment'. Jackson called him 'Little Walter'; 'Great Walter' being Pater himself. "He is full of original fire and what a sweet way he has of looking at men and things," said Jackson, and further: "He is a most sweet child—a prose Chatterton, an eternity of consolation to me." A portrait shows a beautiful youth with curling lips, deep expressive eyes and a fine profile.

Not all their hopes for him were in vain. Walter Harte did not qualify as a prose Chatterton but emigrating to America he became in the 1890s a successful journalist and leader-writer and a book of his essays *Meditations in Motley* published in Boston in 1894 is not without interest. 'A Bundle of Papers Imbued with the Sobriety of Midnight' he ominously called the essays. It appears from the preface that for two years Harte kept a bookshop called Dodsley's 'in the literary slums' but 'a certain literary bumbailiff who objected to my existence and occupation upon principle, finally put the shutters up one fine winter morning'.

The essays are wordy and pseudo-Addisonian, in keeping with the oddly eighteenth-century tone of much American journalism of eighty years ago, but they are not without humour.

Disasters came to Harte and he died in the same year as Oscar Wilde, at the age of thirty. From America he used to send Pater neckties—'to make him cut a jaunty figure', he wrote with friendly irony. Perhaps they produced a revival of Pater's burst of brilliant apple-green and peacock blue gaiety of the 1870s? It seems unlikely for in his last few years Pater became more retired and disinclined to move about. He rarely went up to London, finding that the 'trains of the underground railway belched smoke and blacks at him, the omnibuses roared in his ears, ugly buildings obtruded their hideousness before his eyes. Everybody hustled him, shook him, trod on his toes, puffed cigar smoke into his face.' Yet this is Thomas Wright talking, perhaps only drawing his own conclusions. Who knows what Pater felt about the changing London of the Nineties, or about anything else?

CHAPTER NINE

Wilde, Gray and Raffalovich

MUCH fable and invention about Wilde was destroyed in 1962 when Sir Rupert Hart-Davis published his edition of *The Letters*• a book in which with thoroughness and care he collected all the extant letters and supplemented these with the results of researches into the lives of the people addressed and mentioned. For half a century one writer on Wilde after another had been swallowing stories from frivolous memoirs or handed down by word of mouth or started by Frank Harris or invented by the whimsy of some would-be authority, and a whole mass of seemingly solid material was piled on Wilde's memory, even the more conscientious biographers like Hesketh Pearson adding weight to it. Much of this was destroyed by *The Letters*, sometimes because they show incidents to have been factually impossible, sometimes because they reveal a Wilde incapable of acts and words attributed to him in the myths.

The whole fatuous conception of Wilde at Oxford, for instance, an aesthete living up to his blue china, a notoriety already, answering reprimands from the dons with cheeky sophisticated epigrams, giving famous parties in his rooms to aesthetes whom he charmed with his

• *The Letters of Oscar Wilde* edited by Rupert Hart-Davis, 1962.

brilliance, defeating in combat large gangs of hearties who had come to mob him, all this is swept away by Wilde's correspondence with his intimate friends William Ward and Reginald Harding. These show him to have been very much an undergraduate of the time, with his own small circle of friends, fairly industrious, in no way precious or a victim of philistine elements and of no particular fame in the university. He may have invented his blue china as a conversational prop in later life; this is what he tells Ward about the rooms he inherited from him: "I enjoy your rooms awfully. The inner room is filled with china, pictures, a portfolio and a piano—and a grey carpet with stained floor. The whole get up is much admired and a little made fun of on Sunday evenings." As for the parties of aesthetes in Wilde's rooms, the intensity and the advanced conversation which Oscar led with startling paradoxes: "I have been doing my duty like a brick," he writes to Ward, "and keeping up the reputation of these rooms by breakfasts, lunches, etc.: however I find it is rather a bore and that one gains nothing from the conversation of any one." Then, of his unforgettable repartee he gives an example of which he was evidently most proud. "Now of course Jupp and I are not on speaking terms, but when we were I gave him a great jar; the Caliban came into Hall beaming and sniggering and said 'I'm very glad they've given the £15 Exhibition to *Jones*' (put in all the beastly pronunciation for yourself) so I maliciously said 'What! the old Jugger got an Exhibition! very hot indeed.' He was *too sick* and said 'Not likely, I mean Wansbrough Jones,' to which I replied 'I never knew there was such a fellow up here.' Which confined Jupp to his gummy bed for a day and prevented him dining in hall for two days." If more were needed, a photograph appears in which Wilde, with a curly-brimmed bowler hat set square on his head, a butterfly collar and a vulgarly loud check suit, stands in a group of similarly dressed sportsmen looking as horsy as they.

His letters, like those of any undergraduate to his intimate friends, concern chiefly college affairs, his own religious doubts, gossip about other undergraduates, his home and his father's death, girls he has met and his work and hopes for a First. There is a good deal of boasting about his proficiency in shooting, salmon- and trout-fishing, his love of riding and swimming and his dash and success with 'stunning' girls. There is a scandalous story of how he found a mutual friend in a box at the theatre with 'Ward the choirboy'. "I believe Todd is extremely moral and only mentally spoons the boy." But everything is written not in the famous Wilde manner, which did not develop till much later, but with the heavy-handed humour and leg-pulling of the least aesthetic of undergraduates.

Whatever Wilde was, or knew, at this time—and he had been abroad with Mahaffy the Hellenist and had already met Lord Ronald Gower and Frank Miles—he was determined not to reveal it at least to William Ward ('Bouncer') in whom he confided everything else. He could be a little sentimental about their friendship—'those dear rides through the greenwood', 'dear old boy, I wish I could see you again'—but such remarks might appear in any undergraduate letter.

With Reginald Harding ('Kitten') it was evidently another matter. A photograph shows Harding as having just the sort of face Wilde adored—thick blond hair fluffed up across the head and over the ears, deep-set dark eyes, straight nose and a lush but sensitive mouth. Wilde wrote to William Ward about him—"I am quite as fond of the dear Kitten as ever but he has not enough power of character to be more than a pleasant affectionate boy. He never exerts my intellect or brain in any way. Between his mind and mine there is no intellectual friction to rouse me up to talk or think." Then what was there? For it is plain that Wilde was devoted to him.

Three years younger than Wilde—a considerable gap between two undergraduates—he was a slim, dreamy boy of not very profound character, conventional, devoted to music and to his comfortable middle-class family. Not too much notice must be taken of the affectionate nickname of Kitten for it was an age of nicknames and among Wilde's friends they were fashionable, 'Hosky', a jocular corruption of Oscar being used for Wilde. 'Kitten' came from a music-hall song of the time

> Beg your parding, Mrs. Harding,
> Is my kitting in your garding?

and Kitten's brother and sister were known as 'Puss' and 'Miss Puss' respectively.

Oscar and Kitten seem to have become friends, making a trio with Bouncer, during Wilde's first year. Their letters in the vacation have grown intimate by the summer of 1876, though Oscar is always complaining of the Kitten's failure to write. "I suppose you are too much occupied with croquet and loafing and playing the organ to write to me." Wilde's letters are gossipy, boastful, affectionate but read as though they might have been written to a younger brother. References to the Kitten in Wilde's letters to Ward are more indicative—'the dear Kitten', 'his thoughts and ink rarely last beyond one sheet'. But there becomes noticeable after a time an undercurrent of tenderness in Wilde's letters to the Kitten himself (he always sends 'love to Puss') which is not in his letters to Ward. He begs the Kitten for flowers when he is ill and the Kitten responds with a 'charming basket of flowers and a delightful letter'. "You are the nicest of kittens." Their correspondence faltered and ceased only when Wilde had settled in London.

But before then Wilde had become friendly with two men outside the university who went about together a great deal and were both conscious and uninhibited homosexuals, Lord Ronald Gower and Frank Miles. Of Gower this might not be stated except by those who knew him intimately if it were not for Phyllis Grosskurth• who speaks so emphatically that she must have learned the facts from John Addington Symonds's Journal which she had been privileged to examine at the London Library. In relation to Symonds's 'sexual activity with a wide variety of men,' she says that Symonds did not approve of treating the working-classes as 'fair game for sexual exploitation' and 'unlike Wilde and Lord Ronald Gower' did not find perverse pleasure in slumming. He was shocked by the 'defiantly unsentimental approach of Roden Noel and Lord Ronald Gower'. In his last days he grew less squeamish and became very intimate with Lord Ronald Gower of whose abandoned sensuality he had never quite approved.

Gower, in fact, was a thorough-paced queer who liked rough trade and found time, in spite of a public career, to enjoy it prodigally.

Younger son of the Duke of Sutherland (his full name was Sutherland-Gower) he is described by Hart-Davis as 'sculptor, politician, author and art-critic'. He was ten years older than Wilde and died in 1916, and although his activities were common knowledge and he was remembered for them for years after his death, he avoided any public scandal and wrote a book of respectable memoirs.

Frank Miles, on the other hand, had a short and tragic life. He and

• *John Addington Symonds* by Phyllis Grosskurth, 1966.

Wilde were on intimate terms while Wilde was at Oxford and shared rooms in London afterwards, and Miles, with his early sophistication, his dangerous libertinism and his wide homosexual acquaintance probably influenced the *fate* of Wilde, though not Wilde himself, more than anyone in his young manhood. A characteristic piece of clumsy misrepresentation by Robert Harborough Sherard, who to the end of his long life could never believe that such a thing as homosexuality existed, has given biographers a wholly false idea of this somewhat degenerate, talented, seducer of the young, both boys and girls. Sherard told Hesketh Pearson: 'Miles had a predilection for Exhibition natural enough in a struggling artist but reprehensible, *parait-il*, where only small girls in single spies are invited to contemplation. Wilde told me how he had saved Miles's bacon, but never referred to him again. Poor Miles could have shaken hands on a common taste with Victor Hugo."• Miles was an exhibitionist in the pathological sense, but he was also homosexual and had much in common with his friend Ronald Gower.

Miles was probably up at Oxford during Wilde's first year, for he was known to both Ward and Harding, and in the summer of 1876 Wilde and Ronald Gower went to stay at Frank's home at Bingham, Nottinghamshire, where Miles's father was the Rector. Wilde wrote from there to Kitten and Bouncer, mentioning that he is going to a garden-party at the Duke of Rutland's but saying nothing of Frank Miles and Ronald Gower. In August Frank went to stay with Oscar at a cottage on Lough Carrib and had 'a royal time of it'. In September Wilde was to have gone to Rome with Miles and Gower—'we would have been a great Trinity'—but at the last minute Gower could not get away. In March of the next year, Wilde confides in Bouncer that he has been to tea with Frank Miles to meet Ronald Gower and his sister the Duchess of Westminster. Wilde had 'a delightful time in town with Frank and a lot of friends' on his way home from Greece and in the following year, his last at Oxford, after his First in Greats had been announced he rowed to Pangbourne with Frank Miles in a birchbark canoe 'and shot rapids and did wonders everywhere'.

It was understandable that when Wilde came down from Oxford he and Miles should agree to share rooms. Miles was making money as a fashionable portraitist and Wilde had recently inherited his patri-

• *The Life of Oscar Wilde* by Hesketh Pearson.

mony. They found pleasant apartments at the bottom of Salisbury Street from which they overlooked the river.

Miles was twenty-seven years old, Wilde twenty-five. Both were ambitious socially and professionally. Miles had his talent for portraiture and Wilde the few articles he had written for Dublin magazines and his poetry (with which he had won the Newdigate Prize that year). Between them they had a wide acquaintance.

Wilde set out to conquer the town. Like many young writers he had faith that somehow, mysteriously out of vacuum, success would come to him. He and Miles invited to their at-Homes a remarkable collection of stage stars and artists, specializing in beautiful women of whom Miles did brilliant pencil sketches. Genevieve Ward, Lily Langtry, Walter Sickert and his sister Helena, Mrs Alfred Hunt the painter's wife and original of Tennyson's 'Margaret' with her daughter Violet ('the sweetest Violet in England, I call her,' said Oscar, though in later years he would not have found many to agree with him), Mrs Bancroft, wife of the actor-manager Squire Bancroft ('Dramatic art in England owes you and your husband a great debt') and most triumphantly Ellen Terry. Madame Modjeska was expected to come but declined because it would be unwise to visit so young a man, even for tea. Especially, perhaps, when that young man was seen about at first nights and some private entertainments in his own fanciful version of Court dress, with silk stockings and lace ruffles.

But all this did nothing, in vulgar terms, to bring home the bacon and Wilde and Miles moved to more modest rooms in Chelsea. Number One Tite Street had once been inhabited by a Miss Elizabeth Skeates and Wilde ingeniously shortened the word and wrote from Keats House, Tite Street. There may have been other reasons for their move for Miles was frequently in trouble over his behaviour with young people and on one occasion Wilde had to hold the police at bay while Miles escaped.

Whether or not the two of them, and perhaps Ronald Gower, joined forces in nocturnal adventures is not known, but it must be concluded that Wilde was fully aware of his friend's nature and behaviour and with some of it at least sympathized. It seems scarcely likely that his reputation as an aesthete would have grown as quickly as it did in those two years if it had not been aided by the gossip of the queers, one of publicity's most powerful mouthpieces then and today.

And in his letters to one man in this period may be heard tones of highfalutin admiration, tempered with humour, which are remarkable in his love-letters to Bosie of ten years later. They were addressed to Norman Forbes-Robertson, the handsome younger brother of Johnston.

> I don't know if I bored you the other night with my life and its troubles. There seems something so sympathetic and gentle about your nature, and you have been so charming whenever I have seen you, that I felt somehow that although I knew you only a short time, yet that still I could talk to you about things, which I only talk of to people whom I like—to those whom I count my friends. If you will let me count *you* as one of my friends, it would give a new pleasure to my life.

and

> Here from the uttermost end of the great world I send you love and greeting, and thanks for your letters which delight me very much. But, dear boy, your hair will lose its gold and your cheek its roses if you insist on being such a chivalrous defender of this much abused young man. It is so brave and good of you.
> Tonight I am escorted by the Mayor of the city through the Chinese quarter, to their theatre and joss houses and rooms, which will be most interesting. They have 'houses' and 'persons'.

To suggest as some innocent biographers have done that Wilde knew nothing about himself in his early years and suddenly took to homosexuality, as a man might take to stamp collecting, after meeting Robert Ross in 1886 is nonsense. He may have been too occupied with the nebulous career he was trying to make, or too cautious, or too mindful of the idealized comradeships of Oxford to do more than dream, but the notion that he was ignorant of his own sexual constitution is unrealistic or wilfully blind.

At some time during Wilde's year in Tite Street he and Miles quarrelled, nobody has discovered or even guessed why. Miles left Wilde and six years later was confined in a lunatic asylum where he is believed to have committed suicide. Alfred Douglas told the present writer that Wilde could never be induced to speak of him. But Wilde's friendship with Ronald Gower continued and in 1888 Wilde went down to Stratford to speak at the unveiling of Gower's statue of Shakespeare in the gardens of the Memorial Theatre. ("The volunteers played God Save the Queen in my honour", wrote Wilde ambiguously to Robert Ross.)

2

When W. S. Gilbert wrote the words of *Patience* he had probably never heard of Wilde. English satire, as usual out of date, was concentrated on the aesthetes who had been a name in London for ten years, precious young men who adored Rossetti's pictures and shuddered deliciously at the decadence of Swinburne. If Bunthorne, in fact was intended for anyone, it was Rossetti himself. To the honest Britishers of the time Ruskin with his *Sesame and Lilies*, Pater with his *Renaissance* if they had heard of him, Morris with what was considered his repulsive mixture of Socialism and Mediaevalism, the High Churchmen with all this damned incense and frippery, Swinburne perceptively satirized in those surprising lines of *Patience* 'The pain that is all a pleasure will change For the pleasure that's all but pain,' but above all the Pre-Raphaelites: these were equally nauseating and ridiculous. Gilbert had at them all, and even more viciously at their followers.

Curiously enough it was the supposed sexlessness of the movement that Gilbert attacked—

> Then a sentimental passion of a vegetable fashion must excite your languid spleen,
> An attachment à la Plato for a bashful young potato or a not too French French bean:
> Though the Philistines may jostle, you will rank as an apostle in the high aesthetic band,
> If you walk down Piccadilly with a poppy or a lily in your mediaeval hand. . . .

He saw it all as bloodless and emasculated, seriously supposing that a devotion to mediaeval art was wishy-washy and out of keeping with the virile age of imperialism.

> Francesca di Rimini, miminy, piminy,
> Je ne sais quoi young man:
> A greenery-yallery, Grosvenor Gallery,
> Foot-in-the grave young man.

Wilde was less than two years down from Oxford, an obscure young Irishman who had paid for the publication of a book of unoriginal poems, whose greatest daring had been to wear at night, but never in daylight, somewhat eccentric evening dress and entertain stage stars for tea. If Gilbert knew of his existence he was, as in all his operettas, out for far bigger game—a whole tendency of the times which he intended to reduce to a laughing-stock.

But Wilde was clever enough to see that he could corner the publicity. *Patience* was first produced in April 1881 when Wilde was living in Chelsea and must have been conceived by Gilbert at least two years earlier when Wilde was an unknown undergraduate, but audiences, always in the know, decided that it satirized that oddly dressed young man they had seen at first nights and Wilde did nothing to disillusion them. He was carried to a kind of fame on the Savoyard band-waggon and, when an offer was made to him to go to New York (where *Patience* was to be produced on January 2nd, 1882) and actually lecture as Bunthorne, he at once began to order his wardrobe, no limit now to the singular drag he might put on by day or night. He sailed on the *Arizona* in time to give his first lecture just one week after the first night of *Patience.* That instead of merely adding to the publicity of the operetta he secured lasting fame in America for himself was all to his credit.

There is no evidence that his sexual experience was enlarged by his stay in America. He visited Walt Whitman and the two got pickled on elderberry wine and milk punch, Whitman describing Wilde as a great big splendid boy, and Wilde telling Whitman in a letter afterwards, "There is no one in this great wide world of America whom I love and honour so much." He wrote amusingly about his experiences to Norman Forbes-Robertson.

He spent most of what remained of the takings from his lectures on staying for three months in Paris. He had a certain reputation now, but not as a writer in which capacity he had only his book of *Poems* to show. He sent copies of it to prominent French authors who might be sympathetic and received in return a number of invitations from the great, none of which led to any future acquaintance. But he met an Englishman, a gauche, selfconscious young man who was determined to be a writer. Wilde—he must have smiled about it in after years—was violently attracted to him. This was Robert Harborough Sherard, the son of a parson and the great-grandson of Wordsworth, then a blond not ill-looking youngster of twenty-two. They spent many hours together in Paris, Sherard supposing that Wilde was interested in him as a promising writer, Wilde not yet realizing that all Sherard had for him was youth and a pleasant face. For Sherard it was a more fateful meeting than for Wilde because when Wilde's fall came Sherard, who claimed never to have seen or suspected anything of *that* sort in Wilde, spent the rest of his life in championing him with a blundering ineptness which made Robert Ross's task of salvaging Wilde's reputation doubly difficult. Sherard, that flaxen-haired hero-worshipper of Wilde's early visit to Paris, to whom Wilde wrote soon after his return to England that they should seek perfect friendship together, that he accepted the dedication of his poems 'fashioned by one I love so much as I love you,' was to become one of the great bores of Wilde's life. 'I think of you often wandering in violet valleys with your honey-coloured hair', he wrote in 1883, but fourteen years later, after Sherard had long been shouting indiscreetly about his friend Oscar, meaning painfully well but stirring up trouble wherever he went, Wilde wrote him from Naples: "When you wish to talk morality—always an amusement—and to attack me behind my back, don't, like a good fellow, talk so loud, as the reverberation reaches from the (Authors') Club to Naples; also, it is easy—far too easy—for you to find an audience that does not contain any friends of mine; before them, play Tartuffe in the style of Termagant to your heart's content; but when you do it in the presence of friends of mine, you expose yourself to rebuke and contempt, and of course I hear all about it."

If they had gone to bed together it would all have ended as many other affairs of Wilde's did with no calamitous sequel. But Wilde's attention to young Sherard, who had not the remotest idea of what it was all about, woke such response in that heterosexual breast that Sherard gradually lost all other interests and instead of the books he planned produced little but a series of hero-worshipping, blind, rabid books on Wilde.

Back in London Wilde's situation was serious. His little property in Ireland was mortgaged to the limit, his American earnings were spent, his attempts to write plays for various well-known actresses had ended in nothing except a one-week run in New York of *Vera: or the Nihilists*,* and he was reduced to ill-paid lectures in the English pro-

* In one of his pithy footnotes to *The Letters of Oscar Wilde* Rupert Hart-Davis describes its reception: "*Vera* opened at the Union Square Theatre on 20 August but ran for only a week. It was described as 'a foolish, highly-peppered story of love, intrigue and politics' (*New York Tribune*), 'unreal, long-winded and wearisome' (*New York Times*) and 'long-drawn dramatic rot' (*New York Herald*)."

vinces in order to live in furnished apartments in London. It was while lecturing in Dublin that he met again Constance Lloyd and they became engaged to be married. She had a sufficient income and they set up a home in Tite Street.

He gave her all that a man not primarily heterosexual could give to his wife, splendid companionship, exciting love letters and some physical love. He designed her clothes, designed (in consultation with E. W. Godwin and James Whistler) the decoration of their house, took her about somewhat over-gallantly for a time before leaving her to her own friends, whom she seems to have preferred to his, while he returned to something like his bachelor life made less penurious by her money. He was an attentive husband when they were together and an affectionate father to their two sons. But his own life scarcely changed with his marriage and he would have smiled at J. A. Symonds's attempts to 'be a natural man' during the first years of his married life.

Just two years after the marriage he received a letter from a Cambridge undergraduate of twenty who as a fifteen-year-old boy he had known when he lived with Miles in Salisbury Street. His answer to this and three other letters to Harry Marillier happen to have survived and were printed in a book of memoirs,• but they are probably among many which Wilde wrote to young men during the years before his private life came under the scrutiny of the police. They are worth reproducing as they stand, for they tell their own story and it is one which can be read in the lines themselves without looking between them.

5 November 1885
Of course I remember the blue-coat boy, and am charmed to find he had not forgotten me.
Your letter gave me great pleasure and if possible I will come down to see the *Eumenides*—which I suppose will look like Hamlet surrounded by the witches of *Macbeth*—but you have not told me the date of the production yet, so I cannot say if I will be really free.
I have a very vivid remembrance of the bright enthusiastic boy who used to bring me my coffee in Salisbury Street, and am delighted to find he is devoted to the muses, but I suppose you don't flirt with all nine ladies at once? Which of them do you really love?
Whether or not I can come and see you, you must certainly come and see me when you are in town, and we will talk of the poets

• *All That I Have Met* by Mrs Claude Beddington, 1929.

and drink Keats's health. I wonder are you all Wordsworthians still at Cambridge, or do you love Keats, and Poe, and Baudelaire? I hope so.

Write and tell me what things in art you and your friends love best. I do not mean what pictures, but what models and modulations of art affect you most.

Is it five years ago really? Then I must almost sign myself an old friend, but the word old is full of terror.

Oscar Wilde

8 November 1885

Harry, why did you let me catch my train? I would have liked to have gone to the National Gallery with you, and looked at Velasquez's pale evil King, at Titian's Bacchus with the velvet panthers, and at that strange heaven of Angelico's where everyone seems made of gold and purple and fire, and which, for all that, looks to me ascetic—everyone dead and decorative! I wonder will it really be like that, but I wonder without caring. *Je trouve la terre aussi belle que le ciel, et le corps aussi beau que l'âme.* If I do live again I would like it to be as a flower—no soul but perfectly beautiful. Perhaps for my sins I shall be made a red geranium!!

And your paper on Browning? You must tell me of it. In our meeting again there was a touch of Browning—keen curiosity, wonder, delight.

It was an hour intensely dramatic and intensely psychological, and, in art, only Browning can make action and psychology one. When am I to see you again? Write me a long letter to Tite Street, and I will get it when I come back. I wish you were here, Harry. But in the vacation you must often come and see me, and we will talk of the poets and forget Piccadilly!! I have never learned anything except from people younger than myself and you are infinitely young.

Oscar Wilde

? January–February 1886

Dear Harry, I am away in the region of horrible snow and horrible note-paper! Lecturing and wandering—a vagabond with a mission! But your letter has reached me, like a strain of music wind-blown from a far land. You too have the love of things impossible—ἔρως τῶν ἀδυνάτων—*l'amour de l'impossible* (how do men name it?). Sometime you will find, even as I have found, that there is no such thing as a romantic experience; there are romantic memories, and there is the desire of romance—that is all. Our most fiery moments of ecstasy are merely shadows of what somewhere else we have felt, or of what we long some day to feel. So at least it seems to me.

And, strangely enough, what comes of all this is a curious mixture of ardour and of indifference. I myself would sacrifice everything for a new experience, and I know there is no such thing as a new experience at all. I think I would more readily die for what I do not believe in than for what I hold to be true. I would go to the stake for a sensation and be a sceptic to the last! Only one thing remains infinitely fascinating to me, the mystery of moods. To be master of these moods is exquisite, to be mastered by them more exquisite still. Sometimes I think that the artistic life is a long and lovely suicide, and am not sorry that it is so.

And much of this I fancy you yourself have felt: much also remains for you to feel. There is an unknown land full of strange flowers and subtle perfurmes, a land of which it is joy of all joys to dream, a land where all things are perfect and poisonous. I have been reading Walter Scott for the last week; you too should read him, for the last week; you too should read him, for there is nothing of all this in him.

Write to me at Tite Street, and let me know where you will be. Ever yours

O.W.

That is all, and Marillier's name does not appear again in Wilde's correspondence or in any biography of Wilde. He became an art critic and authority on Beardsley and on tapestry and died in 1951. It would be interesting to know whether in his old age, remembering Wilde, he ever spoke his *Ronsard me celebrait du temps que j'étais jeune* as in the Thirties and Forties of this century more than one gouty old gentleman did.

It does not need these letters to Marillier, with their irresistible implications, to see that in the years after his marriage, Wilde was wilfully fusing what had been two separate lives. Ronald Gower and Frank Miles had shown him his way into one, the other was his professional and social life in which nothing intruded from *les bas profonds*. But again, it is in his letters, which are the one quite reliable source of information, that something may be seen which is only describable as 'camp'.

'Camp', a word once used by no one but the more exclusively homosexual sophisticates has now gone into the language and it can be no more than a question of time before the Oxford Dictionary gives its proper connotations. Derived, it is said, from 'camp-followers', many of whom in the fifteenth, sixteenth and seventeenth centuries were 'mollies' or 'queans', especially in the armies of the pederastic William of Orange, it now denotes something far livelier than merely having certain sexual tendencies, something which the present writer, at least, can only explain by clumsy and inadequate definition and a number of examples. It suggests, first, a quality both pretentious and feminine. A woman's hat could be camp, or a man's tie. It has an element of comedy particularly at the expense of a queer, so that a situation can be camp. It can be applied to artificial emotions—or to artificial almost anything—so that forced tears in a small crisis, sulks and petty melodrama can be camp. Outrageous behaviour, over-dressing, exhibitionism are all camp, but so are flashy humour and over-acting. Perhaps most frequently the word is used of appearance and speech.

Many things about Oscar Wilde must have been thought camp by knowing contemporaries, his button-holes, his fur coat, his elaborate walking-sticks, his hair-do, his manner of speech. This does not mean that he was an effeminate man, for he was not, but those artificial metaphors in his conversation, his addressing of some young renter as 'honey-sweet boy', his fastidious avoidance of coarse Rabelaisian smut, his air of moving as though he was on the stage, all this was camp. And now his letters, especially those to young men in whom he was interested, began to be adorned with the humour, the absurdity, the exaggerated endearment, the smiling romanticism, the half-bantering flattery of High Camp. He was a master of it. One must read the later letters and his plays to realize how much his wit depended on it, but already he was using it with a skill and individuality which no one had achieved.

It is at least arguable that to it we owe the capricious humour, the irreverent, the preposterous flippancy of his plays, the delicious gaiety and inconsequence of *The Importance of Being Earnest.* What could be camper than the characters of Lady Bracknell and Miss Prism? Wilde as a romantic in costume, a self-advertising poet, had exhibited camp of a different kind and he would have been grossly insulted at the word, even if he had understood it. But the man who could write 'They played God Save the Queen in my honour' knew exactly what he was doing. As a playwright he was a superb technician and he subjected the camp of his humour to the rigours of technique without pricking any of his bubbles. It was an age of humour, the glorious noisy humour of the music-halls, and he conquered it by humour of another kind which he had learned, in its elements, from wise-cracking queers. This is not to suggest that his was not creative genius—it is rather to assert it. But if he had never known those sadly gay segregated people with their hysterical self-mockery, if he had not been one of them however much a lord of life he defensively called himself, he could not have been the master of playful ridicule he was.

In those years, that is in the Eighties, he was learning to laugh at himself and at others and it can be seen in the letters. These were of two kinds, written in two styles, or in two tones of voice, that used towards professional acquaintances, men and women connected with the paper he edited, *Women's World*, theatre managers, editors, strangers and those who approached him formally, and that he adopted towards intimate male friends, most though not all of whom were, as it were, in the secret. It is in these that the camp becomes with the years increasingly evident.

To Douglas Ainslie of his friend Lord Albert Osborne: "He is quite charming, with his low musical voice, and his graceful incapacity for a career. He is a little like the moon." To Robert Ross after the publication of *The Portrait of Mr. W. H.*: 'Write me a letter. Now that Willie Hughes has been revealed to the world we must have another secret." To Charles Ricketts after he had presented Wilde with a clever fake portrait he had made of the supposed Willie Hughes: "It is not a forgery at all; it is an authentic Clouet of the highest authentic value. It is absurd of you and Shannon to try and take me in! As if I did not know the master's touch, or was no judge of frames! Seriously, my dear fellow, it is quite wonderful, and your giving it to me is an act so charming that, in despair of showing you any return, I at once call upon the gods to shower gold and roses on the Vale where the De Morgans do not live. I am really most grateful (no! that is a horrid word: I am never grateful) I am flattered and fascinated, and I hope we shall always be friends and see each other often." To a young actor after a production of *A Midsummer's Night's Dream* in which he had played Oberon: "Of course you looked quite wonderful—like a marvellous Dionysus—and you moved with infinite grace." To Edgar Saltus the American writer: "Your strange book, so pessimistic, so poisonous and so perfect." To Norman Forbes-Robertson, after a gossipy reference to André Raffalovich of whom we shall hear more:

"Augusta's party was a great success, but there was a virgin of some ninety winters who hid haggard blushes behind a tattered fan! She was quite dreadful, and must not be asked again."

To the Prosecution in Wilde's case, when it came, these letters would not have been nearly as useful as those he wrote to Alfred Douglas which were produced in Court. But to a psychologist they would have been just as pregnant.

3

Wilde brought in the Nineties with his publication of *The Picture of Dorian Gray*. For him this bridged the two periods of his work; the first of his poetry, short stories and selfconscious aphoristic philosophizing in all of which he took himself seriously, the second period of his plays in which he had learned to laugh at himself as well as others. There is deliberate comedy in *Dorian Gray* which is often funny but not nearly so funny as the seriously intended drama. Wilde forcing himself into the role of a modern novelist, describing 'foul' scenes in the slums and the reactions of 'real' people is absurd and shaming, but Wilde writing the first of the frothy unforgettable dialogue which he would polish to be the stuff of his plays shows the beginnings of genius.

But the book has another significance. In it Wilde gave the most audacious expression to his theory of 'the artist' being free from the obligations and exigencies of life, a theory sometimes miscalled art-for-art's-sake. It was, as we have seen, largely a personal concept adapted from many others, but with *Dorian Gray* he formulated it as a doctrine. It was caught at desperately and followed by the minor figures of the time whose lives were mostly vicious and feckless. It is true that Dorian is not the artist in the book and that the artist, a painter in this case, is shown as a man of boring virtue. It is true that Dorian's superiority to mere human ethics is finally punished and that right is made grudgingly to triumph.• But in the meantime Wilde obviously enjoys himself describing the life of a man who has escaped a sense of guilt, who experiments with all the 'strange sins' in the list, who exploits his own lavish and extraordinary taste in all the arts—particu-

• Wilde afterwards wrote in answer to a newspaper criticism: "Yes; there is a terrible moral in *Dorian Gray*—a moral which the prurient will not be able to find in it, but which will be revealed to all whose minds are healthy. Is this an artistic error? I fear it is. It is the only error in the book."

larly that of the jeweller—who imperiously flouts all notions of decency and those who respect them, who smiles with infuriating loftiness at bourgeois efforts to reclaim him, who commits crimes for their kick and ruins lives to watch the effect, all with a des Esseintes fastidiousness and elegance. The reader is left in no doubt as to where Wilde's sympathies lie.

The book is grossly over-written. The word 'strange' is used fifty-one times in it, 'wonderful' forty-one, 'curious' forty, 'horrible' thirty-five, 'hideous' twenty-two and 'monstrous' twenty. Its melodrama is clownish, its attempts at realism slapstick, its style novelettish. Its most artificial character Lord Henry Wotton is the only one with any life—the rest are dummies. Yet it has a certain drive behind it, even a certain power which explains its appeal at the time it was published and its continuing popularity. If the decadents of the Nineties existed as a clique this was their oracle.

Wilde prefaced it with a number of maxims culminating in his unattributed rendering of Gautier's '*la peinture, la sculpture, la musique, ne servent absolument à rien*'. Moreover in letters to the editors of various daily newspapers whose critics had attacked the book he reiterated quite brilliantly the opinion, which now seems an obvious one, that no work of art should be criticized on ethical grounds. "I am quite incapable", he wrote to the editor of the *St James's Gazette*, "of understanding how any work of art can be criticized from a moral standpoint. The sphere of art and the sphere of ethics are absolutely distinct and separate; and it is to the confusion between the two that we owe the appearance of Mrs Grundy, that amusing old lady who represents the only original form of humour that the middle-classes of this country have been able to produce." Some of his retorts to newspapers were read at the trial of Queensberry by Wilde's Counsel Sir Edward Clarke when Carson put in the book as evidence.

The book had immediate impact. "Even in the precincts of the Savile nothing but praise of Dorian Gray though of course it is said to be very dangerous," wrote Robert Ross ecstatically to Wilde. "I heard a clergyman extolling it he only regretted some of the sentiments of Lord Henry as apt to lead people astray. Spriggie tells me that Lippincotts has had a phenomenal sale. 80 copies were sold in one day at a Strand booksellers, the usual amount being about 3 a week in that part."

"*Dorian Gray*, with all its faults, is a wonderful book," wrote W. B. Yeats. It was moreover a fateful one, for Wilde himself and for a number of young writers who accepted its barren hedonism.

4

The first of these was a namesake of Dorian's, John Gray, whom Wilde met in 1889, that is nearly two years before he knew Alfred Douglas. Gray as a poet was very much of the Nineties and although his story went far into the next century it may be told here, at the point when he and Wilde met. It is a story with a happy ending, one pleasing to moralists and in contrast to some other better-known life-stories of that time.

It opens with a situation that is traditional in metropolitan life and a form of it that has been particularly common in London in the last hundred years or so. The 'artistic one' in a working-class family leaves his dull home to find a place in the flashy and pretentious circles of 'the West End'. With good looks, a flair for conspicuous clothes and social graces and with willingness to be accessible to men or women who can help them, young men from all regions and classes achieve a certain sophistication and if they have any talent learn to exploit it among others of their kind and many in time enter a world beyond the imagination of their own parents. From unsympathetic families who find them frivolous or effeminate in their love of elegance and artistic effects, they go to enjoy the admiration and patronage of their elders in what seems to them a dazzling background. Their lonely ambitions are for a time fulfilled and though their destinies are often pitiful they sometimes triumph and rarely regret the initiative which took them first to certain streets, certain bars, restaurants, music-hall promenades, cafés, in which they met a more interesting fate than could ever have been theirs at home.

John Gray was just such a young man, the eldest of the nine children of a journeyman carpenter. He was born in 1866 in Woolwich where his father worked in the Docks or Arsenal. From the first he seemed something of a prodigy to his Scottish parents but lovably so, a pretty and graceful child with a remarkable aptitude for learning and for what his family found esoteric and useless occupations. At thirteen years he was sent to work in the Arsenal as a metal turner's mate but determined to better himself and being of a naturally artistic disposition he taught himself French and drawing and became a passable violinist. Ambitious for clerical rather than manual work as a means of livelihood, he passed an examination for a clerkship in the General Post Office and in his early twenties, working in the library of the Foreign Office, he was able to take a room in the Temple and spend his nights in the cheerful gas-lit streets and bars and music halls of central London. There is no record of his returning to Woolwich or, except for his friendship with one sister who became a nun, of further association with his family.

By 1889 when he was twenty-three years old he had tuned his voice to his new surroundings, dropping the dialect as he had dropped the companions of boyhood, and had learned to dress and act the part of what he would doubtless have called a young man about town. He was writing short stories and poems in the manner popular at that time, translating from the French Decadents, and spending more money than he could afford on going to the theatre.

At this point, in a bar near Shaftesbury Avenue one night, he was picked up by Oscar Wilde. There has been a good deal of discussion as to whether or not he was the 'original' of Dorian Gray and the point is an interesting one as Wilde certainly wrote the novel in the year of their meeting. Hesketh Pearson in his *Life of Oscar Wilde* tells how another character in the book Basil Hallward was named after an artist called Basil Hall and it may well be that Wilde, attracted by the handsome Gray, used his surname for his protagonist, though as to 'character' speculation seems futile with such a cipher as Dorian, who does a great many things without having any perceptible character at all. It may also be that Wilde had finished his book before meeting John Gray and finding him beautiful enough to match his hero affectionately called him Dorian. It is certain that Gray signed letters to Wilde as Dorian and was spoken of thus by other young men.

Wilde took him up with enthusiasm. He first introduced him to Ricketts and Shannon, that matrimonial pair of artists who lived and worked together for forty years and were just then about to issue the first number of their decorative periodical *The Dial*. They, like Wilde, found young Gray irresistible and accepted for publication an article of his called *Les Goncourt* in which the French brothers are discussed as novelists in an enthusiastic schoolboyish way. In the same issue they printed a short story by Gray called *The Great Worm*, the sort of odd affected stuff that was being turned out by young writers anxious to be in the swim: A city 'upheld by silver columns, trunks of the birch; its battlements, daring minarets in the shape of palms, towers like the cypress, domes like masses of foliage, golden all in the setting sun'.

Wilde took John Gray about with him but this was before the production of Wilde's first plays or his years of great prosperity and they went chiefly to the less extravagant eating-houses. There is no record of Gray's having been to Wilde's home in Tite Street to meet Constance but there is no reason to doubt it when Lane's office boy, Edward Shelley, who was even younger than Gray and from a similar background was taken there soon afterwards.

Wilde also introduced Gray to friends he thought might be useful to the young man in the literary career to which he aspired, friends like Frank Harris and the Sphinx, Ada Leverson. Frank Harris showed no particular interest in Gray at the time and certainly published nothing of his in *The Fortnightly Review* which he was then editing, but he wrote of him many years later, *after* he had read Wilde's claim in *De Profundis* that his real life, his higher life, was with such as Gray. "For Gray", Harris said, "had not only great personal distinction, but charming manners and a marked poetic gift, a much greater gift than Oscar possessed. He had besides an eager, curious mind, and of course found extraordinary stimulus in Oscar's talk. It seemed to me that intellectual sympathy and the natural admiration which a young man feels for a brilliant senior formed the obvious bond between them."

As for the Sphinx, she seems to have taken to Gray, though she made a gaffe some years later in attributing to him the authorship of that disgusting little story *The Priest and the Acolyte* which was published in an undergraduate paper called *The Chameleon* and used with effect against Wilde in his trial since he had contributed to the same number. It had in fact been written by the editor, a future clergyman named J. F. Bloxam, who did nothing to correct the general impression that Wilde was responsible. "Dear Sphinx," wrote Oscar gaily when the paper was first published and no trouble threatened, "Your aphorisms must appear in the second number of the *Chameleon*: they are exquisite. 'The Priest and the Acolyte' is not by Dorian: though you were right in discerning by internal evidence that the author has a profile. He is an undergraduate of strange beauty."

The year 1892 was a great one for the Woolwich boy. In spite of Wilde's growing infatuation for Alfred Douglas, Gray was still the frequent companion of Wilde who since the enormous success of *Lady Windermere's Fan* on February 20 had become a famous dramatist. Seen in public with him while Bosie was still at Oxford, Gray became known to the poverty-stricken young poets of the time as a man of fashion, 'incurably given over to social things', as Ernest Dowson wrote contemptuously in a letter to Victor Plarr.

In that year Gray read a lecture to the Playgoers' Club on 'The Modern Actor' for which Wilde took the Chair. "Delicacy is developed to an extent almost abnormal in Mr John Gray", wrote a critic. "His view is that of the artistic pagan, and is vaporously expressed. His thoughts, if I may parody Meredith, are sensuous, but so delicately that to consider them so were to expose oneself to the charge of sensuality. His language is iridescent, or perhaps scented would be a better word. His method of delivery is very gentle. He ceased; he did not conclude."

This was a preliminary to a production by J. T. Grein's Independent Theatre of a one-act play which Gray had translated from the French. Already, towards the beginning of the year, he had been sent up in the *Mainly About People* column of *The Star* for his Introduction to an Italian play translated by J. T. Grein.

> "Mr. John Gray, who writes the 'too-too' introduction to the latest dramatic novelty, Emilio Montanaro's *In the Garden of Citrons*, is said to be the original Dorian of the same name. Mr. Gray, who has cultivated his manner to the highest pitch of languor yet attained, is a well-known figure of the Playgoers' Club, where, though he often speaks, he is seldom heard."

Gray saw an opportunity for a rewarding libel action here and wrote to the *Star* on the subject. Again Dowson wrote Plarr

> . . . the latest news—that Gray of whom I am seeing a good deal just at present, pursues *The Star* for libel asserting him to be the original Dorian of that name.

But the *Star* evaded the issue by calling their recent paragraph an example of the New Humour. "Mr Wilde would be as likely to draw a character from life as to call a photograph an artistic production." At the same time Wilde himself wrote to the *Daily Telegraph* who had told the same story and denied that John Gray was his protégé.

The one-act play which Grein produced at the Royalty Theatre on March 4 was *Le Baiser* by Theodore de Banville and Gray had rendered it in rhymed couplets. It was the first of three one-acters produced that night. The *Star* now gushed:

> The Royalty has never been more crowded than it was last night at the performance of the Independent Theatre, though there was room in the house for the east wind who came uninvited. Literature was represented in the stalls by Mr. J. M. Barrie, Mr. Henry James and Mr. Kennedy, whose play 'The New Wing' last night reached its fiftieth performance. A number of pretty actresses were in the stalls, among them Elizabeth Robins with her inseparable friend Marion Lee, and Estelle Burney sat among the critics of the old school who made quite a compact little body on one side of the stalls . . . Mr. George Moore entertained a party of friends in a private box and had for 'vis à vis' Mr. Oscar Wilde and a suite of young gentlemen, all wearing the vivid dyed carnation which has superseded the lily and the sunflower.

In that same spring Pierre Louÿs, a French poet nearly five years younger than Gray wrote him from Paris a fan letter in the form of a facetious prose poem before coming to London and meeting him. Further letters from Louÿs during and after his stay leave little doubt that the two young poets, in spite of the Frenchman's large moustache and subsequent marriage, had some sort of affair. Gray's side of the correspondence has not come to light but before returning to France in July Louÿs, of whom a great deal can be learnt from his own work, his relationship with Wilde and Alfred Douglas and the writings of André Gide, wrote this:

> My dear John,
>
> When I told you last evening about a letter I had received from you, I meant only the first one and I did not know you had written to me such a beautiful second letter. I know now you are quite a *friend*, such a terrible word! how many have you? how many have I?
>
> Do we know?
>
> You shall go in Paris. We will meet again and often. I wish now one thing: to be for you what you have been for me during that short month.
>
> Give me your hand.
>
> Pierre Louÿs.
>
> Chelsea, 18 July.

Seven years later when Gray had decided to become a priest and Louÿs had married, Louÿs wrote to Gray as though the two decisions were comparable.

> "Oui, mon cher ami, je me suis marié, on ne t'avait pas trompé. Nous sommes arrivés toi et moi, presque la même année, à un tournant de notre vie. Es-tu content de ta decision? Moi, je suis heureux de la mienne."

It was also in that year of 1892 that Wilde, stricken with compunction perhaps at his recent tendency to neglect Gray whenever he could be with Bosie Douglas, agreed to bear the whole cost of issuing Gray's first book of poems *Silverpoints* which was accordingly taken to John Lane for publication in the following year. Gray was viewed with some suspicion by his earnest fellow poets for his association with Wilde and other smart and wealthy people. Though he assiduously attended meetings of the Rhymers' Club he was never made a member, and though he could be seen at the Crown, much frequented by what were still and justly called Bohemians, his dress which like Wilde's had grown conventional but elaborate, and his manner which was confidently camp, were putting-off to penurious and alcoholic writers like Dowson, Lionel Johnson, Plarr and the rest who were mostly public school and university men rejoicing in their new seediness.

Gray's poetry, dated and emasculated as it seems now, was not without grace. One senses the adolescent desire to be bold and wicked, to shock and attract attention, which reduced much verse of the Nineties to sickly English imitations of Baudelaire. But with it there are some genuine metaphysical fancies and some pretty tricks of prosody. The vocabulary is at times archaic and single lines or couplets extracted look absurd and naked in their banality—

I was a masseur and my fingers bled
With wonder as I touched their awful limbs

Or

How very pale your pallor is!

The translations in the book are better, but Gray's choice of originals is significant. Of the twenty-nine poems in *Silverpoints* sixteen were original and thirteen were translations from the French (seven from Verlaine, one from Mallarmé, two from Rimbaud, and three from

Baudelaire). The book designed by Charles Ricketts is in form and content a very parody of all that has come to be considered Ninetyish, but there is a delicacy and campness about it which distinguish its verse from the honestly voluptuous and bacchanalian poetry of Dowson or the scholarly sincerity of Lionel Johnson.

Silverpoints, however, was only projected and its backing guaranteed by Wilde when John Gray, in the autumn of 1892, met André Raffalovich and his life was at once changed. The two were introduced by Arthur Symons in his flat in Fountain Court and Raffalovich, two years older than Gray, instantly fell in love with him and never wholly recovered from it.

Marc-André Raffalovich was the offspring of a Russian Jewish banking family, minor Rothschilds of international finance. André showed no taste for his father's profession and was educated privately in Paris, partly by an English governess Florence Gribbel or Gribbell who remained a dominant figure in his life. His father, Hermann Raffalovich, was much older than his wife Marie who was also his niece and had been promised to her husband in the oriental manner for financial reasons while she was still a child. Both André's parents came from Odessa and had been forced to leave Russia during a pogrom but Hermann afterwards became the Czar's banker in Paris.

André from childhood was grotesque in appearance, beaky, heavy-lipped with beady dark eyes and a thick and ugly speaking voice. His mother, who was a beautiful woman using her riches to make herself a fashionable hostess in Paris, could not bear to have her second son in her presence and sent him to England with Florence Gribbell. Coming of age he inherited a large fortune and set out to conquer artistic London. He was well-read and had a dilettante devotion to the arts and paid for the publication of his verses, *Cyril and Lionel and Other Poems: A Volume of Sentimental Studies* in 1884 and *Tuberose and Meadowsweet* in 1885. The second was reviewed by Wilde with other collections of verses by unknown writers in *The Pall Mall Gazette*, Wilde complaining fractiously that he pronounced tuberose as a trisyllable. ("To say of these poems that they are unhealthy and bring with them the heavy odour of the hot-house is to point out neither their defect nor their merit but their quality merely.") Soon after this the two men met and Oscar threw off that careless epigram which he afterwards adapted, as he did most of his better remarks, to use in a play—'Dear André! He came to London to found a *salon* and only succeeded in opening a saloon.' Raffalovich never forgave him for this and later took his revenge.

André's elder brother remained in Paris where according to Fr Brocard Sewell who wrote a biographical outline of the two friends for a memorial volume• he was well known as the author of books on economic subjects and as translator of standard English works of the same kind. In 1888 he became financial editor of the *Journal des Débats*. André's sister Sophie married the Irish Nationalist William O'Brien. But André, for whom the very English Miss Gribbell had taken the place of a mother, was an anglophil and continued to entertain lavishly in his house in South Audley Street, to cultivate writers and artists and to contribute social gossip to long forgotten magazines of the time, *The Hawk*, *Modern Society* and *The Gridiron*. He was dressy and in spite of his extravagance unpopular, as Vernon Lee's references to him in her letters suggest.

Wilde's crack about opening a saloon was not his only one at André's expense. Something about him seems to have brought out a little malice in Wilde who rarely said anything that could hurt an individual, but André had an ostentatious way of entertaining and there was a suggestion of patronage in the manner in which he treated his guests who were not usually as prosperous as he. Once Wilde with five other men asked to lunch was kept waiting at André's front door in a rainstorm and when he was at last admitted by the butler said: "We want a table for six, please." It was not very funny and was said to amuse his fellow-sufferers rather than to annoy André who was out of sight, but it was overheard and not forgiven.

In the beautiful John Gray with his over-polished manner and literary ambitions André saw all he could never be, all he most admired. A snob but not a genealogical snob, he thought the young man with his self-confidence, good looks and promising place in the only kind of society they both knew, a heroic figure and he at once threw himself, with all his large resources, at Gray's feet. Determined to win him from Wilde he invited him to move to quarters in Park Lane at his expense and carried him triumphantly to his mother's house in Paris where Gray met Mallarmé and other French writers. He bought a

• *Two Friends: John Gray and André Raffalovich: Essays Biographical and Critical.* St Albert's Press, 1963.

yacht and took him cruising in the Mediterranean. He persuaded Miss Gribbell to accept him as a second adopted son and these two became lifelong friends. He later persuaded him to give up his rather menial job at the Foreign Office and gave him all the money he wanted to spend. The two of them, so grotesquely contrasted in appearance, were seen everywhere together, be-jewelled and over-dressed, very consciously men about town but with an inevitable touch of vulgarity about them.

Wilde does not seem to have been more than amused. He was now entirely taken up with Bosie Douglas on the one hand and the stable-boys and other rough youths provided by Alfred Taylor on the other, and friends like Gray, Louÿs, Ross, Turner who had not the *éclat* of the former or the animal attraction of the latter were either neglected or treated as mere recipients of confidences in the years immediately before his fall. He was never a jealous or malicious man and probably heard of the new friendship with a tolerant smile. He could afford to do so. His sudden and immense triumph as a playwright, his exhibitionistic friendship with Bosie Douglas, his success in ridiculing the forces of convention and propriety convinced him that he occupied an eminence, a throne, from which such things as the friendship of André and John could be seen as mere antics.

No, the jealousy, if any, was on the other side. Raffalovich had succeeded in drawing Gray from the dangerously devout circle round Wilde but neither he nor Gray had achieved anything in literature more than the subsidized publication of their verses. Wilde's sudden rise as a dramatist turned poor André's efforts in a new direction and in January 1893 he paid for a production by the Independent Theatre of a play of his. This was a tawdry little piece called *Roses of Shadow* which anyone professionally concerned with play production would have told him to destroy, but Raffalovich, his ears ringing with the applause that had greeted *Lady Windermere's Fan*, insisted on putting it on at the Athenaeum Hall in Tottenham Court Road, a barn of a place which Grein occasionally hired for his productions. Then he and John Gray started work together on a play which would, they believed, have an instant success, comparable perhaps with Oscar's.

So during the spring and summer of 1893, while *A Woman of No Importance* was filling the Haymarket, the two worked away at their drama *The Blackmailers*, and on June 17th, 1894 it was tried out at a matinée performance at the Prince of Wales's Theatre. The press was frankly contemptuous and *The Times*, though more indulgent than most, spoke for the rest:

> "The description 'new and original' was hardly needed in connexion with *The Blackmailers*, a play by Messrs John Gray and André Raffalovich, which was tried at the Prince of Wales's Theatre yesterday afternoon. It would be hard to name any source to which the authors could have been indebted, or, indeed, any society which their sketch could be said to resemble. Like Jean-Jacques' 'Confessions' their work is without precedent and may very well hope to remain without imitators. The story is a sordid and repulsive picture of blackmailing practises carried on in society. The principal adventurer is one Claude Price, but he has obtained a sinister influence over, and makes a tool of, a foolish youth, Hal Danger, a member of an influential family, who has vainly tried to solve by honest means the distressing problem of how to live on an allowance of four hundred a year. By these two scoundrels, whose game appears to be perfectly well understood by the society in which they move, and which, nevertheless tolerates them, blackmail is levied right and left; there is nothing but that in the play. In the last act the young culprit is soundly rated for his offences by a sort of family council who propose that he should emigrate. He thinks of taking poison, but in the end, being left to himself to consider the situation, he merely walks out of the house, leaving the family council, which is headed by a garrulous old admiral, to its own devices. The greater culprit apparently escapes molestation of any kind. The curtain thus descends upon the 'note of interrogation' beloved of Ibsenites. Of the acting in the piece it is unnecessary to speak, though it was in the hands of such an excellent company as Miss Olga Brandon, Mrs. Theodore Wright, Mr. W. L. Abingdon, Mr. Colnagni, and Mr. Julian Cross."

Undeterred by this, Gray and Raffalovich continued to write for the theatre and early in the following year printed privately two duologues which (suggests Alexandra Zaina in an article on Gray's prose writings•) were probably produced in a drawing-room, perhaps as privately as they were printed. The passages which Alexandra Zaina quotes from them chill the marrow. There is in them a plodding deliberate attempt to produce animated and smart dialogue but the speeches go to and fro as ponderously and wearily as the flappers of an old-fashioned punkah. Yet reading the lines one knows that they could only have

• Included in *Two Friends* op. cit.

been written by someone familiar with the crackling wafery dialogue of Wilde, someone who had seen and read his plays, someone who had mistaken Wilde's spontaneity for facile slovenliness and said to himself, Why, I can do this sort of thing just as well. Someone, it is hard not to infer, consumed with envy for the brilliant much-publicized Irishman.

Nothing is heard of the two friends during the protracted hearings in the Wilde case. Raffalovich was living still at Number 72, South Audley Street and there is no reason to think that either he or Gray found it necessary to travel for a time after the verdict as did so many of Wilde's circle. No great blame would have attached to them if they had merely kept discreetly away, for there was little they could do for Wilde and it was three years now since Gray, once so proud of Wilde's company, had made his choice and followed André beckoning towards Park Lane. But André was not content to keep quiet. This was his moment to kick the fallen Wilde and at the same time exploit the circumstances of his fall to get a book professionally published at last. Within three months of Wilde's conviction was published in Paris the small book on which he had worked furiously since Wilde's arrest, *L'Affaire Oscar Wilde*.

Of all Wilde's acquaintances and fellow homosexuals the only one who had attempted at the time to defend him in print—ineptly and unfortunately certainly, but with the best of intentions—was Bosie Douglas. Not until after his death did other friends begin to cash in on their acquaintance with him. No one in England dared to publish a memoir till 1905 when R. H. Sherard started, with *Oscar Wilde: The Story of an Unhappy Friendship*, to write book after book on the strength of his acquaintance with Wilde. But Raffalovich had nothing to lose, and with an assumption of high-minded disapproval and a pseudo-scientifically inquiring attitude towards what he called Wilde's 'crime' he wrote a filthy-minded little pamphlet in a tone of moral indignation. A couple of quotations will show its tenor:

> Quand je l'accuse de criminalité, je ne m'occupe plus des actes sexuels qu'on lui a reprochés, mais du rôle qu'il a joué, de l'influence qu'il a prise et si mal employée, des jeunes vanités qu'il a faussées, des vices qu'il a tant encouragés.
>
> Seulement l'opinion publique m'inspire peu d'estime à ce sujet; elle l'a supporté, soutenu, entretenu, elle l'a subi, ce malheureux

prêtre de Priape, malade de la manie des reclames; l'opinion publique lui a passé bien des mauvaises paroles qui étaient de mauvaises actions, et aujourd'hui c'est sa culpabilité qu'elle attaque plus que sa criminalité.

Raffalovich continued, with a bitchiness almost unmatched, to write of Wilde's sensual lips, discoloured teeth and tongue *qui semblait lecher ses paroles*, to call him a buffoon who vaunted his egotism, idleness, vanity, inconstancy and all imaginable vices. So on for forty-odd vituperative pages. If Wilde, then with shorn head and broad-arrow slops tramping round the silent exercise yard of Reading Gaol, could have read it he would have been baffled by its malignancy. It was not in his nature to understand how his off-hand epigram about 'dear André' could have festered for years in that mean little mind to burst in this current of pus.

In the following year Raffalovich enlarged his pamphlet into a full-length book published in a series *Bibliothèque de Criminologie*. He called his work *Uranisme et Unisexualité* and gave it the pretentious appearance of a scientific handbook. It is in fact little more than an anthology of case histories culled from literature, from Ulrichs, Krafft-Ebbing and such, stale self-righteous stuff presented as a serious study. Its opening words give the measure of its sheer silliness, "On peut diviser les uranistes en ultra-virils, virils, effeminés, passifs" and its quotations from Sainte-Beuve, Goethe, St John of the Cross and Plato of its pretensions.

He quotes a passage from the memoirs of Victor Alfieri about his admiration (at eight years old) for certain innocent Carmelite novices, and from this categorizes Alfieri's as a case of '*Heterosexualité étouffant des penchants uranistes avant la puberté*'. An incident in the youth of the Emperor Baber when he adored a young officer makes his 'case' that of '*Uranisme avec tolerance sexuelle*' and Jean-Jacques Rousseau exemplifies '*Heterosexualité malgré masturbation et masochisme*'. To passages from Casanova is attached the label '*Heterosexualité congenitale malgré des actes unisexuels commis apres la puberté*'. These are followed by many pages of phoney generalizations about 'Uranistes' chiefly based on Krafft-Ebbing's observations, passages from novels, a large slice of the *Satyricon*, passages from de Grimarest's Life of Molière suggesting an unusual relationship between the dramatist and the young actor Baron, and a long account of the Diaries of Platen-Hallermund of which only a part had then been published. The whole book is a superficial and salacious hotch-potch drawn from most of the known sources of the time.

But fortunately a new life was beginning for the jealous and unhappy Raffalovich. John Gray had become a Catholic six years previously, baptised at SS Anselm's and Cecilia's in Lincoln's Inn Fields near the Temple when he lived there. The truth about this conversion is unknown. Many of the Decadents were Catholics or converts to Catholicism and it may not have been the result of any revelation or even of overwhelming conviction, for he continued to lead his mundane and meaningless life and showed no sign of having accepted any discipline. Neither at the time nor in the years thereafter did he give the smallest explanation of this and the religious poetry he wrote before the turn of the century was as artificial and flighty as the rest of his verse. But after the Wilde case he seems to have grown more serious in his work as in his life and he must have confided in Raffalovich the way his thoughts were leading him for in February 1896 Raffalovich joined him in his creed and chose the fashionable Jesuit church in Farm Street for his baptism. Two years later Gray decided that he wished to become a priest and in October 1898 entered the Scots College in Rome as a candidate.

Raffalovich and Miss Gribbell spent part of each year in Rome to be near him during his studies, and during the annual closure of theological schools in Rome Raffalovich would invite the priest-to-be for tours on the continent or back to England or to see Gray's sister Beatrice (afterwards Sister Mary Raphael Gray, O.S.B.) at her convent school at Regensburg in Bavaria. The devotion Raffalovich showed to the priest was different in kind from that shown to the young and graceful disciple of Wilde six years earlier, but it was no less whole-hearted.

It was about to be tested. When Gray was ready to be ordained the Church authorities felt a certain anxiety, not because Gray had failed to show himself a devout and earnest aspirant, but because of certain unfortunate precedents. There had been the dissolute charlatan Frederick Rolfe who had been at the Scots College only ten years previously and some of the conversions of English Decadents were suspect as hysterically induced or acts of deathbed panic. Fr Brocard Sewell even suggests that the Pope himself may have intervened in the case of Gray and decreed that as a priest he must not work in England, least of all in London, and Gray, remembering that he was of Scottish origin, sought a title to ordination from the Archbishop of St Andrews and Edinburgh.

He was ordained priest by Cardinal Respighi a few days before Christmas 1901. After another four months in Rome and three at Fribourg he took up his work as a curate at St Patrick's Church in the Cowgate at Edinburgh, a tough area of Irish workers.

Raffalovich followed him there and in 1905 persuaded the Archbishop to let him build a church and clergy house for Gray in the Morningside district of Edinburgh and purchased for himself a house, 9 Whitehouse Terrace, near the site on which St Peter's began to rise. Miss Gribbell accompanied him as housekeeper and Gray lived in the house till his presbytery was completed. In 1906 Fr John Gray was appointed first parish priest of St Peter's and in April 1907 the church was blessed and a High Mass sung in it.

For twenty-seven years, till the death of Raffalovich in February 1934 and Gray's death four months later the two friends kept up an extraordinary relationship of daily visits and formal greetings which has been described by many who knew them.

Raffalovich whose piety may have been no less real because it was a mite demonstrative, achieved a maturity and a recognizable character of his own and eventually succeeded in founding if not a *salon* at least a most hospitable household to which he attracted a great variety of people, eminent visitors to Edinburgh, stage and literary celebrities enough to belie, in his own mind, that long-ago casual remark of Wilde's which had rankled for half a century. It was Wilde who was 'poor Oscar' now when Raffaolovich referred to him complacently at his luncheon table.

He never lost his ugly guttural speech and he deliberately followed the fashions in men's clothes of the 1890s, which gave him in old age and oddly over-dressed appearance, but with the years his very ugliness took on character and though he could be thought gross and ill-favoured nobody could call him plain, as Eric Gill's drawing of him shows.

Every morning he rose early and went to John Gray's church for Mass where he occupied the same seat daily for more than a quarter of a century. He had a great devotion to the Dominican Order, as Fr Brocard Sewell explains:

A Dominican preacher each Sunday—not at all the services, of course—was the rule at St Peter's. John Gray had known the Order from his boyhood, more or less, and no doubt it was he who introduced André Raffalovich to the Friars Preachers. André was admitted to the Dominican Third Order by Fr. Pius Cavanagh, O.P. in May 1898. He took the name of Brother Sebastian, and preferred thenceforward to be known as André Sebastian Raffalovich. John Gray was received as a Tertiary by Fr. Cavanagh in July 1899, taking the name of Brother Albert. Raffalovich became an outstanding benefactor to the Dominicans, for whom he built St Sebastian's priory at Pendleton, Manchester; and he was also the founder of the small priory and university chaplaincy in George Square, Edinburgh.

His religion, though very much that of a convert to Catholicism, was not obsessive or tiresome to those who did not share his faith. It was perhaps from his mother that he had inherited the ambition to entertain lavishly and gain a reputation for it and in Edinburgh with enterprise, patience and a high rate of expenditure over the years he was successful.

He gave a luncheon party every Sunday at which Champagne was invariably served. Opinions differ about the food as they do about the food in any restaurant; it has been called delicious and merely 'Scotch'. He was a meticulous host, taking endless precautions about the juxtapositions of his guests, showing irritation at the smallest unpunctuality, trying to convey reproofs to those who expressed opinions which were not his, taking his guests aside for whispered confidences, too watchful and anxious to set the good example of hearty eating. He was capable of showing displeasure when a guest cut a rose in his garden to give to a woman in his presence and he had no talent for remaining unruffled by a small social crisis. He does not seem to have sought for his guests in Burke or tried for foreign royalty or Ambassadors, but he did manage to attract respectable celebrities like Lady Margaret Sackville, Eric Gill, Gordon Bottomley, Walter Sickert, Father Robert Hugh Benson, Compton Mackenzie and once at least Max Beerbohm, so that summoning the ghost of Wilde he could ask defiantly if *this* was no more than a saloon.

His dinner-parties on Tuesday evenings were more intimate and André was then expected to recall the past. Under pressure he would talk of 'dear Aubrey Beardsley' and 'poor Oscar', of Lionel Johnson,

Ernest Dowson and the rest, but he much preferred to describe the period glories, perhaps a trifle idealized, of his mother's Paris *Salon* with its hot-house flowers and heavy draperies among which it seemed Sarah Bernhardt, Colette, Robert Louis Stevenson, Huysmans and Mallarmé had been very much at their best. André had no great gift for evocation of the past but he would usually answer his guests' questions.

The atmosphere in his home, says one writer, was 'rather like acting in one of Oscar Wilde's plays produced by Cecil Beaton in slightly off-period costume'. It would have made an ideal setting for an Edinburgh version of Proust's novels. The furniture, though of the best quality, might have been ordered from Maple's or Waring and Gillows and the paintings, by later Impressionists, were dominated by a seated portrait of André as a young man wearing evening dress complete with white waistcoat and a white camellia in his button-hole. The writer adds quaintly that 'a reminder of one of his earlier interests' was a shelf of textbooks on homosexuality.

After the turn of the century Raffalovich published no more books. He was not creative by nature and perhaps realized that it was his not altogether unrewarding function to subsidize the dreams of others, so that St Peter's church, with its baroque high altar, its reredos by Frank Brangwyn, and the Persian rugs in its chancel, was conceived by other men but might never have risen without the djinn-like André and his cheque-book. But he practised one minor art, perhaps the most ephemeral but instantly rewarding of all, flower arrangement. He must have been something of a pioneer for in Great Britain Gertrude Jekyll was at that time the only known authority, and though none of his set pieces have been described the impression is left that he produced some splendid harmonies.

But with this facility for flower arrangement and in spite of his beginnings and early years, Raffalovich as he grew older became more British than the British. The more oriental were his features and the more thickly foreign his speech, the more overbearingly John Bullish was his attitude. Like so many of his race in England he became a vociferous patriot and though there was something extravagant and un-English about this Englishness he was outraged by anything which seemed to flout it. Peter F. Anson recalls how 'after Compton Mackenzie had expressed strong opinions in favour of Scottish

Nationalism at a Sunday luncheon party, André was so shocked at this want of loyalty to Empire that he told me he did not think he would invite him again'. A young girl visitor to Raffalovich's house tells how he would beg her in a guttural voice and with a middle-European accent not to marry 'some horrible foreigner'.

John Gray, on the other hand, became proudly Scottish as the years passed and spoke of regions south of the Border as though they were in a foreign country. Ageing in the 1920s he grew solemn, even a little pompous, very much Canon Gray, a paragon to his curates and a conscientious but somewhat remote parish priest. When he was first given his church and comfortable presbytery other Catholic clergy in the city and diocese were jealous. 'For a long time even the local clergy failed to appreciate him', writes Fr Brocard Sewell, and one can scarcely wonder when they saw the de luxe atmosphere of his church and home and knew that any of the things they had so dearly wanted for so long —a new sanctuary lamp or furniture for a spare bedroom in their cold clergy houses—would be supplied to Gray, before his need had occurred to him, by the ever attentive and munificent Raffalovich.

Gray's presbytery has been more than once described. The leaded windows filled with semi-opaque glass, the Art Nouveau appearance of the place, the twilit atmosphere of the rooms, the drawings by Ricketts and Shannon, the black linen bedsheets, the well-ordered kitchen and good wine, the domestic 'treasure' and excellent staff and Gray himself being considered 'remote', 'inscrutable', 'courteous' but 'stiff' by his various priestly visitors.

He never seems to have lost his literary ambitions though they became less eager with the years. In 1904 Longmans published *The Last Letters of Aubrey Beardsley* edited with an introductory note by the Rev. John Gray and it is ironic that this was the only book, with which he was connected, to be issued by a professional publisher without a subsidy. Most of the letters had been addressed to Raffalovich who had helped to support Beardsley in the last months of his life, and a few to Gray himself. For fifteen years after this publication nothing appeared in print then Gray started contributing to the Dominican Monthly *Blackfriars*—essays chiefly in a style that fatally attempted to echo that of Chesterton and Belloc. He continued to contribute to *Blackfriars* till he wrote, between the date of Raffalovich's death and his own, a tribute to his friend. His book *Poems* (1931) was printed by Eric Gill who had become a friend of Gray and Raffalovich. There is little that is likely to survive in either poetry or prose; from first to last his work was stamped with amateurism. There is a hungry straining after originality of form and expression which ends in feeble eccentricity.

It was typical of his attitude in the years after he had become a hard-working parish priest that though he did not part with his elaborately bound books of the Nineties he kept them on a shelf with their titles to the wall. He could not forget the past and may not have wished to do so. It is unlikely that he ever knew of Wilde's reference to him in *De Profundis* for only Ross's non-committal selection from the book was published in his lifetime, but if it came to his ears he may have felt whimsically and retrospectively flattered. "When I compare my friendship with you", Wilde wrote to Bosie Douglas, "with such still younger men as John Gray and Pierre Louÿs I feel ashamed. My real life, my higher life was with them." In fact Gray was four and a half years older than Bosie, and Louÿs of exactly Bosie's age, but Oscar was making a case untroubled by considerations of accuracy.

Gray, unlike Raffalovich, avoided reminiscences of the past, though he said Mass once a year for Paul Verlaine, and when he was induced to speak of the Nineties remembered the Catholics, Lionel Johnson, Beardsley, Dowson. Nobody has recorded and perhaps nobody ever heard what he had to say about Wilde or Douglas, or his own young manhood. Peter F. Anson had the feeling that Gray was 'wearing a mask' which never once, in his fifteen years' acquaintance with the Canon, was removed. He was also wearing a wig as his later photographs show.

Most vivid, most memorable and most significant are the descriptions given by many observers of the outward relationship between Gray and Raffalovich in later life. Gray's writings were not without a certain wit but neither he nor Raffalovich had much sense of humour, and the solemnity with which they treated one another, the monstrous conventions they observed, must have been uproariously funny to anyone who had known them in their salad days. Gray allowed himself to address Raffalovich and speak of him to intimate friends as 'André', but to Raffalovich in speech and correspondence Gray was 'Canon Gray', or occasionally 'dear Canon'.

When Gray went to Raffalovich's house, ten minutes from his own, as he did on most days during the twenty-seven years they lived in Edinburgh, the parlourmaid would announce him and Raffalovich would rise, with a faintly surprised air, to greet him and enquire after his health. 'How kind of you to call!' he would say as though this were a rare and unexpected visit. Gray on his side would say to a priest who had stayed with him over many years and knew the customs of both houses, "André has been kind enough to ask us to luncheon on Sunday," as though there could ever be a Sunday on which Gray and his guest would not join the invariable luncheon party. "How very kind of André," the guest would be expected to reply. Yet when Gray was away from home he would send a daily telegram—the men of the Nineties were great telegraphists—reporting on his welfare and movements, and Raffalovich would be in a visible tizzy until he received it.

What, one cannot help wondering vulgarly, did they say to one another when they were alone? What had they said, what resolutions had they made or taken for granted when the great change in their lives came? Did they regret their first few years together or merely repent of them? Did they ever, in spite of the validity and potency of their faith and self-dedication, have secret moments in which they saw their conversion as a sacrifice? What was behind that 'mask' of the Canon's and that broad-lipped smile of André's?

Certainly, whatever their relationship before and after Gray's entering the priesthood, they were almost the only two of all the Nineties men who made something constructive and beneficent of their later lives, however remote it was from their early ambitions. And theirs was the only one of all those passionate friendships and love-affairs that lasted more than a season or two. Its offspring was of bricks and mortar but that is better, surely, than no offspring at all.

CHAPTER TEN

Wilde, Lionel Johnson, Ernest Dowson and Count Stenbock

THOUGH there was properly no school, or literary period, or group of 'The Nineties', it was certainly an epoch of its own in London life.

The streets seemed to have been awakened to gaiety by the brilliant lighting and the people to have a new animation. The population and the prosperity of the city had both increased and there was already talk of traffic problems.

Large and luxurious hotels were opening up and restaurants with famous names were sparkling and rather Parisian, everyone thought. Eating in restaurants at night was something the English had only done by necessity or on their way to the theatre; now they caught the continental trick of supper parties or dinners *à deux* in one of the plush-seated, gilt-mirrored places where French or Italian waiters gave them ostentatious attention, and they could eat foreign foods like 'ortolans wrapped in Sicilian vine leaves', as Wilde called them, with lashings of 'Tom' or 'Bubbly' at five shillings a bottle. They might even go on, if there were no ladies in the party, to the Café Royal and look at the famous artists and writers of the day quarrelling, laughing or taking up noticeable poses.

It was the day of the music-hall. A chairman, not yet called a compère, introduced the acts and accepted a drink from those near him. The acts had not degenerated into vaudeville which came with the new century but were true music-hall acts, crude, heartrending, blatantly funny. There were muscular acrobats in black woollen tights who wore fierce waxed moustaches and jolly old drunks in white waistcoats and top hats watching them. There were musical-hall stars, too, whose pictures with those of famous actors and actresses were sold all over London, the ladies big-busted, tight-waisted with loops of hair and pleading eyes, the gentlemen sternly handsome in their tall stiff collars. But in spite of the Englishness of the music-hall people did not only talk about the Continent, they went there and came back to give a flashy new foreign air to London and more than one Soho pub fixed a drip-trap on its counter for those desperate characters who drank absinthe.

It was the day, too, of the illustrator, even novels appearing with at least a frontispiece showing the heroine registering fury and the hero, sometimes clean-shaven now, in an attitude of pleading and adoration, or else facing his rival armed with a six-shooter and wearing a Norfolk suit. Or of a lesser kind of illustration, that of coloured postcards having vulgar jokes on them, which came in with the fashions of the period and showed gentlemen in striped bathing costumes to the neck and ankles, a fashion which the postcards kept for forty years. The illustrator could do as much as the author to create a character in those days and every month or so one could not only read about Sherlock Holmes and Dr Watson but *see* them up to some benificent devilry in the *Strand Magazine*.

It was still the day of the horse and everyone could be sentimental about the cabby devoted to his own. Brewers' drays, doctors' broughams, four-wheelers and buses had their several kinds of heroic horses stumbling over the cobbles, while racing, in that last proud flush before it fell into the hands of crooks and dopers and gang-protected bilkers, was still the sport of kings.

It was the day of millionaires, American or South African—rarely English because 'millionaire' was a harsh word when applied to fellow-countrymen and nobody would think of mentioning that a Duke was a millionaire, that went without saying. The day of dim lodgings in long monotonous streets but of lodgers who went 'up

West' at night. Of Inverness capes, and above all of hats—opera hats, silk hats, bowlers of many shapes, billycocks, deerstalkers, straw hats, mostly hard and all heavy. The day of sticks and umbrellas, too, when a man was expected to carry something protective. Of boots, for shoes were improvident in the muddy streets, of goloshes, and in the country of gaiters.

It was the day when all London, outside 'the City', 'the West End' and 'the East End' was a network of solid Victorian streets undisturbed by more than a few carriages or respectable passers-by, where the errand-boy's whistle or a German band or a barrel-organ woke the deathly quietness of the middle-classes at home, where no one hurried and where minor characters like housemaids might appear briefly in cap and apron at the top of the area steps. If the people there wanted noise and movement they had to go and find it in the glittering not-quite-nice West End.

It was the day of Oscar Wilde, for now that his smart risqué plays began to fill the theatres no one could ignore the name, which became an irritation on the ear-drums. For four years he was a prodigy.

2

The circumstances of his trials and the trials themselves have been often described• and form no part of this book. His extraordinary friendship with Lord Alfred Douglas has been considered in detail•• and is only incidental to the present purpose. His phenomenal success as a playwright and his relations with the theatre are carefully studied by Hesketh Pearson. There remains only what has been unctiously called 'the *other* side of his life', as though it were the darker side of the moon. In fact, as he himself stated, it became life itself. "I let myself be lured into long spells of senseless and sensual ease. I amused myself with being a *flâneur*, a dandy, a man of fashion. I surrounded myself with the smaller natures and the meaner minds. . . . Tired of being on the heights, I deliberately went to the depths in the search for

• Notably in *Oscar Wilde Three Times Tried* (1911), *The Trials of Oscar Wilde*, edited by H. Montgomery Hyde (1948) and in *The Life of Oscar Wilde* by Hesketh Pearson (1946).

•• *Bosie: The Story of Lord Alfred Douglas his Friends and Enemies* by Rupert Croft-Cooke, 1963.

new sensations. What the paradox was to me in the sphere of thought, perversity became to me in the sphere of passion. Desire, at the end, was a malady, or a madness, or both."

The *Letters* are not very helpful for an understanding of this. Doubtless many of his letters written in this period were destroyed in the time of panic that followed, but Wilde had not in any case reached those years of indiscretion after his imprisonment when he wrote without restraint to Robert Ross and Reginald Turner about Edmond, golden Maurice whose upper lip was like a rose leaf, 'the Florifer' who sold violets, Léon, Eugène 'that wonderful harvest moon', Sir John's little friend Joseph who was 'quite an imp though attractive in love-scenes', Georges 'so like Antinous', Eolo, André 'with wonderful eyes', Pietro 'like a young St John', Didaco 'a beautiful young actor', Eduardo, Rollo 'one of the sea-farers', Henri 'with the sweetest and most compromising smiles', Casquette, 'Le Premier Consul', Maltchek, Armando 'a very smart elegant young Roman Sporus', Arnaldo, Omero, Dario and Le Boucher. These he was to view later with indulgent amusement, recording their crimes and brief imprisonments, enjoying their mischievous company, for in his life as in his work he outlived melodrama. Whereas if he had left such souvenirs of the London years he would have spoken with a ghoulish awe of his friends' 'infamous war against life'.

When the Marquess of Queensberry employed two retired police detectives to assist his search for boys to give evidence against Wilde (that is, evidence to justify him in a grave charge of libel), they found over a dozen, some of whom were not called, their researches going back three years. It is possible in the nature of things and remembering Wilde's admissions in *De Profundis* that these were no more than a small proportion of his associates, for sexual curiosity, a powerful impulse, was driving him and he spent most of his nights, in the last three years before his case, in search and pursuit. It will be remembered that the Savoy servants gave evidence of five boys having stayed the night with Wilde whereas the prosecution identified only one.

There were erotic or semi-erotic friendships, and there is evidence of these in the *Letters*—that with Norman Forbes-Robertson which ended in a difference of opinion about a play, that with H. C. Marillier, with an actor named Roland Atwood, with Robert Ross and at last, most conspicuously, with Alfred Douglas. But these were not what Wilde primarily wanted. He did not like affairs with intellectuals or young men of his own class. Even with Bosie the merely sexual side of the relationship was negligible. He liked—and he used the word in one of his letters—'roughs'. Not as John Addington Symonds had done, with womanish devotion, but to tame them briefly to his will. Of the earlier of these, from the time of his friendship with Ronald Gower and Frank Miles down to 1892, we can know nothing except that they must have existed. From there onwards, thanks to the Scarlet Marquis, the efficiency of his private detectives and perhaps some voluntary informers, we know a great deal, but not all.

Wilde needed spectators for all he did, not of course *voyeurs* in the literal sense, but friends who could hear of his adventures, watch him making difficult contacts, dine with him in the private room of a restaurant when he had invited some entertaining young blackguard to meet him there.

With Bosie the case was somewhat different for Wilde and Bosie adored one another, were proud to be seen together, talked poetry and conducted their relationship on a level of ostentatious romance. But there is plenty of evidence that—sometimes together, sometimes alone—they went cruising after new and dangerous contacts and in conversation and in letters used the vocabulary of high camp. They were introduced by Lionel Johnson and though neither would forgo formality and good manners they were soon on terms of such familiarity that they could talk about renters and roughs. In the first year of their friendship Wilde—through the lawyer George Lewis—had to rescue Bosie from some blackmailer in Oxford, and in one of the first surviving letters Wilde wrote to him (from Babbacombe to Salisbury where Bosie was staying with his mother) he said facetiously of the poem which Bosie had published in his paper the *Spirit Lamp*: "My charge for the sonnet is £300. Who on earth *is* the editor? He must be rented. I hear he is hiding at Salisbury." He uses the word a month later in a letter from the Savoy after one of their violent quarrels. "I would sooner be blackmailed by every renter in London than have you bitter, unjust, hating." In the next year he writes telling Bosie of a 'frantic telegram' and request for money from one of the boys who was later to appear against him, adding lightly: "As he betrayed me grossly I of course gave him money and was kind to him." From

Worthing in the year before the disaster Wilde writes of the boys they had known together there. Although these letters were interspersed with extravagant love prose to Douglas himself they were, it can be seen, exchanges of confidence concerning adventures. Whatever else they quarrelled about they were never jealous of one another's young friends. Moreover one of the chief witnesses against Wilde, Alfred Wood, who stole the letters with which Wilde was blackmailed, had been sent to him by Bosie and there was other evidence that Wilde and Bosie had shared boys and occasions.

The same could not be said of Ross. There was some sort of affair between Wilde and Ross at first; thereafter Ross, who lived among educated inverts, was a friend of Edmund Gosse, talked sex with dainty young men of the Bohemian fringes but at this time never went slumming, introduced to Wilde not 'renters' and 'trade' as Bosie had done, but—scarcely less dangerous—the audience Wilde needed, intelligent queers like Maurice Schwabe, Arthur Clifton, Tom Kennion, More Adey, Reggie Turner and the Horniman brothers, Roy and B. G. Of these only Maurice Schwabe shared Wilde's uninhibited enthusiasm for the lower orders and was responsible for one of his most fatal introductions.

3

Among those who knew Wilde at this time were four men who are usually considered poets of the Nineties. One of them, John Gray, has already been discussed. Two more, Lionel Johnson and Ernest Dowson, were poets without being Ninetyish and the fourth, Count Eric Stenbock, was Ninetyish without being a poet.

Physically Lionel Johnson was little more than a dwarf. From glandular or other causes he grew only to five-foot-two and for many years kept the appearance (though not, seen from close at hand, the fresh complexion) of a boy of fifteen. This was, naturally enough, the first thing that everyone who met Lionel Johnson noticed and most commentators on his poems start by quoting Oscar Wilde's remark about Lionel's going out and hailing the first passing perambulator. Pictures show an almost triangular face, a broad brow narrowing to a point of chin, not particularly attractive though the eyes are kind and frank. Until he was nearing thirty he was actually taken for a schoolboy on many occasions. Richard Le Gallienne, seeing him first at the Rhymers Club,* supposed he was the son of one of the members.

The second thing remembered of him by the memoir writers was his scholarship which seemed to most of them prodigious. He himself in a well-known letter to Le Gallienne denied this:

> My Dear Le Gallienne,
>
> Very many thanks for your kind and welcome praises of my book; they are refreshing, after the somewhat savage, and slightly silly, utterances of our friend, the *Chronicle*. What do these dear people mean by 'learning'? Some of my critics while saying pleasant and cordial things, yet raise hands of amazement at my 'learning', or bend brows of reproach at my 'pedantry'. And yet I am neither learned, nor pedantic, but simply fond of literature. It is as natural to me to quote Aristotle, or Aeschylus, as to quote Stevenson, or Bridges, just because I like them: but I begin to believe, I must be lean, pale, spectacled, stooping, bent over dusty folios, great at Arabic, and hating frivolity. It must be a dream, that I love walking tours, whisky, dogs, the Alhambra, and a joke. Seriously, I am the poorest of scholars: to take the Oxford test, I got a first in 'Greats', but a bad second in 'Mods'. I read the classics, and foreign literatures, for mere love of them: my memory is good, and when I sit down to write, quotations pour in upon me; Pascal jostling Mr. Sims, Goethe tumbling over Zangwill, Cicero elbowing John Morley. I was lately walking at the Land's End, and found myself, unconsciously declaiming Virgil and Arnold to the seagulls. And this perfectly natural instinct, neither a merit, nor a fault, is put down, as laborious and affected pedantry. One would think, a writer were bound to apologize, should he dare mention an author of more than fifty years since: and that, if he do so dare, it must be the result of painful research. No one ever reproaches an architect, painter, musician, for being decently acquainted with the history and triumphs of his art: it is only natural, that he should be. Doubtless, I overdo quotation: but it is from mere exuberance of delight, not in any spirit of pedantry. How can one help knowing things so delightful, or making use of them? I won't say, that my reproachful critics are ignorant, but, assuredly, I am not learned. I will only say, that they do not know what learning is: I do.
>
> 'Casual commas': I thank you: no, you are right, my commas, Heaven be praised, are *not* casual. What right has anything, in any

* The Rhymers Club which has been too often written about was a very miscellaneous collection of poets, not necessarily Ninetyish, which met at intervals at the Cheshire Cheese. Wilde went once or twice with Gray but was never a member.

> work of art, however slight, to be casual? Oh, for the scholarly graces of Addison and Goldsmith![•]

But his poetry, drilled to a classic precision, owing nearly as much to literature, Latin and English, as to imagination, suggests that if not a profound scholar he was essentially a man of books, certainly one of the best-read younger poets who have written in English. His letters, written between the ages of sixteen and eighteen to his school friends and edited anonymously by Lord Russell[••] are almost incredible in their precocity and he had a name as a learned conversationalist while still at Oxford.

The third characteristic, no longer glossed over in accounts of him, was his alcoholism which was, in his last years, of a piteous lonely kind and even in the early Nineties more like drug-taking than jovial tippling. For a time he fought against it, at Oxford and afterwards, and had some of Swinburne's belief that it was not really stronger than he was. We find him writing to his landlord Arthur Mackmurdo who let rooms to members of the Century Guild[•••] at 20 Fitzroy Street—

> I am exceedingly distressed by your letter, though I fully recognize your just cause of complaint. But I may ask for a further trial, upon the condition that I take the pledge at once—which I should have done long ago—and that upon giving the least disturbance I go. Also, I promise to have no drink in my rooms but for friends. As long as it depends upon my own will, I am quite hopeless: but the pledge is different. I once took it temporarily, for a month, and kept it rigidly: and should have taken it for good and all, but for falling ill. If you will consent to this, it will be the greatest of many kindnesses. Of course, should you be willing to do this, the Frasers must be told. I can't tell you how sorry I should be to leave the house where I have lived for five years and had so many friends. Medically speaking, I am not hopelessly given up to drink: it is easy for me to abstain altogether, though very hard to be moderate. At home and elsewhere, where I am not my own master, I drink nothing: it will be quite as easy here with the pledge. I shall be leaving town fairly soon, which will be best for me. If you will give me this last chance, I and my people will be more indebted to you than I can say.[••••]

• *The Romantic Nineties* by Richard le Gallienne, 1926.

•• *Some Winchester Letters of Lionel Johnson*, 1919.

••• An association of craftsmen which included Arthur Mackmurdo, Selwyn Image and Henry Horne and issued *The Century Guild Hobby-Horse* in which much of the poetry of the Nineties appeared.

•••• *The Complete Poems of Lionel Johnson* edited by Iain Fletcher, 1953.

It was not till he had been living in London for three years that he wrote that curious poem *Vinum Daemonum* which he dedicated to Stephen Phillips who was also a drunk:

> The crystal flame, the ruby flame,
> Alluring, dancing, revelling!
> See them: and ask me not, whence came
> This cup I bring.
>
> But only watch the wild vine glow,
> But only taste its fragrance: then,
> Drink the wild drink I bring, and so
> Reign among men.
>
> Only one sting, and then but joy:
> One pang of fire, and thou art free.
> Then, what thou wilt, thou canst destroy:
> Save only me!
>
> Triumph in tumult of thy lust:
> Wanton in passion of thy will:
> Cry *Peace*! to conscience, and it must
> At last be still.
>
> I am the Prince of this World: I
> Command the flames, command the fires.
> Mine are the draughts, that satisfy
> This World's desires.
>
> Thy longing leans across the brink:
> Ah, the brave thirst within thine eyes!
> For there is that within this drink,
> Which never dies.

The fourth thing about Johnson which has not been openly discussed until recent years was his homosexuality which seems to have been of a rare and esoteric kind. Professor Iain Fletcher who edits Johnson's poems with an understanding preface which is all that so far exists as a biography, says that Johnson's pale oval face cast him for the role of Giton at Winchester and that for his last two years there he was 'one of the leaders of a homosexual circle'. He thinks there was no doubt that after Johnson became a Catholic 'such practices were discontinued' but he gives no reason for this beyond Johnson's conversion and this seems a dubious one. If his Faith could not prevent him from committing the greater sin of destroying his genius and eventually his life with alcohol, why should it have suddenly made him sexually ascetic? We can gather, in fact, that it did not; he certainly continued to associate with fellow-homosexuals—some of them contentedly extrovert and uninhibited—like Alfred Douglas, Oscar Wilde, Campbell Dodgson, William Theodore Peters, William Percy Addleshaw, Edward Marsh and More Adey. His capacity for strange sins was probably not great but in 1891, the year of his conversion, he was rhyming to Wilde on the publication of *The Picture of Dorian Gray*:

Amat avidus amores
Miros, miros carpit flores
  Saevus pulchritudine:
Quanto anima nigrescit,
Tanto facies splendescit,
  Mendax, sed quam splendide!

Hic sunt poma Sodomorum;
Hic sunt corda vitiorum;
  Et peccata dulcia.
In excelsis et infernis,
Tibi sit, qui tanta cernis,
  Gloriarum gloria.•

Johnson's life recalls Swinburne's, his poetry not at all. Like Swinburne he was the son of a retired naval officer and like him undersized and frail. They both had extraordinary memories for what they had read and both impressed their fellows with it. They both, by natural choice, by instinct, dedicated their lives to literature. Swinburne was a masochist, Johnson an invert but they were both dipsomaniacs. At the age of thirty-five they were both at the point of death from alcoholism and self-starvation. The difference between them in life was that Johnson had no Watts-Dunton to take him away to Putney and by patience and self-sacrifice help him to defeat his own weakness. In a state of debility and drunkenness after lying neglected for some time in a room at Clifford's Inn Johnson staggered round to a pub called the Green Dragon, looking, according to evidence at the inquest, 'extremely ill'. He 'went to sit in a chair and in trying to do so fell slightly on his

• Rough prose translation:
He loves strange sins avidly, he gathers strange flowers, fierce with beauty. The more dark his spirit the more radiant his face, false but splendid! The apples of Sodom are here and the very heart of vice and sweet sins. In heaven and hell be glory of glories to you who perceive so much.

head'. A fracture of the skull resulted from this and he died five days later in St Bartholomew's Hospital. According to evidence at the inquest, from a laundress named Annie Jenkins who had tried to do what she could for him, he had been drinking two pints of whisky every twenty-four hours.

This was in 1902, two years after Wilde's death in Paris. The two met when Wilde was visiting Pater at Oxford in February 1890. Pater had told Wilde of the brilliant little poet and Wilde decided to meet him. Johnson wrote afterwards to his friend Arthur Galton

> On Saturday at mid-day, lying half asleep in bed, reading Green, I was roused by a pathetic and unexpected note from Oscar: he plaintively besought me to get up and see him. Which I did: and I found him as delightful as Green is not. He discoursed, with infinite flippancy, of everyone: lauded the *Dial*: laughed at Pater: and consumed all my cigarettes. I am in love with him. He was come to visit Pater; and to see *Strafford*.

Wilde wrote almost as enthusiastically to Johnson.

> I hope you will let me know when you are in town. I like your poetry—the little I have seen of it—so much, that I want to know the poet as well.
>
> It was very good of you getting up to see me. I was determined to meet you before I left Oxford.

They used to meet at the Crown, a pub with a clientele like one of the pubs of Fitzrovia sixty years later, and it was Johnson, with the best intentions in the world, who decided that his older friend Oscar should meet his younger friend Bosie Douglas, and brought the two together.

He never forgave himself for this. He had been devoted to Bosie ever since they had been at Winchester and Johnson had been detailed to hold up Bosie's shirt—a part of the ritual of a Winchester flogging—when Bosie was thrashed by the headmaster, Dr Fearon. They had been friends at Oxford, but when Bosie came under the fashionable spell of Wilde, Johnson found him unbearable and wrote a sonnet to Wilde who had once been his idol.

The Destroyer of a Soul

I hate you with a necessary hate.
First, I sought patience: passionate was she:
My patience turned in very scorn of me,
That I should dare forgive a sin so great,

As this, through which I sit disconsolate;
Mourning for that live soul, I used to see;
Soul of a saint, whose friend I used to be:
Till you came by! a cold, corrupting, fate.

Why come you now? You, whom I cannot cease
With pure and perfect hate to hate? Go, ring
The death-bell with a deep, triumphant toll!
Say you, my friend sits by me still? Ah, peace!
Call you this thing my friend? this nameless thing?
This living body, hiding its dead soul?

He remained on friendly terms with Bosie and his mother, however, and was able to secure for his friend Dodgson the task of tutoring Bosie which led to some amusing comments from Wilde. But he was never reconciled with Wilde and there is a story that when the trials came he told Katherine Tynan somewhat hypocritically that 'he could not forgive Oscar's marriage, his having brought that poor girl into it'.• This could be true but it sounds very much out of character. Katherine Tynan (Hinkson) was a poet and adored Johnson somewhat blindly. "Johnson stands out with an austere light behind him like the aureoled head of a little saint." One can believe her description of his arriving at her house 'carrying his infinitesmal top hat in his hand, all fine manners and gracious courtesies', but when she says 'the grosser sins never touched him. He remained *snow-white*', and goes on to say that it is time to prick the legend that has grown up about Johnson once and for all, one finds her syntax truer than her intention. When she adds that in the last years of his life she saw him under the influence of drink only twice and knew of one other occasion, one is reminded of the inquest evidence and concludes that Katherine Tynan's acquaintance cannot have been very close. She may have thought her repetition of the remark about bringing the 'poor girl into it' presented Johnson in an amiable light, at least to women, but it is far from doing so.

4

Johnson has been claimed as a Nineties poet for no better reason than that he lived in the Nineties and died young. For Ernest Dowson there seems, on the face of it, a better argument. But Ernest Dowson

• *Memories* by Katherine Tynan, 1924.

has become far more of a legend than Johnson. There have collected round him more stories and theories, more vivid but contradictory personal recollections, more sheer fiction, than around any poet of the time. It is hard to know who is to blame for this—Arthur Symons or Robert Sherard or that high-pitched American writer Frances Winwar or Frank Harris again or Desmond Flower or one of half a dozen more who have seen in Dowson's indecorous life, with its corny motif of unrequited passion, material for imaginative biography or editing. It is an excellent example of the tendency by biographers, critics and historians to make all the facts fit with some preconceived pattern.

According to the long-accepted myth, Ernest Dowson was the Pessimist, the end-of-century death-wisher, fated in life to be beyond consolation and only in an early death to find peace. Everything he did was touched with hopelessness and despair, everything he wrote was full of dejection. At Oxford, instead of taking a degree he took hashish. In London he let his family business fall from inert fingers while he found oblivion in absinthe. Falling in love with a Polish waitress in a Soho restaurant he wrote *Cynara* to her and broke his heart when she married a waiter. He even failed to interest Wilde in the treats of a Dieppe brothel. Finally, worn out with drugs, disease, under-nourishment and drink, he died, a Keats, a Chatterton, in the arms of Robert Sherard.

If that were the truth one might be able to talk of the Decadent Nineties and of Dowson as their apogee. But Dowson thoroughly enjoyed himself in the earlier years of the Nineties and his more tragic poetry, like most good tragic poetry, was usually written and discussed in the best of spirits. His first concern with the *Cynara* poem, for instance, was—would it shock? In a high-spirited letter to a friend he wrote, "I have just seen the proofs of my Cynara poem for the April *Hobby*.• It looks less indecent in print, but I am still nervous! though I admire Horne's•• audacity." His hashish at Oxford was an isolated experiment with some undergraduates in taking *kif* which led on repetition to emetics at the chemist's. He did not stay up to take a degree because he was urgently needed by his father in the business. The business, a small dry dock in Limehouse was a failure and a

• *The Century Guild Hobby-Horse.*

•• Herbert Horne, the editor of *The Century Guild Hobby-Horse.*

financial genius with capital could not have made it pay, let alone an inexperienced undergraduate—though Dowson was quite conscientious about it. As for the waitress, she was not one, but the twelve-year-old daughter of a Polish father and a mother of unknown nationality who to Dowson, when he wrote *Cynara*, was a delightful little innocent with whom he played Halma. When eight years later she was to marry a young French tailor he seems to have accepted the situation without any attempt to change it. He died at thirty-two of tuberculosis while a lodger in a house Sherard had in Catford. He was a good poet with the poet's usual unstable character and he died of a disease which even with the medical knowledge of those days need not have killed him so soon. But much that is sunny in his story remains, and 'unrequited love' was a small part of it.

Both his parents were consumptive. His father had inherited his dry dock, but during Ernest's lifetime the business declined and finally gave out altogether. His parents' health sent them abroad a good deal and Ernest grew up almost as much in France as in England. He loved France all his life, spoke and wrote French as though it was his language and during his bad times in London felt that he needed only to escape to some French village to regain his equilibrium, as though he were returning to his boyhood.

He went up to Oxford but remained at Queen's College for less than two years. During that time he started writing and occasionally publishing verse, chiefly about the innocence of girlhood with which he had an almost Dodgsonian obsession. In London he lived at the Dock till his parents' death in 1894 and for the rest of the decade he hung out in London or France, neglecting the tuberculosis that was killing him, writing at times feverishly, drinking far too much and whoring indiscriminately. Perhaps it has been English envy of the French, who do this sort of thing much better, which has made Dowson's biographers invest this sad, sordid life-story with a grandly tragic air which it only half merits. Mr Longaker's* insensitive and laborious book, for instance, goes over each trivial incident with demure and wordy considerations, and shorter essays are no better. They make one doubt at last whether there was any *grande passion* at all.

But it is one of the dearest fictions of the western world that poets

* *Ernest Dowson* by Mark Longaker, 1944.

should die young after lives of broken health or gross excess of alcohol, or sorrow, if possible with a *grande passion* thrown in, meeting contempt from an unsympathetic world in their lifetimes and being honoured after their deaths. A good many in England seem to have obliged by conforming to this pattern. Keats, of course, is the prime type but there are Shelley, Marlowe, Chatterton, and a late-comer, but none the less welcome to keep the myth alive in the twentieth century, Dylan Thomas. (War poets do not count.) Dowson's life, suitably recorded and considered, makes an excellent example of this, and even readers of it today insist on the *grande passion*. The story of this, for some parts of which the present author was given information by an eye-witness, the brother of A. B. Miall the Nineties poet, is not without interest even when the elaborations and false drama have been removed.

Dowson, aged twenty-three, just down from Oxford, his head full of literature and the ambition to write, went into an eating-house kept by a Pole and his family. It was on the edge of Soho being just across the street from what became later the main entrance of the Regent Palace Hotel. It consisted of one rather bare room with a fireplace or continental stove in front of which the family washing used to be hung to dry at night, so that the atmosphere was more domestic than that of most restaurants open to the public.

There were three in the family, Foltinowicz himself who spoke very little English, his wife—who according to Derwent Miall was not Polish but, he always understood, Italian—and a child of twelve named Adelaide. Dowson who had already written poetry about little girls adored this one and went every night to eat at the place which he and his friends called 'Poland'. He watched her movements as she flashed about between the tables and listened to her pert slightly un-English speech. His emotions were involved but—at first at least—in a slightly forced and sentimental way.

He wrote his best poetry at this time and it was in a sense inspired by Adelaide, known as Missie, to whom it was dedicated, as a knight-errant in the most romantic tradition might dedicate his quest to the service of his etherealized lady-love. It was of the contemporary we're-all-damned, *carpe diem* variety which his own line 'they are not long, the days of wine and roses' so ruefully expressed, but he did it better than any one else then living. When he wrote his poem to Cynara *Non Sum Qualis Eram Bonae Sub Regno Cynarae* he knew he had hit the jackpot or as Arthur Symons less vulgarly put it 'one of the greatest lyrical poems of our time; in it he has for once said everything and he has said it to an intoxicating and perhaps immortal music'. Like all he wrote at that time it was 'inspired' by Missie, if there is such a thing as inspiration—and to Dowson there was—but to suggest that its theme has any direct or personal connection with her, that Cynara does not represent innocence, or a man's one great love, or the ideal of womanhood, or some other nebulous figure-head, but a child of twelve with whom he played Halma every night is plum silly.

At first amused and enchanted by Adelaide, who was a pretty little dark thing, he found in two years during which he rarely missed an evening in the restaurant he called 'Poland', that she was rapidly growing physically mature and the kind of poetic child-worship he had been giving her had to change with her development. He himself was far less callow. Spending parts of his evenings with other young writers and actors at the Cock, the Crown and the Café Royal, he drank absinthe, picked up women and slept with them, joined his friends in their would-be Parisian whoring, had mild affairs with girls of character who went about with his friends like Dulcie and Marie, and was sincerely ambitious. He took seriously all the literary coteries and reviews of the time, belonged to the Rhymers Club where Lionel Johnson used to read out his poems because Dowson was too diffident, wrote for *The Century Guild Hobby-Horse* and edited the few issues of a mushroom periodical, knew all the young poets and stayed up most of the night talking literature with them, though he continued to work at the Dock during the daytime.

He became a Catholic in the same year as his friend Lionel Johnson, probably through his influence and almost certainly in collusion with him. It may even have been on the same day or in the same church.

His letters during the early Nineties are full of literary matters and chit-chat about writers and publications, but there are occasional references —often no more than afterthoughts—to his perplexities over Missie. He could no longer treat her as a child but he seems to have had no impatient desire to possess her. He had only to present himself to Missie's mother to be accepted as her future husband, but dithered over this for a long time, unwilling, perhaps, to give up the joys of perpetual remote adoration. He had not the callousness of a Dodgson who could coolly dismiss his little favourites as soon as they reached the age of fourteen or fifteen. He wrote to his friend Sam Smith—

> I go on in precisely the same situation in Poland. I can't somehow screw myself up to making a declaration of myself to *Madame*, although I am convinced that it is the most reasonable course. Any day however with favourable omens it may arrive. She herself is sometimes very charming, sometimes not! But in the latter case it is merely my own abominably irritable temper which is to blame.

There are letters about Rhymers Club meetings and the *Book of the Rhymers Club* in which some of his poetry was printed, about a girl called Marie who had a breakdown and had to be nursed in turns by the men who had enjoyed her, and about various revelries. By the winter of his second year in London he was writing to Sam Smith lightly, almost jocularly, about the situation with Missie. (He always referred to her mother as 'Madame'.)

> Things are coming to a crisis, *cher vieux*! I go to have *tête-à-tête* teas with *Madame*! We talk intimately, we talk of Her—*natürlich*—and we are constantly on the verge of an understanding. Yesterday it was the nearest shave of all. She gave me an admirable occasion. I am sure she expected it. I was just coming out with a protestation, to the effect that my one object and desire in life was to be of service to her admirable daughter—when we were interrupted. We were both curiously moved! I went out and had a gin and bitters and poured it tremulously down my shirt, and passed a perfectly wide-awake night—damning this interruption. This morning I saw that it would have been foolish; but this afternoon I shall be in precisely the same state, and I feel certain that it is only a question of days now. To think that a little girl of barely fourteen should have so disorganized my spiritual economy.

Finally, in the following spring Missie being now less than fifteen, he spoke to Missie herself. "She took it with a great deal of dignity and self-possession; I don't think I have ever admired her more. She reminded me very properly that she was rather too young: but she proceeded to admit that she was not surprised at what I had told her, and that she was not angry." On the following day he had it out with Madame.

> Nothing could possibly exceed her extreme kindness and delicacy. She didn't in the least appear to resent, as she might very reasonaby have resented, my proposing to her daughter, without her permission

a couple of days before her 15th birthday; on the contrary she seemed rather pleased—in short, she was perfect.

These do not appear to be the letters of a passionately impatient lover and Dowson was more obsessed by what Symons called the 'exquisite and appropriate impossibility of the situation' than with any desire to possess Missie herself. He was a fully sexed and vigorous young man but he knew other women and one cannot resist the conviction that his love for Missie was emasculated by his long sentimental worship of her. At least when he wrote to Smith rather sadly about his horoscope ("I always have a sort of feeling upon me that I am doing certain things for the last time. Therefore I am particularly anxious for you to come to Brittany with me this year . . . I must have one month more in Brittany before the Ides if only you could manage it"), it is as an afterthought that he adds, "in Poland there is no material alteration—perhaps we are a little troubled by the approach of anniversaries".

His father died in 1894, of an over-dose of chloral according to the 'final judgment of those who made the grim investigation', as Mark Longaker says, meaning, I suppose, the Coroner's jury. A few months afterwards Dowson found his mother hanging dead from the bedpost. This double tragedy and his awareness that he was suffering from the same disease strangled much in him, his enthusiasm and some of his ambition as a writer, his gusto and for a long time his friendliness towards his fellows.

He settled up his father's affairs, sent his younger brother to Canada, lived for a short time at the Dock then took a room in Bloomsbury. He had always been somewhat moody among his friends at the Crown and with Missie—he now grew morose with both, and saw them less frequently. So little did Poland mean to him that with an advance from Leonard Smithers who had just set up as a publisher in London, he set out with Charles Conder• the artist to live in Dieppe. He was to translate for Smithers and Conder was to illustrate Balzac's story

• Both Leonard Smithers (1861–1909) and Charles Conder (1868–1909) are figures of the period of wellnigh irresistible interest who have no place in this book because it deals with Wilde and certain of his associates before his imprisonment. There is a portrait of Smithers and some notes about him in Rupert Hart-Davis's *Letters of Oscar Wilde* and William Rothenstein (*Men and Memories*, Volumes 1 and 2) and Augustus John (*Chiaroscuro*) write entertainingly of Conder.

La Fille aux Yeux d'Or—a very Ninetyish proposition for all three.

During the months before they left, the Wilde case was filling the newspapers with a ghastly hotch-potch of misinformation in flagrant contempt of court which roused no protest at the time. (To examine it now curdles the stomach and makes one realize that the Press in the 1890s, while finding synonyms to avoid any offence to its readers, was capable of a dirty-minded beastliness almost incredible to a modern reader. To those who think the Press of today as occasionally unrestrained a reading of some of the comments on Wilde's trial is recommended.)

Dowson had met Wilde at the Rhymers Club. During the fortnight when bail was at last allowed to Wilde, Dowson asked Sherard to take him along to Lady Wilde's house in Oakley Street where he was staying. Sherard has nothing significant to say of the meeting, but there has been so much 'supposing' in Dowson's case that we may suppose that Dowson, never very articulate in difficult situations, could not do much more than show, by his call, the sympathy he felt. He had never been one of Wilde's immediate circle and had certainly never been in his confidence, but he was entirely free from the vice of condemning every habit of life but his own. He would be one of the first of Wilde's friends to see him after his imprisonment.

He spent the summer in Dieppe, but did not finish his translation and a visit to England in the autumn brought him only small advances from his dry dock and perhaps from Smithers, and an assurance that Lane would at last issue his short stories *Dilemmas* in the Keynotes Series. He may have called at Poland on one or two occasions but he never again revived the matter on which he had once approached both Missie and Madame. From a letter to Smith written after his return to France in December it can be seen that he was relieved not to be taken very seriously now by mother or daughter. In a previous letter to Smith he had spoken of a crisis, meaning in his health or pocket.

> You mustn't imagine, as I gather from your letter you perhaps did, that my 'crisis' was sentimental. God forbid. I have just answered my *damigella's* last letter and we are on the most affectionate terms—at least I think so—that we have been on for years. You must go and see her when you are in London—*Please* do that, and speak of me as freely as you like, *only do not* speak of my exile as being so prolonged

> as I presume it will be. I always write to her with the intention of returning in a month or two—and so I may—*for a fortnight*! but I doubt if ever I shall make my home in England again. My great desire is that the Foltinowiczs will carry out their long-conceived idea of returning to Germany. Then I would go there and join them. But I have taken a great dislike to London.

This letter, which ends by asking Smith to tell Missie that Dowson's chief pleasure in life was to get a letter from her and in doing so only to fall short 'of the extreme truth which it is perhaps not yet seasonable to say' disposes of the supposition that he was, if he had ever been in any ordinary sense, in love with Missie and a story that he quarrelled with her, based on an incident in a totally unautobiographical short story of Dowson's, is without any logical basis. (He dedicated the story, as he did so much else, to A. F.)

Except for a few months in Brittany he spent the next two years, 1896 and 1897, in Paris. It is difficult for us who know Paris under de Gaulle, a city of sheepish tourists conducted to standardized places of entertainment, an expensive, regimented and commercialized city, to realize what it meant to the English writers and artists of the Nineties. It was their refuge and their paradise, dreamed-of from boyhood as inspiring, civilized, free from Grundyism, Bohemian, gay, a creative and intellectual centre in which one could live well on a few shillings a day. Wilde had visited it in his first flush of success and returned to it to spend his last days on the boulevards uninvigilated by the police and unmolested by those who would have persecuted him in London. It was essential for a writer of his time to be conversant with the culture, the literature and if possible the *litterateurs* of Paris, to talk of the Café de la Paix and the Place de l'Opera or the Rive Gauche as though they knew them better than the Café Royal, Piccadilly Circus and Soho, to read the *Mercure de France* as they read the *Yellow Book*, to boast of having met Verlaine as they had boasted of a greeting from Wilde. There was none of the sentimentalized Gay Paree, Last-Time-I-Saw-Paris nausea in their conception of the city, it was a place to know, to live in, to be part of, not an essential stop on a tour of Europe. It was a hospitable, tolerant city where madcap artists, writers who lurched home after talking and drinking the sun up, Britons who had suffered from the incomprehensible laws of their country, refugees from puritanism, impecunious or not, were welcomed or at least accepted.

Moreover it was the City of Light even then, glittering bravely till long after the citizens of London were in bed, a city of music where little orchestras and spontaneous singers were everywhere, a city of wine and cheap delicious food, a cosmopolitan city where vice was for the most part elegant and inviting. One might be sad in Paris—indeed it was rather fashionable to complain of solitude amid the laughing crowds—but one could not be bored.

Ernest Dowson loved it and was more truly at home in Paris than in London. For of all Englishmen whose lives have been chronicled or remembered he was the most thoroughbred, perhaps the only true Bohemian. There might be drunks, drug-takers, tramps, men of uncontrolled and shiftless life utterly beyond the limits of convention, but they all kept some secret tie with everyday existence, some small connection with the happy folk in housen which kept them from the last excesses and the last breakaway. There was a sister somewhere to whom they wrote, or a past they regretted, or a scrap of vanity or respectability which acted like a clothes-brush on their shabby lives, or a friend, or even the woman who kept their lodgings, someone who felt enough concern about them to try to keep them to orderly habits and insist on a clean under-vest. Dowson, deliberately it seemed, freed himself of all that.

There was nothing defiant or rebellious about this. Nor was it in the least a pose or a costume drama like that of the modern beatnik. Dowson was quite docile. If anyone took him to the public baths or a hairdressers he made no protest. He simply could not be bothered with these things himself. He was known to stink like a polecat till Conal O'Riordan took him in hand at one point, and before he died at thirty-two he had lost most of his teeth from sheer neglect. He was drunk for much of the time, he slept out frequently, he was unconscious of his appearance rather than defiant of criticism. He worked at times quite hard and was not without natural good manners or consideration for others, and knew what obligation and gratitude were. He was even capable of making sudden and erratic decisions. But the ordinary senses, of time, of direction and of proportion were dead in him. He wrote letters, but not in answer to letters; he was often glad to see his friends but did not keep appointments. He met Verlaine 'quite by chance' and left no account of the acquaintance. He was not dishonourable about money, he did not affect to be contemptuous of it in the way of those who live by cadging, but he never felt he had any right to it and regarded what came his way, however hard he might have worked for it, as fallen from heaven.

To the pseudo-Bohemians of the English artistic colony in Paris and their visitors he was beyond redemption. Beardsley, a dressy young man, found his drunkenness and disreputable appearance a disgrace and in answer to Vincent O'Sullivan's protest that Dowson was a great poet said: "I don't care. No man is great enough to excuse behaviour like this."

That was not the only occasion on which Beardsley spoke bitchily about Dowson, but he *was* bitchy about his acquaintances and said of Wilde and Douglas that they were both 'really very dreadful people'. O'Sullivan did not approve of Dowson's appearance either.

> Dowson's neglect of his personal appearance went to lengths I have never seen in anybody else still on the surface, and hardly in bums and beats and down-and-out tramps forced by hardship to a condition which they have not the means to remedy. The thing about Dowson was that he did not want to remedy it.

That *was* the thing about Dowson, as he showed soon after when a well-meaning woman tried to tidy him up. In her memoirs* Gertrude Atherton gave an account of this, unconsciously but wildly funny. She tried to 'reclaim' him when he was staying in Brittany. A male novelist of the time Horace Annesley Vachell had seen him as a prospect for reclamation, rather as a Sally Army lass might have spotted a candidate for reform, and spoken to Mrs Atherton.

> He really is a genius—and what a fate! Only twenty-nine and already an outcast! If one could only keep him from drinking he might pull up and become a brilliant figure in London. He is terribly poor, but what he has written has been received with such acclaim by the critics that anything he wrote would be well paid for, and he could soon reinstate himself. But he won't even write . . . If you would only let me bring him over. It must be years since he has spoken to a decent woman—if he ever knew one! If he thought you took an interest in him . . . who knows? . . . it might mean a rebirth.

Vachell watched Dowson 'slink into the hotel with averted eyes' and

* *The Adventures of a Novelist* by Gertrude Atherton, 1932, quoted by Mark Longaker in his *Ernest Dowson*.

realized that Dowson's dusty black sweater, unshaven chin and gap-toothed mouth would not make a good impression but introduced him to Mrs Atherton on the terrace. Dowson's 'shifty eyes moved like a wild creature's'. He accepted a cup of coffee, but when his hostess talked of writers he must have known he 'looked confused' and soon slipped away. He was next dragged to a party in the studio of an American lady named Mrs Trulow appearing with 'white collar and cuffs attached to his sweater' which seemed to everyone a hopeful sign though it sounds now like Dowson's only symptom of lunacy. This time he drank three cups of tea before he left. Mrs Atherton decided he needed 'proper companionship' and they went on walks together, the lady tactfully allowing him 'to open her parasol and assist her over difficult places in the road'. When Vachell had to quit Pont-Aven he left Dowson to Mrs Atherton as 'a solemn responsibility'. She discharged this by showing him an empty house 'in which they could write and judge each other's work'. She had to leave for London and wrote to him from there but received no reply. "Your poet has been drunk ever since you left", wrote Mrs Trulow, and probably did not exaggerate. The relief to poor Dowson was too much, and soon after Mrs Trulow wrote with complacent insolence: "Your poet left today to pay a farewell visit to Aubrey Beardsley, who is said to be dying. His only luggage was an extra sweater, which he carried under his arm. He may have had a toothbrush in his pocket, but I doubt it."

He went back to London in the early summer of 1897 and calling at Poland for the first time in two years heard that Missie was to marry a man named Auguste in September. He wrote to Smith: "I know you must think me a fool, but I am suffering the torture of the damned. I ought to have drowned myself at Pont-Aven, or having come back to London, I ought to have had the strength of mind to have kept away." He did not go to the wedding but sent Missie a present by his friend Arthur Moore and almost immediately returned to Paris where he planned to furnish an apartment.

In the meantime he had spent some months at Arques a village near Dieppe where he saw quite a lot of Wilde who was now released from prison. One gathers from Wilde's letters that both were in high spirits and Dowson introduced a soldier called Achille Fromentin who was described by Wilde as 'one of my best friends'. Wilde wrote extravagant little notes to Dowson, as he did to most young men—"I am looking for the green costume that goes so well with your dark hyacinth locks"—that sort of thing. But there is not the smallest reason to believe, unless one pleases to do so, a story which Yeats told on the merest hearsay about Dowson taking Wilde to a brothel in Dieppe to improve his mind, or something of the sort, and even if there is truth in the story itself the disgusting comment on the visit attributed to Wilde is certainly fictitious. If Wilde had wanted to remark on his experiences in a brothel he might have done so in his mock-poetic terminology, or wittily, or frivolously. He would not have said something banal and coarse, as Yeats suggests. Nor would a crowd have followed him.

Dowson spent the rest of his life drifting between London and Paris, working at intervals, living on small advances from Leonard Smithers, leading a down-and-out's hand-to-mouth existence and growing weaker from his diseased lungs. In December 1899 Sherard went to a garret in which Dowson was staying in Euston Road and took him back to his own inadequate quarters in Catford. Sherard's wife, herself discovered in a poor-house in 1939, looked after him for two months. He died on February 22nd, 1900, eight months before Wilde.

5

A figure which conforms far more closely to the popular notion of the Nineties as interpreted by Richard Le Gallienne was Estonian by blood though British by upbringing and preference. His name was Count Eric Magnus Andreas Harry Stenbock.

The Slav is apt to overdo things as the Kremlin shows architecturally and politically and Stenbock certainly overdid the Nineties in his brief, hectic and thoroughly asinine career, overdid them in all their aspects of sex, literature, personal appearance and rehearsed eccentricity. So much so that he became a sort of living parody of Ninetyism, an exaggeration both in himself and his work, of the more rabidly fantastic aspects of the epoch. A zoolatrist with a live snake encircling his neck in public, an opium-eater and alcoholic who killed himself with drugs and drink in his thirty-fifth year, a homosexual who paid for the publication of his love poetry to boys and affected the dress and movements of a professional catamite, an occultist and Black

Magician who claimed to perform odious rites, the author of stories of witchcraft, demonology, werewolves and yawning graves who actually had in his possession a lonely castle in Russia in which he had spent mysterious years, a dilettante in prose and person who copied Wilde's worst excesses in both so that he could write to a friend 'send me a winged herald in the shape of a telegram' and publicly scent his hands and hair before greeting his hostess, he was yet reputed to be a tool of the Jesuits and—like so many others of the Nineties—died a Catholic.

Facts are known about Stenbock and Mr John Adlard has assembled these conscientiously and entertainingly in a biography.* But of the man himself, of his inner life or even of his conversation nothing has been revealed. He is a mask, or perhaps a Pierrot, a figure absurd and tragic of whose excesses and background we are told but who quite eludes us as a credible human being. He is like one of the characters in his own stories, the merest cipher, and it seems doubtful whether the most perceptive contemporary account of him would have revealed much more, for he was eccentric without being original, merely exaggerating in his own person the eccentricities of others, while his writings however bizarre were under analysis derivative.

He was unfortunate, admittedly, in almost his only contemporary chronicler, Ernest Rhys, the first editor of the Everyman Series, who was unfitted by temperament to do more than gape at his outrageous behaviour, acknowledge his kindness and recall both in a name-dropping book called *Everyman Remembers*. Bernard Muddiman in *The Men of the Nineties* gives a footnote to Stenbock's writings and quotes a lurid description of a Black Mass from his story *The Other Side*. ("There are things the top half like black cats, and the bottom part like men only their legs are all covered with close black hair, and they play on the bag-pipes, and when they come to the elevation then—. Amid the old crones there was lying on the hearth-rug, before the fire, a boy whose large lovely eyes dilated and whose limbs quivered in the very ecstacy of terror.")** Arthur Symons wrote a short sensational but inaccurate article on him after his own period of insanity which tells us almost nothing. Lord Alfred Douglas who published a story of his in *The Spirit Lamp* knew him slightly and told

* *Stenbock, Yeats and the Nineties* by John Adlard, 1966.
** *The Men of the Nineties* by Bernard Muddiman, 1920.

me a little about him but left no written record. More Adey knew him better and collaborated with him in translating a book of Balzac's short stories and Robert Ross was well acquainted with him and transmitted a little money from him to Simeon Solomon when the painter was a drunken outcast but neither of these two friends of Wilde have mentioned him in their writings. Even descriptions of his appearance are contradictory, Ernest Rhys saying 'he was short' and Symons calling him 'tall and slender'. There remain only legends from descendants of his Estonian family and English step-relations which Mr Adlard has brought to light, and Stenbock's own books, not all of which are in the British Museum Library.

Eric Stenbock was born in 1860 at Thirlestaine Hall near Cheltenham, the home of his mother's family the Frerichs. A year later his father, who had bought a castle in the Tyrol which had belonged to Ludwig I of Bavaria, died there. This father was known as a *quartalstrinker* (quart-mug drinker), the equivalent presumably of an English four-bottle man. The title and Estonian estates then reverted to Eric Stenbock's grandfather till he himself inherited them on the old man's death in 1885.

Meanwhile Eric's mother had married again, a man named Francis Mowatt, a friend of the Churchill family who later became Permanent Secretary to the Treasury. Eric Stenbock had no affection for his step-father or (with one exception) for the six half-brothers and half-sisters who were born during the next few years. He was sent to study at Wiesbaden where he remained till he was seventeen. He then went up to Oxford and was at Balliol under Jowett. In 1881 a volume of verse he published called *Love, Sleep and Death* describing the pursuit of a male 'beloved' by a 'poet' revealed too much of his nature for the comfort of his family and two years later another collection of verse *Myrtle, Rue and Cypress* (issued by Hatchards) was openly dedicated to three men, Simeon Solomon then a convicted sex offender, Arvid Stenbock a young naval officer of whom Eric's own family disapproved and to the memory of Charles Bertram Fowler the son of an Oxfordshire vicar whom Stenbock had loved during his time at Balliol and lost when the boy died of tuberculosis in his seventeenth year.

For two years after this publication in 1883 Stenbock moved penuriously between England and the Continent until in 1885 he came into his estates in Estonia and remained for two years at his home at Kalk.

His life there was outrageous to his neighbours and many of his family, yet there is a certain staleness—not in Mr Adlard's account of it but in the story itself. A rich young man indulging in intemperate gestures and selfish exhibitions of luxury is a theme wearily familiar both in literature and life and recalls des Esseintes and Dorian Gray among others in the former, and the Baron Fersen of Capri, Ludwig II of Bavaria or William Beckford of Fonthill in the latter. Even with an ancestral home and countless adoring dependents and the means to satisfy all his whims, Stenbock does not seem to have achieved more than ostentatious unconventionality and would have been considered a milk-and-water eccentric by many contemporary Russian noblemen whose excesses are still a legend.

He arrived in a green suit with an orange silk shirt, his blond hair shoulder long, curled and parted in the centre. His favourite costume thereafter is described as a loose red tie, a silk shirt of some dazzling colour and Moroccan slippers. He collected and wore Oriental costumes and had many elaborate dressing-gowns, used potent scents and was in the habit of carrying about with him a volume of his own poems—not over-enterprising when one remembers his transvestist and macaronic competitors even in London at the time.

Nor does his menagerie of animals seem too curious in view of some of the creatures which have been led by publicity-seekers about Oxford and Paris. A favourite monkey named Troscha who wore a scarlet shawl and cracked nuts in the dining-room during dinner-parties was reputed, not surprisingly, to be 'smelly'. Tortoises crawled about the floor of his sitting-room and there was a snake which coiled down his arm to protrude at his cuff. There was also an aquarium in which toads, lizards and salamanders thrived and a greatly loved dachshund named Trixie.

Stenbock lived with one personal servant, of whom nothing is known, in a suite at the top of the house. His sitting-room was papered a lurid red—the megalomaniac's colour—and furnished with a writing-desk and piano, having low Oriental seats and cushions covered with skins and rugs. There were also caged birds and oppressive hothouse plants in great numbers. It was lit with a red lamp. The bedroom was painted peacock blue and, says Mr Adlard, "Over the marble chimney-piece a great altar had been erected, tricked out with Oriental shawls, peacock feathers, lamps and rosaries. In the middle stood a green bronze statue of Eros. There was a little flame that burned unceasingly, and resin in a copper bowl that scented the air. The floor was covered with thick Smyrna carpets, and over his bed was a big pentagram to keep the evil spirits at bay. (He had, in fact, evolved a religion of his own, compounded of Buddhism, Catholicism and idolatry.) On this bed, in the middle of the room, he would lie smoking opium, watched by a swinging parrot." These rooms Stenbock called 'my aesthetic chambers'.

Stenbock seems to have been fond of children and wrote nonsense verses for them, but when a neighbouring landowner with nine daughters brought two of them for his inspection he pointedly caressed his monkey.

In about 1887 he returned to London and took rooms at 11, Sloane Terrace. He had several friends from his Oxford and post-Oxford years in England including More Adey and Simeon Solomon, but Adey was not to be found just then and poor Solomon had sunk to being a drunken pavement artist and was, Stenbock wrote, the bane of his life.

Stenbock soon had other friends and acquaintances, chiefly literary or artistic youths much his juniors. He met Beardsley, Ernest Rhys a keen young Welshman and, on the top of a Piccadilly horse-bus, a sixteen-year-old boy named Norman O'Neill who was to become in time, with the assistance of a bequest from Stenbock, the popular composer of the music for Barrie's *Mary Rose* and Maeterlinck's *The Blue Bird.*

Rhys never got over the shock of what he considered the enormity of Stenbock's individualism and more than forty years later was to recall their acquaintanceship with awe and some unction as a startling incident in his life. 'Look what a funny one I found when I was a young man', he seems to say, writing of Eric playing the piano so that the Russian Steppes appeared beyond the window-panes, while another evening spent with Stenbock was 'like an Arabian Night's dream'.

Rhys stayed with Stenbock, observed his opium-taking, went with him to luncheon parties at Mrs Ostell's where they met Bertrand Russell and Edward Carpenter, listened to him reading his short stories, and remained his protégé, and perhaps more, for some years. Yet he can communicate absolutely nothing which would begin to bring Stenbock to life and all his perceptions are merely visual.

Mr Adlard cannot give us much more about the man himself during his seven or eight years in London. Stenbock remained at 11, Sloane

Terrace till 1890 when he moved to 21, Gloucester Walk, not very interesting or significant addresses though Arthur Symons, infected with the tendency to inflate and colour Stenbock's reputation, wrote of the second as 'a certain house, rather out of the way, one of a row of houses where degenerates lived'.

Stenbock seems to have existed in England on money inherited from his maternal grandfather, money which may have been controlled by his step-father Mowatt. He left the Estonian estates to his relatives making them over before his death to his cousin Count Michel. He did not live extravagantly in a monetary sense though to the penurious men of the Nineties he seemed to be rich.

Two particularly improbable stories about him have been invented with nothing whatever to support them. One, for which a poisonous little gossip-monger called Percy Colson was responsible, suggested that Stenbock wrote a set of verses popular at the universities at the time of the Jubilee which open with a promising couplet

> There is a thing which no one knows
> How the Queen looks without her clothes

but tail away into bathos. Stenbock's humour, such as it was, appealed chiefly to children, and he was incapable of that sort of pawky undergraduate joke. The second story is retailed by Rhys and has the smack, familiar to those who have studied Wilde's character, of one of the many travesties attached to it. Wilde is supposed to have lit a cigarette at one of Stenbock's sanctuary lamps and when Stenbock fell on the floor in alarm or rage Wilde is said to have spurned him with his foot before leaving. It is difficult to say which is more improbable, Stenbock shrieking and falling to the floor or the kind Oscar kicking his prostrate body.

The truth is that Stenbock lived obscurely in London, too outré to be socially acceptable. That he had a malodorous reputation for his sexual habits, a reputation known to his step-father Mowatt, is shown by a letter from a friend of Stenbock's who is protesting to Mowatt himself: "Dr Flanagan . . . states that you took leave of him with the remark that when certain unnatural courses were charged against Count Stenbock I had not in your opinion regarded it as a serious matter . . . You are doing me a monstrous injustice . . . I simply abhor anything of the kind."

Stenbock seems to have been known to a number of writers and artists, but like others of them he talked of what he would write, mulled over it in his cups, wrote letters about it and got very little on paper. He wanted to lead the life of a writer but hazed with opium and booze could rarely concentrate. He wrote captions for some drawings of Beardsley's, knew Herbert Horne of the *Hobby-Horse* and Lionel Johnson who wrote to a friend that the Count had inflicted devilish drinks on him and poems even worse. He met Yeats who called him 'scholar, connoisseur, drunkard, poet, pervert, most charming of men'. He was acquainted (through Rhys) with Arthur Symons who said he was 'one of those extraordinary Slav creatures who . . . live in a bizarre, fantastic, feverish, eccentric, extravagant, morbid and perverse fashion after their own will, whim, caprice or fancy; self-centred, quite crazy enough to be aware of his singular madness which was always on him, always around him, like some cruel and poisonous exhalation that arises out of a mist-covered valley where assassins hide themselves in the act to slay him. Besides this he had weird propensities'. He also knew Logan Pearsall Smith and was intimate for a time with More Adey and Robert Ross who lived near him. His only known contribution to a periodical was the story in *The Spirit Lamp* already mentioned.

But he published two books in his last three years, the first, of poetry, he issued himself through the Leadenhall Press and the last, a collection of stories, was published by David Nutt. These were *The Shadow of Death*, 1893, and *Studies of Death*, 1894. The poems are quite appalling, melodramatic and banal, and have pretentious Latin or Greek texts. The stories are arty and derivative; the first called, inevitably, *Hylas* is about an artist adopting a boy who drowns himself. It is painfully reminiscent of the most maudlin in *Dorian Gray*.

In his last two years Stenbock aged suddenly, grew ill and vague and came very near to certifiable insanity. He wrote morbidly to Norman O'Neill, the young musician for whose studies in Frankfurt he was paying, in 1894:

> This is a sort of anniversary—the date when I first met you—I remember I afterwards consulted a penny in the slot devil (they were really devils in those days not merely smiling Gypsies as now) and the answer was 'Happiness'—but that is a form of humour which the Devil is rather fond of . . . But this is verging on the sentimental—

is it the effect of the weather, or the red hawthorn tree before the window which always affects my nerves?

In another letter to the same he wrote:

The highest odds on my life now is five weeks, I would advise you for a bet to say 3½ to four—so it is not likely that you will see my by no means improved physiognomy again—as a last chance I am going to some village on the coast of France or Belgium as Dr Ord insists on the neighbourhood of the sea—I shan't go to Withdeane—my sisters are nice enough, but I can't stand my brothers. (I wonder your brother can) but I can't die under the contemptuous pity of Puppies like Frank and Charlie—meanwhile I shall amuse myself by completing a novel I am writing, in which there will be some quite original situations—5 weeks is not long—but may you live and enjoy life as far as it *can* be enjoyed—and don't become an English Masher or a German Sot.

Rhys meeting him after a break found him much changed for the worse. He gave Rhys and his wife dinner at Gloucester Walk but looked very ill, his clustering yellow curls faded and thin, his lips colourless and his eyes dull. He could eat only bread and milk and was too tired to play the piano.

He travelled abroad for some months with Flanagan, a doctor, (who was an old friend) to the Riviera and Abbazia. By this time he was suffering from delusions and would not be parted from a life-size doll which he believed to be his son and heir, referring to it always as '*le petite comte*'. Brought back to the home of his mother and step-father in Sussex he was confined to his room and there on April 26th, 1895 in a drunken rage he attacked someone with a poker and in doing so fell into the grate. It is not known whether this killed him but he certainly died the same day.

By an ironical chance it was the day on which Wilde's trial opened at the Old Bailey.

Arthur Symons said of Stenbock: "He was one of the most inhuman beings I have ever encountered: inhuman and abnormal; a degenerate who had I know not how many vices." This is big talk to apply to a weak, unhappy man, kindly disposed to his fellows while he sought to shock them, uncreative and posturing but more pitiful than evil. All his vices were of weakness—alcoholism, drug-taking and a morbid hankering kind of homosexuality. He wanted to appear a monster but succeeded in being little more than a freak and a portent of his times.

CHAPTER ELEVEN

Wilde Before the Trials

To examine Wilde's life during the years before his trials may seem an unrewarding, unoriginal and unnecessary thing to do. Surely in these last ten or twenty years we have heard enough of Wilde. Apart from the question, a pertinent one, as to whether readers will ever have heard enough of Wilde, whose name they would not speak for many years, there is the singular fact that no scrupulous, complete and documented biography has yet appeared, for no biographer before 1962 was able to examine the letters in their entirety. There have been many popular versions, of which Hesketh Pearson's is the best; there have been two films and much other fiction, but nearly everything has been founded on Harris or hearsay or both.

As to those last years and Wilde's life among the male prostitutes and blackmailers of London in the Nineties, no one has yet tried to disentangle the curious and complicated story. The trials have been read in both versions,• but from them it is difficult, without the closest study, to follow what actually happened or see how Wilde went his

• *Oscar Wilde Three Times Tried* (edited anonymously by Christopher Millard), 1911, and *The Trials of Oscar Wilde* edited by H. Montgomery Hyde, 1948. Penguin Edition with additional material, 1962.

incredibly blind way to the dock. There are many inaccuracies in them, not on the part of their editors, but because the lawyers were deliberately misleading and sometimes mistaken over dates, and the witnesses lied and contradicted themselves and one another.

Another, more valid, objection might be raised. If we have had enough of Wilde we have had more than enough of every kind of literature dealing with homosexuality, which is not a subject in itself of remarkable interest and nearly always a bore in fiction. To follow an intelligent man's besotted passage through a labyrinth of homosexual vice and crime might have been worth while at the time, but today, when every man is his own psychologist, it promises no novelty. Yet that is what gives it its peculiar relevance and interest in this book. The story of Wilde in the underworld is essentially a period piece full of the colour and scent of the Nineties, full of contemporary touches in background, costume and social mores, and yet as one comes to examine events one finds that dated as they are they have a harrowing comparability with those of our decades. The behaviour of all the principals, accused, witnesses, police and judiciary, was repeated in the 1950s. One event, the police raid in Fitzroy Street, had its counterpart (down to such details as the accused being forced to appear in the light of day in court in the bedraggled women's clothes they had worn) in Holland Park in 1932, and the blackmailing gangs whom Wilde knew are as busy today as then.

Indeed the story has the double attraction of many good stories, that of a period piece or an episode in social history, and that of timelessness. It shows as one the Giton of Petronius, the Charlie Parker of Wilde and the youth, perhaps as yet unborn, who will give evidence against the next great artist to stand in the dock for being what Wilde called a born antinomian.

Anecdotes about the trials, moreover, have been so blown up, so grossly sensationalized, that the thing itself has become scarcely recognizable as what you may hear any day if you drop in at the Old Bailey. Wilde, at first the victim of exaggerated execration and later of no less exaggerated hero-worship, has always been an outsize figure and his fall from grace has taken on Luciferic proportions. He saw himself and made others see him as first a lord of life then as one sitting 'in the lowest pit of Malebolge'. The only unique thing about his prosecution was the worldwide publicity it received and has been receiving ever since. The charges were commonplace and need to be seen as such, for similar ones are reported in local papers every week.

It is not however the charges and scenes in court which will be dealt with here but the events in Wilde's life which they partially exposed. They show him to have been in many ways a rather silly man, perhaps somewhat over-sexed and pleased with himself for being so, and childishly self-indulgent, yet no more of any of these than many others who have stood where he did. The young men who were called against him have been seen as the lowest blackguards who ever gave perjured evidence for money or from fear, but they have turned up with the same sort of shameless stories in every prosecution since the Labouchère Amendment became law.* They were a particularly desperate and unscrupulous lot by modern standards, but they were poorer than their type today and they lived in a crueller age and Wilde, whether rich or not, behaved as though money fell from the skies. A boy who saw a working household's expenses for a month spent on a single dinner-party cannot be blamed too severely for wanting a small share of that affluence. One or two of them were frankly evil but as one remarked to Wilde 'there's good and bad in every one of us'.

The first chapter in the story, and the last chapter before it became public, are separated from the rest because the youths they concern, Edward Shelley and Alphonse Conway and two others, were unconnected with the main body of witnesses.

2

When Elkin Mathews and John Lane formed their partnership in January 1892 the first book that was to bear their joint imprint was *Poems* by Oscar Wilde. This was not in fact a new book. Bogue, who

* This amendment to the Criminal Law Amendment Act, 1885, from its passing has been known as the Blackmailer's Charter. It was only a few years old when Wilde met Alfred Taylor and blackmailers were joyfully realizing its immense potentialities. Before the end of the century the police had begun to see the necessity of giving some protection to those it laid open to the most blatant forms of blackmail and two of the men involved in Wilde's case were prosecuted and imprisoned for later offences though no action was taken against them at the time. But this protection depended then, and has depended ever since, on the whims or prejudices or scruples of the police themselves and no guarantee exists for the complainant. It remains to be seen whether Mr Abse's Act will provide any.

had first issued it in 1882, had gone bankrupt and 230 sets of sheets had remained unbound in his stock. These were now issued with a new title page and pale violet cloth boards designed by Charles Ricketts. The edition was to be limited to 220 copies (ten had been damaged) and signed by Wilde on his own insistence.

Although he was busy with rehearsals of his first play to be produced in London, *Lady Windermere's Fan*—'one of those modern drawing-room plays with pink lampshades' he called it—he found time to go down to the offices of Elkin Mathews and John Lane, 'At the Bodley Head', in Vigo Street to put his splaying signature in these 220 copies and while doing so he noticed that the new firm had taken on a good-looking office boy.

Three years later this boy, Edward Shelley, was described by the press as a tall heavy-framed young fellow with a square jaw and distinctly 'intellectual' face. But in spite of this disability and his passion for literature, expressed in hurried confidence at the office, Wilde liked the look of him and stopped at his desk to chat on a number of occasions.

It is interesting to notice that three-quarters of a century ago Londoners were not so ignorant of queerness that this could pass. "It would be a terrible thing for society at large", proclaimed Mr Justice Wills solemnly in this connection, "if it were to be considered unnatural for a man to ask a younger man of good character to dine with him." But the irreverent employees of Mathews and Lane were not easily deceived and pulled Shelley's leg mercilessly about it, calling him 'Miss Oscar' and 'Mrs Wilde'. Or perhaps Wilde's reputation had spread to Vigo Street. Or perhaps Shelley at eighteen was camp and obvious. Anyhow it caused quite a sensation when in the weeks that followed Shelley showed his fellow clerks presentation copies of Wilde's books, and rather fatuously a copy of *The Sinner's Comedy* by John Oliver Hobbes (Mrs Craigie) inscribed 'From the Author to dear Edward Shelley'.

Wilde should have known better. Shelley was not, in any case, his cup of tea. Coming from a respectable home, a product of State education, he had literary ambitions and affected some refinement. His brother was of sub-normal intelligence and had to be kept at home. Edward had what were known then as 'ideas above his station' and was put into a great flutter by Wilde's notice of him.

One day as Wilde was leaving the offices he stopped and spoke to

Shelley. Would he like to have dinner with him that evening? Oh, Mr Wilde! Thank you, Mr Wilde. Seven o'clock then, at the Albemarle Hotel.

They dined in the public room but Wilde ordered champagne. Then they went to Wilde's suite and after a whisky and soda Shelley found himself kissed and taken to bed as he must have anticipated. On the following night they went to a theatre together.

Wilde in the next weeks saw much of Shelley, taking him to the Earl's Court Exhibition, the Lyric Club, the Café Royal, Kettner's and to a first night at the Independent Theatre. He considered him presentable enough to be invited to Tite Street and introduced to his wife. And when the first night of *Lady Windermere's Fan* (Saturday, February 20th, 1892) approached he sent Shelley a ticket. The boy was to sit next to Pierre Louÿs, André Gide's friend who had helped Oscar draft *Salome* in French, "*Vous serez à coté d'Edouard Shelley*", he wrote Louÿs, and some acquaintance may have sprung up between the two for in one of Shelley's letters to Wilde he said that Louÿs was 'of the same opinion' about Wilde's work and added that he was 'a charming fellow'.

Shelley heard Wilde make his unfortunate curtain speech congratulating the public on the intelligence of their appreciation. He must have been in that group of 'admiring disciples' at the bar in the interval which Le Gallienne noticed 'over whom (Wilde) towered head and shoulders'. Next day Shelley wrote Wilde a gushing letter.

> Dear Mr. Oscar Wilde,
>
> I must again thank you for the 'House of Pomegranates' and the theatre ticket. It was very good of you to send them to me and I shall never forget your kindness. What a triumph was yours last night! The play is the best I have seen on the stage, with such beauty of form and wit that it adds a new phase of pleasure to existence. Could Lady Blessington live anew the conversations would make her jealous. George Meredith might have signed it. How miserably poor everything else seems beside it! Except, of course, your books—but then your books are part of yourself.

For the rest of that year they met at intervals and when in the autumn Wilde took a farmhouse for his family at Felbrigg near Cromer he asked Shelley to come and stay. Shelley was still working for Mathews and Lane and had to refuse.

To think of Wilde in that year of his first success in the theatre, so famous that his every movement was followed in the press (his stay with Bosie at Homberg that summer and their address there was duly reported), taking his publishers' ambitious office-boy about with him must have been more discomforting to his friends than many of his later indiscretions. It was the year in which the Lord Chamberlain refused to license *Salome* after Sarah Bernhardt had begun to rehearse it and Wilde threatened to become a French citizen to the delight of *Punch* who pictured him as a Légionnaire. It was the year when (at Homberg) Wilde first met the Prince of Wales. *Lady Windermere's Fan* made him a pot of money and he was being extravagant in every sense of the word. Shelley was an indiscretion and he soon began to realize this.

Shelley was intense, highly strung and demanding. Already that October he began to be tiresome.

> My dear Oscar,
> Will you be at home on Sunday evening next? I am most anxious to see you. I would have called this evening but I am suffering from nervousness, the result of insomnia, and am obliged to remain at home. I have longed to see you all through the week. I have much to tell you. Do not think me forgetful in not coming before, because I shall never forget your kindness and am conscious that I can never sufficiently express my thankfulness to you.

He complained of the 'brutal insults' he was receiving in Vigo Street and the 'horrible harsh existence' he was leading there. He wanted money to live in Chelsea and read with a private coach, and when he finally lost his job and his parents complained of his idleness he said he was 'eating the bitter food of charity and contempt'.

Wilde paid him various sums of money which were never demanded with threats but with hysterical appeals like 'God forgive the past. Do your best for me now'. It seems likely that Shelley told his father of the relationship and was forbidden to see Wilde since for nearly a year nothing was heard of him, but in April 1894 he reappeared. Wilde wrote to Bosie who was in Italy—

> I had a frantic telegram from Edward Shelley, of all people! asking me to see him. When he came he was of course in trouble for money As he betrayed me grossly I, of course, gave him money and was kind to him. I find that forgiving one's enemies is a most curious morbid pleasure; perhaps I should check it.

That Wilde wrote this flippantly has no significance, for Wilde at this time was always flippant, even when he was most deeply concerned. That an excitable young clerk who kept talking about the sins they had committed together,* kept making approaches which were what Wilde called elsewhere a mixture of romance and finance may have disturbed him as much as the open demands of a blackmailer. If so, he was right. He had Shelley to dinner at Kettner's after Queensberry had been charged with criminally libelling him, doubtless to obtain his promise of silence, but Shelley was at first one of the most dangerous witnesses against him, and since he was out of the circles covered by Queensberry's detectives in their researches he may have volunteered his testimony.

3

To disentangle the main story we must leave Wilde himself for a moment and go back to the year 1891.

A man called James Dennis Burton was living in rooms in Lennox Gardens, Chelsea. His ostensible occupation was that of a bookmaker or bookie's tout and he kept at his home a youth named Frederick Atkins then barely seventeen whom he described as his 'clerk'. Burton's name on the racecourses was Watson, and Atkins called himself Dennis, St Denis or simply Denny.

It is possible that they went to race-meetings during the day but at night they were industrious blackmailers. There was nothing very original in their act which consisted in Freddy going to the bar of the St James's, or the standing room behind the circle at the Alhambra, or in bad times on the streets or to the public urinals, and 'copping for a steamer', meeting a mug, or making contact with a prosperous-looking and responsive man. He would bring him home and at the right moment Burton would appear claiming to be Freddy's uncle, so that throughout the little world in which they were both notorious he was known as 'Uncle Burton'.

Freddy's only failing as a stool-pigeon was his uncertain complexion, for he was still at the age of pimples, but with his pale eyes, loose fair

* "Shelley was in the habit of writing me many morbid, very morbid letters which I tore up. In them he said he was a great sinner and anxious to be in closer touch with religion." (Wilde's evidence at his first trial.)

hair and pert profile he was attractive enough for Burton's purpose, Burton himself being 'So' in the language of that time. Occasionally Freddy dressed as a girl, 'wore drag', but both realized that with his cheeky personality (Wilde thought him 'pleasant and good-natured') he was better off in showy male clothing. The two felt themselves suited to one another and as Burton was a police-informer they were able to take chances that others avoided.

Burton had picked up Atkins some months earlier, probably when he was a marker in a billiard saloon with ambitions common at that time to most off-stage female impersonators to 'go on the halls'. Their partnership was running well, but landladies while not being 'particular' disliked disturbances in their rooms and they had to move to Tachbrook Street, Pimlico, which they thought would be more central.

Soon after they arrived there Freddy went out on the game, choosing the Alhambra as his beat. The area at the back of the circle at the Alhambra was for many years—until the 1930s in fact when it became a cinema—a well-known meeting place, as well-known as the Empire Promenade was for ladies of the town, and one can see Freddy in his tight Victorian finery, his tall starched collar and flashy tie, ogling likely prospects among older men, more than one of whom wore evening dress. That night he soon found what he wanted and took his victim—known throughout the trials as 'the Birmingham gentleman' —back to Tachbrook Street.

But he had picked a wrong 'un. Freddy led the way to the bed and encouraged 'the gentleman' to undress as he did. Uncle Burton made his usual appearance but not only did 'the Birmingham gentleman' refuse to hand over any money but demanded the return of his watch and chain which Freddy had thoughtfully appropriated and passed to Burton. Birmingham gentlemen, it appeared, were not to be taken in by this sort of lark and growing noisier and noisier he threatened to call the police.

Burton and Atkins were doubtless prepared for scenes like this but they were not prepared for their landlady who was 'respectable' and wasn't going to have goings-on in her house. She walked in and seeing 'the Birmingham gentleman' and Freddy naked on the bed sent her husband, or went herself for the police.

Everybody's bluff was called now and a sorry procession including

Constables 396A and 500A marched round to Rochester Row Police Station. Uncle Burton and Freddy had their story ready—it had all been a fight over a game of cards—and as the Birmingham gentleman and Freddy had had time to dress before the police arrived there was only the landlady's word for the more objectionable 'goings-on'. "All I want is my watch and chain," the Birmingham gentleman repeated, refusing to prosecute. Freddy agreed to return the watch and chain next day and in view of the police intervention kept his word. So another midnight incident could be written off at Rochester Row until it was exhumed as evidence two years later in one of the most famous prosecutions of the century.

But Uncle Burton and Freddy were only momentarily discouraged. They took nearby rooms at Alderney Street, Pimlico, and their fortunes were soon mended with a cheque for £200 made out to Mr St Denis from another 'gentleman' whom Freddy had picked up while dressed as a woman.

Finding the curiosity of landladies irksome and blackmail more easily levied in hotels, they took respectable rooms in Buckingham Palace Road and worked from there with greater discretion. 'An elderly gentleman from the City' was invited back and robbed of his pocket case which enabled Uncle Burton to discover his address, call on him at his office and extort a large sum. Then there were two American gentlemen whom Freddy took to the Hotel Victoria in Northumberland Avenue where Uncle Burton, deeply shocked, found all three in *flagrante delictu*, and received compensation. This, and another douceur he got from a gentleman at Anderton's Hotel, Fleet Street, enabled him to take Freddy for a holiday to the south of France where they stayed at Gaze's Hotel, Nice and had a day in Monte Carlo, but fell out, presumably over dividends from a profitable stroke while on holiday. It was more than a year before they worked together again.

It was during that year, while the two were separated, that Oscar Wilde met Freddy. Even Wilde might have been discouraged by the appearance of Uncle Burton.

Meanwhile, before Wilde takes the stage we must introduce, as Wilde would wish it, the minor characters, and first a very different and far more sympathetic if more pitiful one, Alfred Waterhouse Somerset Taylor, the son of a wealthy cocoa manufacturer. He had been at Marlborough for a few terms only but denied that he had been expelled. Now thirty-one he was said to have got through a fortune of £45,000 in a few years, not an easy matter in the Nineties, and had been through the bankruptcy court.

He was an empty-headed invert, gossipy and good-natured, a talented pianist, 'artistic' with all the awful implications of the word at that time, and he was to show later that he was capable of a selfless loyalty and courage which made almost everyone in that sorry case look mean and treacherous. But at the beginning of 1891 he was following a life of chattering fatuity. He had just taken rooms over a disused bakehouse in Little College Street, Westminster, and camped them up with fans and artificial flowers and covered the windows—it was almost enough to convict Wilde when it was known that he had visited the place—with *three* sets of curtains through which *the light of day was never seen*. There was only one bed in the apartment and instead of being a respectable brass-knobbed piece of furniture it consisted of the spring-mattress only, slightly raised from the floor. As further signs of depravity he burned scented pastilles or joss-sticks, had no servant and did his own cooking, asked young men to tea and opened the door himself and audibly called them 'dear'. Mrs Grant, who lived in the basement, didn't know *what* to make of it.

Taylor had been going round for years with a couple of queens, also of decent family. One was Ernest Macklin who remains a somewhat dim figure who discreetly left the country before the Wilde prosecution, the other was Charles Spurrier Mason with whom Taylor had lived in the previous year. Mason, said Taylor proudly in court, was a very busy man with shares in a newspaper. He certainly wrote from a Fleet Street address to Taylor in November 1891, but it was not quite the letter one would expect from a newspaper proprietor, at least in this century.

My dear Alfred,

As soon as you can afford it do let me have some money and I will be pleased and obliged. I would not ask you if I could get money myself, but you know the business is not so easy. There is a lot of trouble attached to it. I have not met anyone yet. Come home soon, dear, and let us go out sometimes together. Have very little news. Going to a dance on Monday and to the theatre to-night.

With much love,
Yours always, Charlie

Taylor used to tell, with a good deal of high-pitched laughter, how once Charlie Mason and he had gone through a wedding ceremony, Charlie as the bridegroom and he in a flowing wedding-dress. 'We had a wedding breakfast after it!' he would exclaim.•

Taylor did a lot of cruising in the more notorious streets and meeting-places, and 'frequently walked through Piccadilly' as he was induced to say in evidence to the horror of a London jury. There was a skating rink in Knightsbridge which became famous for young men seeking to be picked up, and there were such meeting places as the Alhambra, the Pavilion, a certain part of the Empire and the bar of the St James's. He was known in them all and would ask the young men he met back to Little College Street for one of the tea-parties he gave almost daily. He had what he described as 'a fancy dress for a female, an Eastern costume' which he wore to carnivals at Olympia, Covent Garden and Queen's Gate, precursors perhaps of Lady Malcolm's Ball in the 1920s and 1930s. He also—it was scarcely credible to the jury when they heard it—had 'lace knickers, and stockings under a long open cloak which fastened at the waist' and a wig made for him when he was going to a ball as Dick Whittington. A vapid innocuous queen, in other words, who under any sane system of legislation would be mildly derided, perhaps, accepted as such an amiable anomaly would be in most other countries where he would exist happily enough with his own kind, but who in England in the Nineties was told by a learned judge that he was guilty of the worst crimes he had ever tried and sent to two years' hard labour.

Wilde might never have met Taylor, and through him the young villains who ruined him, if it had not been for another young man of decent family named Maurice Schwabe.

Now Schwabe was nephew to the wife of Frank Lockwood the Solicitor-General who prosecuted Wilde in his second trial. This bloated, bottle-nosed character, who has plenty of counterparts in the legal profession today, was popular among other lawyers but so

• This led Sir Rupert Hart-Davis into one of the few editorial errors in his almost impeccable edition of Wilde's letters. Mason was genuinely married in 1894 and wrote to tell Wilde of it, perhaps in hope of a present, and Sir Rupert confuses this with the mock marriage which had happened earlier than 1893 when Taylor told the story of it to one of the Parkers. Wilde would never have congratulated him on a silly masquerade and his enquiries about the marriage are quite sincere.

totally irrational on the subject of homosexuality that one wonders if he had not some secret repression. He made a great show of not allowing his nephew's name to be concealed as it had been in the trial of Queensberry and he prosecuted with a bullying violence which—excusable perhaps in Carson who was *defending* his client—was unforgivable in a Solicitor-General.

Schwabe had been sent abroad before the trials and it is scarcely yet realized what a large part he played in Wilde's ruin. Not by intent—he was not much more intelligent than Taylor—but because he was a busy ambitious young man, anxious to please Wilde and careless of the characters of those he introduced to him. A rotund, quick-moving, talkative fellow he was intrepid in making contacts and indefatigable in pursuit. He lived into another generation, the same industrious entrepreneur, who had many stories about Wilde with which he entertained the Edwardians. He was killed in the First World War.

Wilde had met Maurice Schwabe through Robert Ross and occasionally asked him to dinner, chiefly one suspects to listen to his gossip. At some time in the late summer of 1892 Schwabe took Wilde to Taylor's house at 13, Little College Street and the damage was done. From that time onwards Taylor and Schwabe, who had hitherto shared their discoveries, competed in introducing young men to Wilde. Many of them were dangerous; Schwabe seems to have been grossly careless about this and Taylor quite idiotic, but Wilde liked danger and encouraged them both.

> People thought it dreadful of me to have entertained at dinner the evil things of life, and to have found pleasure in their company. But they, from the point of view through which I, as an artist in life, approached them, were delightfully suggestive and stimulating. It was like feasting with panthers. The danger was half the excitement. I used to feel as the snake-charmer must feel when he lures the cobra to stir from the painted cloth or reed-basket that holds it, and makes it spread its hood at his bidding, and sway to and fro in the air as a plant sways restfully in a stream.

Taylor's first introduction was a failure. He had found a young man named Edward Harrington who was wasting his time with a schoolmaster named Court. Harrington, a butch type, was attractive to Taylor but not to Wilde, which saved him from giving evidence later though he was produced in court to intimidate Taylor. Taylor next introduced a youth he had picked up at the Gaiety Theatre. This one was a cut above the criminals to come. His name was Sidney Mavor and his nickname in Little College Street was Jenny Mavor—why is unknown; he would far better have been called Mavourneen. He was a tall, slim young man who lived with his mother in South Kensington. (In later years he became a Church of England parson.)

Schwabe gave a dinner-party at Kettner's for this introduction. Taylor had prepared Mavor by telling him he was to meet an influential man who might help him. "He likes young men when they're modest and nice in appearance." When Mavor called for Taylor on the night of the dinner-party Taylor was delighted with him. "I'm glad you've made yourself pretty," he said, "Mr Wilde likes nice clean boys."

When they arrived at Kettner's, where Wilde had been known since his Oxford days, they found a private room had been reserved and Mavor had his first sight of luxury—pink-shaded candles, Champagne on ice and a dinner-table spread in the overcrowded and ornamental way which passed for splendour in the Nineties. When Wilde came in with Bosie and Schwabe and Mavor was introduced to a 'real Lord' his cup must have been full, and it remained full all the evening. "Our little lad has pleasing manners. We must see more of him," said Oscar in his rich throaty voice when the dinner was over. He did—taking him to the Albemarle Hotel a few nights later and meeting him at intervals till shortly before the case.

Meanwhile Schwabe cruising the Knightsbridge skating rink picked up Freddy Atkins. Freddy's quarrel with Uncle Burton had left him to fend for himself for some months and for the moment he had turned from blackmailing to straight prostitution. Schwabe took him to be a somewhat knowing youth but had no reason to see in this boy, less than eighteen years old, a hardened young villain with a police record. He took him about with him for some months, for Atkins, a tubby youngster with a ready grin, had a certain cockney charm and talked amusingly about his experiences as a billiard-marker, a bookie's clerk and an entertainer in pubs, a recognized way of earning an occasional sovereign. His ambition was still to go on the halls. Schwabe became quite attached to him and Freddy came to his rooms off Margaret Street almost daily but kept a room of his own in

Pimlico. Freddy does not seem to have regarded Schwabe as a prospect but rather as a friend, even a collaborator, for he spoke in court of a 'young fellow named Schwabe'. Schwabe introduced him to Wilde in October 1892.

Wilde was no less susceptible to Freddy's vulgar but sprightly personality. One can see the tall dressy Irishman in his elegant frock-coat beaming down on the cheeky little street rat and indulgently promising to take him to Paris for a week-end as so many Englishmen in the last centuries have promised so many new acquaintances, female and sometimes male. Freddy had passed through Paris on his way to Cannes with Uncle Burton and wanted to see more of the exotic attractions which every young Englishman believed it to possess.

They travelled on the 'Club' train and went straight to an hotel at 29, Boulevard des Capucines where Wilde had discreetly engaged three rooms with communicating doors, for Schwabe was to join them on the following day. Next morning they lunched at the Café Julien and in the afternoon went to Pascal the famous hairdresser under the Grand Hotel where Wilde had once had his hair done in what he called a Neronian style. Freddy was given the nineteenth-century version of a permanent wave. Wilde had to dine with someone connected with the publication of *Salome* and handed Freddy a sovereign with which to go to the Moulin Rouge. It was all very gay and enjoyable and they returned on Wednesday with Maurice Schwabe who had joined them.

Soon afterwards Wilde departed for Babbacombe where he had taken a house for his family. Not surprisingly he was bored. "Are there beautiful people in London?" he asked Robert Ross in a letter. "Here there are none; everyone is so unfinished."

Freddy became an habitué of Taylor's rooms in Little College Street and during the late autumn, most fatefully, took a new friend of his to one of Taylor's tea-parties. This was a youth named Alfred Wood.

Wood appeared to be a pleasant youth, still like Atkins in his teens, fair-haired and frank-looking. In fact he was already a sneak-thief and collaborator with two professional blackmailers named Robert Clibburn or Cliburn (alias Carew, Collins, Harris, Robertson and Stephenson) and William Allen (alias Pea). These were hardened villains who used youths like Wood and Atkins to steal compromising letters with which they could blackmail the recipient or sender. Cliburn, a former telegraph boy in the post office, had already served a prison sentence for blackmail having been convicted at Lewes Assizes in 1890.

Taylor found Wood delightful, as indeed the poor deluded creature found most young men, and like many another temporarily having nowhere to live Wood went to stay with Taylor towards the end of the year. Wilde still being absent at Babbacombe, Taylor introduced Wood to Bosie Douglas which led to one of the most unfortunate episodes in the whole sequence.

Bosie at this time was no less crazy with the uninhibited pleasures of sexual curiosity than Wilde, though he did not regard them as strange purple sins. He was pagan, irresponsible and thoughtless of others, accepting Wilde's doctrine of the artist's right to amorality. He was also youthfully indiscreet or he would not have taken Wood to stay with him at Oxford.

During Wood's stay there ('at the Varsity' Wood called it) Bosie gave him a suit of clothes and according to Wood (who in fact probably stole them) Bosie carelessly left in one of the pockets a number of letters from Wilde which were written in Wilde's most extravagant terms. Back in London Wood showed these to Cliburn and Allen and at a conference it was decided that Wood should sell them back to Wilde or Douglas for the amount of his fare to America, but that Cliburn and Allen should keep one with which to levy further blackmail after Wood had left for the New World. Cliburn made his selection—"This one's quite hot enough," he said—and Wood wrote to Bosie who had been rusticated from Oxford and was staying with his mother at Salisbury. Bosie had already had some warning of Wood's intention, and now asked Wilde to deal with Wood. Wilde, leaving his family at Babbacombe, went up to London to meet Wood for the first time and secure the return of the letters. A meeting between Wilde and Wood at the Café Royal was arranged by telegram.

What followed, as one reads it today, has both comedy and pathos. Wilde, a lord of life and a lord of language, living on the crest of prosperity and fame, an artist above all considerations of discretion or caution, saw before him not a young blackmailer who had come to extort money from him for stolen letters, but an attractive boy. He had already put the case in the hands of George Lewis his solicitor and had probably lost sleep over it, but Wood's fair hair and frank smile made him forget all that. He invited the boy to dinner at the Florence, gave him the usual lavish hospitality, then took him back to his empty house in Tite Street where Wood stayed most of the night, leaving before the milkman, with his great brass urn and jingling harness, came to the door. A few nights later they met again by appointment at the corner of the street and after disposing of a cold fowl in the kitchen they again went up to the bedroom. The little matter of the letters was arranged for thirty pounds at Taylor's a few days later and, after a farewell luncheon party at the Florence and an extra fiver, Wood left for America.

Wilde may have been startled when Cliburn and Allen appeared with the other letter—if so, he did not show it and refused to buy. The pair thereupon made copies of the letter and showed one to Beerbohm Tree who was rehearsing Wilde's second play, *A Woman of No Importance*. Tree handed this to Wilde with a mild comment and when Allen called and asked for £10 for the original Wilde refused 'as he already had a copy', but gave him 10/- for his trouble. Allen conferred with Cliburn round the corner and Cliburn brought the letter back, saying with a grin that it was evidently no use trying to rent Wilde and he might as well have it. "I'm afraid you are leading a wonderfully wicked life," said Wilde and Cliburn made his remark about there being good and bad in every one of us.

Wilde seems to have handled Allen and Cliburn with aplomb however foolish he may have been over Wood but he was more disturbed by the incident than he showed. He did not know how many copies of the letter had been taken and decided to carry it off by asking Pierre Louÿs to turn it into a sonnet which could be published in Bosie's Oxford magazine *The Spirit Lamp*. Louÿs obliged and his poem duly appeared in the May issue of *The Spirit Lamp* as an assurance against any further question about it. In this it failed.•

But Wilde's caution did not last long. Taylor informed him that he had two new acquisitions, the brothers Bill and Charlie Parker, who

• "The turning of one of Wilde's letters to Lord Alfred Douglas into a sonnet was a very thinly veiled attempt to get rid of the character of that letter. A more thinly veiled attempt to cover its real nature has never been made in a Court of Justice." (Edward Carson in his opening speech for the Defence of Lord Queensberry.)

had been introduced to him by Harrington in the notorious St James's Bar. On the strength of Taylor's assurances Wilde engaged a private room at Kettner's and asked Taylor to bring the lads to dinner.

They were the sons of an employee in a racing stable at Datchet and had been working in London, Bill as a groom, Charlie as a valet. Harrington had found them and brought them to the St James's to meet Taylor. Charlie, a dark, slightly built lad with a girlish face, had cheerfully remarked: "If any old gentleman takes a fancy to me, I'm agreeable." They were both without money.

Of all Wilde's dinner-parties at Kettner's this, in the eyes of his guests, most absurdly parodied the kind of Roman feast Wilde dreamed it to be. If Mavor from South Kensington had been impressed these two semi-illiterates who had been sleeping in doss-houses must have had their breath taken away. A large meal, Champagne, Wilde talking about 'poetry and art and the old Roman days,' as Charlie Parker put it, Wilde feeding Charlie with titbits and passing candied cherries from his lips to the boy's, brandy and cigars afterwards and at last Wilde's announcement as he put his arm round Charlie—"This is the boy for me!" Then, a trifle tipsy as he must surely have been, Wilde took Charlie back to the Savoy where he was staying. William was left with Taylor and had the consolation of hearing: "Your brother is lucky. Oscar doesn't care what he pays if he fancies a chap."

Whether or not Charlie was lucky seems doubtful. He afterwards stated in the witness-box that Wilde 'committed the act of sodomy upon me' which caused the prosecuting counsel Charles Gill to put one of the most asinine questions in the whole case. "With your consent?" he asked. Not surprisingly he received no reply. Charlie Parker also gave evidence about Wilde's approach to sex which would tell a psychologist all he needed to know about Wilde's sexual make-up. "I was asked by Wilde to imagine that I was a woman and that he was my lover. I had to keep up this illusion. I used to sit on his knees and he used to play with my privates as a man might amuse himself with a girl. Wilde insisted on this filthy make-believe being kept up."

This was the beginning of another of Wilde's intermittent relationships. He even took the boy about with him for a time, appearing in a box with him at the Pavilion. But when Wilde left London, having taken a house at Goring for the summer, Charlie was picked up by a rich man, mysteriously referred to as 'a famous operatic composer', who took him to Paris for some months. This may only have been a man named Harold Henry, a friend of Wilde's and Taylor's, who was in fact 'a clerk in a music publisher's in Putney'. Charlie was to reappear later.

It was in that year, 1893, that Wilde became consumed with his passion for moving swiftly from one to another of the boys he met. Promiscuity such as his was not unusual and is the aspect of homosexuality which is most shocking to the uncommitted observer, perhaps because it is impracticable when two sexes are concerned. There is a fatal facility about it for homosexuals which produces cases like Wilde's that look like the ravening of wolves of unassuagable appetite but, viewed from another direction, are little more than cerebral excitement finding its outlet in an interminable series of rendezvous and brief encounters. Wilde was hypnotized not by any individual but by his conception of pleasure, of supermanship, a sultan with all the world's delights to choose from crying banally 'Bring on the dancing girls!' He was eating gluttonously, lunching at the Café Royal, dining at the Savoy and having supper at Willis's on most days, drinking too much at meals and between them. He regarded most of the boys who were brought to him by Taylor and Schwabe as figures in what he called painted pageants, paid them and gave no more thought to them than to the hansom cabs he hired. Fate, he thought, had cast him for the part of a Roman emperor and he richly enjoyed it. He was, as he had always been, without the gift of self-criticism. He may have bemoaned his increasing weight—he could not see that his character was becoming gross, too. But as for his promiscuity—there was nothing exceptional in it. It was part of the life he had chosen.

There was some unpleasantness that year with Aloys Vogel the manager of the Albemarle Hotel to which Wilde had often taken young men for the night and he decided to rent some chambers at 10, St James's Place 'purely in order to work undisturbed' as he wrote in *De Profundis* later, and presumably told his wife at the time. Here he was visited by Charlie Parker, Fred Atkins, a friend of Atkins named Harry Barford said to be an actor, Sidney Mavor, and Ernest Scarfe, a young clerk whom Taylor brought in unexpectedly saying that he had come from the Australian gold-diggings. Scarfe was given the two things that seemed indispensable when Wilde began a new acquaintanceship—dinner at Kettner's and an inscribed silver cigarette-case. Taylor had met Scarfe at the Knightsbridge skating rink through a man named Arthur Marling (alias Goff), a thoroughly bad lot who was associated with Cliburn and Allen.

Wilde kept his rooms in St James's Place till March 1894 when he began to be hard up, for it was a year since the production of his last play, *A Woman of No Importance*. Bosie Douglas had been in Egypt all the winter.

Wilde continued to see Atkins and Parker and must have heard that Wood was back from America and sharing rooms with Parker at 72, Regent Street, Chelsea. What he did not know was that the two had joined forces with Cliburn and Allen and were engaged in blackmail, specializing as before in stealing compromising letters. During the spring Charlie Parker had gone home with Ernest Macklin, that old friend of Taylor's, and stolen from his pocket some letters from a silver broker named Clarke who lived at 3, Northumberland Mansions. Parker, by now if not before a hardened blackmailer, went to Clarke and demanded £10 for these at the same time getting possession of his gold watch and chain. Clarke threatened to charge him with the theft of this and at last summoned courage to send for a policeman.

The man on the beat in general seems to have been uninquisitive in cases like this and simply told Charlie Parker to hand the watch back. But Parker still had letters written by Clarke to a man named Durnbach and tried to extort money for these.

He was given notice to quit his rooms at 50, Park Walk by the landlady, Lucy Rumsby, after complaints by another lodger, Mrs Bancroft, that he was being visited late at night by Wilde who kept his cab waiting outside the house.

Meanwhile Uncle Burton and Freddy Atkins had joined forces again and gone to Scarborough where they pulled off their most successful coup. Freddy was appearing at the Scarborough Aquarium earning, he claimed, £4 10*s*. a week as a singer. Freddy 'made the acquaintance' of a foreign nobleman, a Count, who had a big yacht lying in the bay and Uncle Burton managed to relieve him of nearly £500.*

But in London there were events, too, which might have warned Wilde how perilous his position had become as an associate of these

* Could this foreign nobleman possibly have been André Raffalovich? He had a yacht at this time.

people. (He knew for instance that Taylor's rooms had been searched by the police in 1893 and Taylor had moved at a moment's notice to Chapel Street.) Now a man named John Watson Preston with some premises at 46, Fitzroy Street was in the habit of giving drag parties on Sunday evenings and the police decided to raid one of these. The compulsion to certain inverts to appear in public in women's dress is as old as civilization and in some Eastern countries they abandon male dress altogether and live as women. The police would certainly have had the support of the vast majority of the citizenry of the time for what they did and their sympathy for the failure of the prosecution.

Arthur Marling (who had introduced Scarfe to Taylor it may be remembered) was one of the stars of these parties and invited Charlie Parker and Taylor to attend. What happened can best be told by Christopher Millard (who anonymously edited *Oscar Wilde Three Times Tried*) from contemporary newspaper reports.

> Eighteen men were taken into custody by the police in a midnight raid in Fitzroy Street on Sunday, August 12, 1894, two of them being men in feminine clothing. The prisoners were taken to Tottenham Court Road Police Station, and were brought up at Marlborough Street before Mr. Hannay, the magistrate, on the following morning. Amongst them were Charles Parker, 19, of no occupation, 72, Regent Street, Chelsea; Alfred Taylor, 32, no occupation, of 7, Camera Square, Chelsea; John Watson Preston, 34, general dealer, 46, Fitzroy Street, W., the proprietor of the raided premises; and Arthur Marling, 26, of 8, Crawford Street. The last named was described as a female impersonator, and was charged with being an idle and disorderly person. He appeared in court dressed in a fantastic female garb of black and gold.
>
> Detective-Sergeant Kane told how, with Superintendent Sheppard, he proceeded to 46, Fitzroy Street, on the previous night between eleven and twelve o'clock, and saw cabs drive up with men. Two of the prisoners (Marling being one) were in a hansom, dressed as women, one with a fan. A man in ordinary clothes sat on their laps. Mr. Hannay asked Superintendent Kane if he had any idea of the object of the masquerade. Kane replied, 'I have, sir.' Marling said his business was to impersonate women at the halls, and the proprietor of the club at 46, Fitzroy Street, Mr. Preston, asked him to go and sing at his house in feminine attire, and he agreed. Mr. Hannay granted a remand for a week. He said there seemed to be something more than suspicion against five of the men found in the basement, but for the rest he would like to have something

> more definite in the charge when the accused next came before him. Superintendent Sheppard, in reply, said 'They are most of them known, your worship.' Some of the accused were then released on their own recognisances; others had to find sureties in the sum of £5.
>
> On the hearing of the case being resumed on Monday, August 20th, Marling and another were bound over to keep the peace for three months. Taylor and Parker were amongst those who were discharged unconditionally. Five men were ordered to find sureties in the sum of forty shillings each to be of good behaviour for one month. The magistrate said that whatever suspicion there might be, there was no evidence against the majority of the prisoners. He had had a number of letters informing him that many of the men were of the vilest possible character, but no one had come forward to give evidence to that effect.

Taylor's friend Charles Spurrier Mason at once wrote for financial help to Wilde who was staying at Worthing. Wilde replied: "I was very sorry to read in the paper about poor Alfred Taylor. It is a dreadful piece of bad luck, and I wish to goodness I could do something for him, but, as I have had occasion to write to him many times lately, as I have no play going on this season I have no money at all, and indeed am at my wits' end trying to raise some for household expenses and such tedious things."

Wilde was at that time behaving with his usual indiscretion at Worthing where he and Bosie Douglas had picked up a newspaper boy named Alphonse Conway and two of his associates named Percy and Stephen. When Bosie left Wilde wrote to him: "Percy left the day after you did. He spoke much of you. Alphonso is still in favour. He is my only companion, along with Stephen. Alphonso always alludes to you as 'the Lord', which however gives you, I think, a Biblical Hebraic dignity that gracious Greek boys should *not* have. He also says, from time to time, 'Percy was the Lord's favourite', which makes me think of Percy as the infant Samuel—an inaccurate reminiscence, as Percy was Hellenic."

Alphonse Conway leaves one with a happier impression than most of the young blackguards with whom Wilde associated. Wilde explained in court during the trial of Queensberry that he had met Conway when the boy and another had helped launch a boat for him and Bosie Douglas and they had taken him and his friend for a sail. From Wilde's letter it would seem to have been a light-hearted seaside affair, and he said in evidence that Conway had become a great friend of his sons. Wilde bought him clothes and took him to Brighton for the week-end, then tried to get him a job on a ship. Great play was made by Carson of the fact that Conway sold newspapers at a kiosk on the pier. ("The first I've heard of his connection with literature," said Wilde.) It was incredible to Carson and later to most of the jury-men that Wilde should have found this 'happy bright boy', a fit companion for his family when his occupation was selling newspapers. But although Queensberry's solicitors had Conway in court during the trial of Queensberry, the prosecution did not produce him at Wilde's trials. He may, like Mavor, have refused to testify according to the statement he had been induced to make. It would be pleasant to think so. A more cynical view is that Queensberry could bribe him whereas the Public Prosecutor could not.

With him during the Queensberry trial were Grainger and Tankard. Grainger had been Bosie's servant at Oxford and had been engaged to work in Wilde's house at Goring. It was of him that Wilde dropped his famous brick about not kissing him—'a peculiarly plain boy, unfortunately extremely ugly'—which Carson seized on with such advantage. He was never called by the Prosecution, nor was Tankard, a page-boy at the Savoy whom Wilde had shipped to Calais. They, too, may have refused to give the evidence demanded of them.

4

It is impossible to doubt that the men employed by Queensberry to obtain information were thoroughly unscrupulous and deserved a long term of imprisonment for suborning and bribing witnesses on Queensberry's behalf. The solicitors, too, behaved in the most disgraceful way in encouraging or at least turning a blind eye to this.

The full story of how all those young blackguards were brought into court ready to swear Wilde's life away and to admit to being not only male prostitutes but blackmailers will never be known, but several incidents remain on record.

The two men, Kearley• and Littlechild, had been detectives in the

• The policeman who was given the task of arresting Fanny and Stella twenty-four years earlier appeared in reports as Sergeant Kerley. Allowing for variations in spelling names from shorthand notes it is possible that this was the now retired detective at the beginning of his career.

Metropolitan Police and had recently retired to work privately. Whether or not they received any direct assistance from serving policemen they had, or had recently had, access to information which was valuable to them. Moreover, so far as Parker, Wood and the rest of them were concerned they were 'the Police' and could hector and persuade and threaten with police prestige behind them. They also had Queensberry's money to dispense when necessary.

Poor Wilde made some feeble efforts to see some of the boys and win them over, a fact known to Carson who taunted him with it. He and Bosie had stopped on their way through Calais to talk to Tankard, and he asked Shelley and Scarfe to dinner at the Avondale on separate nights. He tried to get in touch with Mavor and consulted with Taylor. He even saw Atkins. But he could offer neither fear of punishment nor hope of reward on the Queensberry scale, and failed dismally to gain any support but Jenny Mavor's and perhaps that of Scarfe who was not called to give evidence.

Kearley and Littlechild found Charles Parker in the Army (the Royal Artillery) and soon roped him in. His brother Bill who disappeared from the London scene soon after meeting Wilde was found in the country and proved a no less eager witness. Charlie had joined up after receiving a small share of £300 which Wood and Allen had obtained by blackmail from a man who had taken him home. Cliburn and Allen were in hiding in Bournemouth but Kearley and Littlechild winkled them out and they were kept at the court on subpoena. Barford, a friend of Atkins who had been to St James's Place, was not found, apparently, but Wood and Atkins were bribed—Queensberry is said to have given his agents £500 for use if necessary.

Kearley admitted to entering Taylor's rooms by a subterfuge and stealing (though he did not call it that) papers belonging to Taylor. No criticism was made of this conduct by anyone in court and the press ignored it though Kearley was acting as a private individual. Another small mystery was Charles Parker's leave of absence from the Army. It lasted, he admitted, three months, from the time he was first brought up to London for the Queensberry trial. This was highly convenient to the prosecution.

All this evidence was collected by Littlechild and Kearley but there is a story about an actor named Brookfield having helped them. In some accounts Charles Hawtrey is associated with Brookfield, surprisingly to those who knew Hawtrey. The story is backed by no very solid evidence and there would seem to be no way in which Brookfield, even had he wished, could have aided the professional work of Littlechild and Kearley. The police were already watching Taylor and had searched his rooms in the previous year.* They also had their informer Burton. The trail was easy to follow.

The course of the trials was a foregone conclusion from the moment that Carson in defending Queensberry said he intended to produce these boys. Yet in the final prosecution the only evidence against Wilde which was not tainted, and known by the prosecution to be tainted, was that of Shelley which was disallowed anyway, on account of his mental condition. Freddy Atkins was caught out in such blatant perjury that he was ordered out of the box and his evidence disallowed. That Wilde had done what he was accused of doing cannot be denied but the case against him was rigged from the start. The witnesses were kept in the private houses of policemen during the two trials of Wilde. In the end, from all Queensberry's display of witnesses against him, the offences for which he was sentenced were those with Wood and Parker, both proven blackmailers. No proceedings were brought against any of the witnesses or their associates though three years later Cliburn got seven years' penal servitude for blackmailing, Allen who informed against him eighteen months' hard labour, and Marling who was concerned with them in the offence was given five years' penal servitude for receiving.

The weakness of Wilde's position was in the prejudice that had been created in the public mind and thus in the minds of the jury. He presented, deliberately it seemed, a most dislikable public image. Fleet Street abominated him for the arrogance he had shown in controversy and the contempt he had expressed for the press. People had no chance to know of his generosity, his charm, his gaiety; in court they saw only a bloated self-assured over-dressed man wisecracking under cross-examination. Queensberry was no popular favourite and if Wilde had been a humble writer defending his good name against a rich and influential peer, the man in the street would have been on his side. But there was nothing Bohemian about him.

* Without a warrant. It may be remembered that in two cases in the 1950s the police admitted to the same offence on the plea that a warrant was not necessary when the occupant had been arrested.

His attempts to befriend Bohemians, his going bail for John Barlas and his visits to the Rhymers Club convinced no one. To him the Dukeries had been an enchanted world and he seemed to be, if anything, in his plays and in his person rather more 'upper class' than the horsy little Marquess. He went to prison for what he was, not for what he had done.

There were only two commendable acts in all that puppet show of cowardice and perjury. One was Taylor's self-sacrifice and courage in refusing to turn Queen's Evidence against Wilde and joining him in the dock to be given the same sentence. The other was Mavor's plucky denial of any misconduct on Wilde's part. He had been bullied into making a statement and startled the whole court by denying it.

Yet once again, all this is commonplace and any similar trial under the Criminal Law Amendment Act produces the same flagrant lying by bribed, or frightened, or bullied witnesses, the same conspiracies on the part of the minions of the prosecution and the same isolated acts of courage. The Wilde Case, comprising two trials, perhaps the most famous prosecution in the last three centuries, has been repeated in essentials a score of times since without attracting more than fleeting attention.

CHAPTER TWELVE

Wilde, the Aftermath

THE influence of Wilde as a writer was short-lived but the effects of his disaster were felt in the literature and life of his time and reverberate to this day.

"And I? May I say nothing, my lord?" asked Wilde when the monstrous sentence had been passed. His lordship made no reply beyond an impatient wave of his hand to the warders who hurried the prisoner out of sight.

And out of mind. Anywhere, to prison, to blazes, to eternity, so long as he was no longer there to embarrass the public, to trouble the conscience of those who thought and the sleep of those who felt. May I say nothing, my lord? Nothing. You have been far too articulate already and for too many years. Are you not silenced for ever, now? Go to hell your own way but do not let us hear your rich beguiling voice again.

In the very vehemence of that wave of the hand, though, there was fear that even yet this irrepressible jester might find a way to make the court ridiculous, to laugh at ponderous Lockwood and his other tormentors, to show the very judge to be a rattling skeleton in a wig and gown, and Justice, British Justice at that, a dance of puppets to the tune of public opinion. Away with him, warders. At least for two years the man will be unseen and unheard. And if in the future, from the grave perhaps, he shows us all, Judge, learned Counsel and the rest to have betrayed the ideal of justice we serve, we at least shall not be here to see it.

So Wilde was hustled out of sight and an invisible following went with him. Not of his imitators, for he had no imitators. In the theatre it would be thirty years before anyone would attempt to gain a hearing for comedy even remotely like his. In conversation no one has ever learned the gay magic of his wit and though some have attempted it their epigrams and paradoxes have dropped like solidly manufactured weights. In his books there was little to imitate.

It was not even the vicious noctambules of the London streets and their patrons who went underground. A week or two, at most a few months, and the back of the circle at the Alhambra would be as crowded as ever, the St James's or whatever bar was by then favoured would be buzzing with introductions and Charlie Parker would be out on the Dilly again.

But something was lost with Wilde's freedom, something that was not to be released in two years' time, or for many years after. Not just that inflated figure of the Artist as Wilde had conceived him, that privileged being above the Boetian hordes. That went, certainly, and was no loss. But with him to the cells below the court Wilde took something visionary and good, something which he himself had only glimpsed. Freedom in the world of ideas? Freedom for mankind to develop not as one progressive mass but as a thousand million individuals? Freedom to create, oblivious of public demand or disapproval? Freedom to live not without obligation to humanity but without reverence for society? Freedom to write, not with Wilde's protestations that beauty was all, but as each writer saw beauty?

Wilde was no David, alone against the Philistine giant. But he had so far assumed the mantle of David in the public eye that his surrender was the surrender not only of the Artist but of the artist. Writers there would be, and greater writers than Wilde, and they were waiting to be heard. But they would have to modulate their voices. None with a suggestion of Wilde's accent would be listened to, for the mood of the audience had changed. The writer might claim indifference to public demand, might prize his independence from its exigencies, but his ear was, consciously or not, to the ground and he was moved by influences which he might not understand or even recognize to learn a new kind of oratory.

Only a few little men made any show of triumph. Henley probably rejoiced bawdily with his sycophants, Jerome K. Jerome who had demanded the suppression of *The Chameleon* made no secret of his satisfaction and the leader-writers, trained to interpret the public mood, thundered self-righteously. The greater men went their way unaware that the ground had been cleared before them. In the very year of Wilde's conviction Thomas Hardy published *Jude the Obscure*, Joseph Conrad his first novel *Almayer's Folly*, Francis Thompson his *Sister Songs*, H. G. Wells *The Time Machine* and Hilaire Belloc *Verses and Sonnets*. There was no sudden or perceptible re-alignment but *fin-de-siècle* became a term of contempt, aestheticism a dirty word and art-for-art's-sake a discredited fallacy. This was valuable. Aestheticism as a cult was played out, as Wilde himself had recognized.

Stevenson, Pater and Symonds had died in the previous year. Stevenson would have shrugged his shoulders very likely, perplexed rather than indifferent; Pater might have jerked back in his shell and peeped out to watch—but Symonds, surely, would have been articulate. He did not like Wilde and had disapproved of *The Picture of Dorian Gray* as the wrong way to treat The Subject, but was he not fighting the very law under which Wilde was being punished? What, above all, was said at the breakfast table at Number Two, The Pines? Did Swinburne speak of Wilde, as he had once spoken of Simeon Solomon, as 'a thing unmentionable alike by men and women' because he had shown no interest in Swinburne's own deviations? Did they shake their heads, those two old gentlemen, and agreeing that it was a terrible thing, calmly set about their literary occupations for the day? Or did Swinburne remember, with mild sympathy for the fallen man, that he once had been execrated and his works publicly damned?

As for the other writers and artists who had known Wilde, not a friendly word was spoken. John Gray who had been Wilde's protégé did nothing to stop Raffalovich from making his attacks almost before sentence was passed. Lionel Johnson who had once said he was in love with Wilde, Aubrey Beardsley who had been his illustrator, André Gide who had taken him to the stews of Blidah, Max Beerbohm who professed an extravagant love for his work even as he caricatured him,

Conan Doyle who would later gain a reputation as a champion of the wrongly convicted, Wilfred Scawen Blunt with whom Wilde had stayed and who had himself been imprisoned, George Curzon once Oscar Browning's young friend who had known Wilde at Oxford and since and was now a Member of Parliament, Arthur Symons to whom Wilde had given encouragement, Oscar Browning who had been his friend and Grant Allen who had thanked him for his 'noble and beautiful' essay *The Soul of Man Under Socialism*, the editors who had published his work in magazines, the publishers who had been proud to have his books on their lists, the people of the theatre whom he had enriched—from all these not a whisper came. Edmund Gosse wrote to Ross who was in France that Wilde's trials would have been comedy or satiric drama if it had not been for his consideration for Ross. John Lane withdrew Wilde's books from sale and cabled from America denying any personal knowledge of the man, while Elkin Mathews actually went into the witness box to say that as soon as he had heard of Shelley's friendship with Wilde he had sacked the boy. The only man to ask, in a bluff sort of way, that Wilde should be given a fair deal was, somewhat anomalously, that very Buchanan who had attacked the Pre-Raphaelites in his article *The Fleshly School in Poetry* twenty-four years earlier. Otherwise silence. The most talked-of man in London could not be mentioned. For some years it seemed that no one had ever known Wilde. The only sound to be heard was a very loud cockcrow.

Of Wilde's intimate friends, Robert Ross and Reggie Turner went abroad on the night of Wilde's arrest, Schwabe had received warning before the case was heard and was in Belgium. More Adey remained loyally in London and Bosie Douglas visited Wilde in prison every day until the eve of his first trial, then joined Ross. Harris's description of the loaded Channel boats was nonsense, of course, but there was some expectation of a witch-hunt and holidays were taken earlier than usual and prolonged.

At first no effects of the trial were perceptible, but soon there began to be audible on all sides instead of Wilde's antonyms 'beautiful' and 'ugly' another two adjectives 'healthy' and 'unhealthy' with meanings having nothing to do with physical salubrity. Wilde, together with all he had stood for, was 'unhealthy', but to be British enough to resent the defiance of Boers was 'healthy'. Low Church was healthy, High

Church with all that lace and bowing and scraping was unhealthy while Popery positively festered. (In Victorian times atheism and anti-Christianity often made themselves presentable to the public by passing themselves off as anti-Catholic.) Bohemianism was healthy enough, but it had to be of the right kind, that was the du Maurier/Trilby variety, wide-brimmed black hats, huge pipes, beefy appetites for food and chorus girls, but nothing aesthetic or precious. Poetry, except for Tennyson and Browning, was unhealthy but a good story such as Rudyard Kipling told about the soldiers he worshipped was healthy. All foreign-ness was unhealthy—the only healthy place to visit outside England were the colonies in which to carry the white man's burden through malarial swamps. Plain dirty stories were healthy enough, subtle ones were an expression of degeneracy. It was all right to like to see a woman well turned out—to know anything about her clothes was poisonous. In art galleries you might 'know what you liked' but any other knowledge of art was suspect. A man could smoke a pipe, large and heavy if possible, but cigarettes were for boys and effeminates. Perhaps the unhealthiest thing of all was to know anything about decor in the home—a healthy man left that sort of fal-lal to the wife.

This passion for healthiness soon made itself felt among writers. The beneficent influence of the French which had enlivened our literature since the eighteenth century died overnight and a whole generation was brought up to think Baudelaire and Verlaine were pornographers and men had to buy even their Rabelais and Balzac's *Contes* in dirty little editions sold in dingy shops in the West End. In English the works of Swinburne and Pater, indeed of anyone who was suspected of knowing Greek, were condemned. It was seen that erotic literature might be splendid, like George Moore's early novels or the *Decameron*; it was this damned, hot-house, scented stuff that had undermined the nation. In urgent demand were open-air poets, good strong adventure-story writers and novelists who wrote about ordinary people. Soon there were plenty of these—Rider Haggard in the forests of Africa, Rudyard Kipling round the barracks of India, Joseph Conrad at sea, Stevenson on a treasure island, Anthony Hope in Ruritania. Heroic types arose who had no weakness in them and never did an unmanly act. Sherlock Holmes was, unfortunately, already addicted to morphine, but this was forgotten as far as possible and characters like Captain

Kettle had no nonsense about them at all. Decent men of the lower middle-classes began to appear in fiction for it was generally felt that decadence was an upper class weakness repulsive to the proletariat, and H. G. Wells created Kipps and Mr Polly, and W. W. Jacobs had his Night Watchman, Jerome his Three Men in a Boat, and slightly comic characters with hearts of gold but no aspirates abounded, making Wilde's Lord Arthur Savile and Lord Henry Wotton and the rest seem in retrospect degenerate aristocrats. There was scarcely a titled man or woman in English fiction for more than twenty years.

It happened that a book called *Degeneration* by Max Nordau appeared in English that year—it had been published in German three years earlier—and it at once became a best-seller. In the civilized world, everyone was delighted to read, there was a 'twilight mood' which led to degeneration and hysteria. The writers of the age exhibited the 'senseless stammering and babbling of deranged minds' and 'what the ignorant hold to be the outbursts of gushing, youthful vigour and turbulent constructive impulses are really nothing but the convulsions and spasms of exhaustion'. This was I-told-you-so with a vengeance and that very dull book ran through many editions. In the next year it was done in verse by Owen Seaman whose *Battle of the Bays* was published by John Lane.

The poets of the Nineties scattered like rabbits. Dowson and Lionel Johnson, as we have seen, were drinking themselves to death already; Dowson would be dead in five years' time and Johnson in seven, while Aubrey Beardsley the 'Fra Angelico of Satanism'* had only three years to live. John Davidson would commit suicide fourteen years later. Alfred Douglas stuck out his chin and published his poems in English and French in Paris and continued to publish them for the remaining fifty years of his life. Theodore Wratislaw who had once written in a sonnet *To a Sicilian Boy*,

> Love, I adore the contours of thy shape . . .
> Ah let me in thy bosom still enjoy
> Oblivion of the past, divinest boy,
> And the dull ennui of a woman's kiss

now entered the Estate Office at Somerset House and remained there till his death in 1933 writing only one poem on the death of Swinburne. Bernard Miall, who had been capable of *Nocturnes and Pastorals*,

* Quoted from Roger Fry by Derek Stanford in *Poets of the Nineties*, 1965.

Black water and black cloudless sky
White stars as cold as Fate.
Beneath the shadowy whispering trees
The women watch and wait.

turned to translation and other literary drudgery and his brother Derwent Miall wrote light fiction and humour for the rest of his life.

Victor Plarr, Dowson's friend and a member of the Rhymers Club became librarian to the Royal College of Surgeons till his death in 1929. Arthur Symons and John Barlas were both confined in lunatic asylums for longish periods, Barlas dying in one. Douglas Ainslie retired to Hollywood, W. T. Peters to Paris. Charles Kains-Jackson who had written

Youth standing sweet triumphant by the sea
All freshness of the day, and all the light
Of thy white limbs, form, bared and bright
For conflict . . .

now wrote *The History of the International Corn and Wool Trade* which appeared in *The Annual Transactions of the Royal Agricultural Society*.

A touch of comedy was provided by Richard Le Gallienne who had clung to the Nineties band-wagon with all the tenacity of an ambitious skouse. He revered Wilde and used to dress up in silk stockings, a green velvet jacket and a floppy hat and wear his hair down to his shoulders to be photographed contemplating nature against a woodland background. Dressed in this rig-out he arrived in New York for his first lecture tour just as the newspapers were full of Wilde's conviction. He found, as his able biographers• say, that English poets with long hair preaching a gospel of decadence were not in demand and hurried back to England to write a bad novel called *The Quest of the Golden Girl*, then spent most of the rest of his life in America as a lecturer and journalist.

There were repercussions of the new healthiness in public life, too. Long hair for men disappeared and something like a crew-cut became popular with a strong moustache, clipped or luxuriant, to go with it. There was a sudden clean-up of the pornography on sale in bookshops and Leonard Smithers's ex-partner H. S. Nichols who had a shop in Charing Cross Road lost two tons of stock and had to flee to Paris

• *The Quest of the Golden Boy* by Richard Whittington-Egan and Geoffrey Smerdon, 1960.

while on bail to avoid imprisonment. William Watson refused to write for the *Yellow Book* unless Beardsley was sacked and both the *Yellow Book* and *The Savoy* which followed it died of starvation. There was a slump in sentimental friendships between men which hitherto wives had encouraged to keep their husbands from other women.

Strangely enough painting and music were unaffected, perhaps because so few people understood what they were about. In both of them French influence, so pernicious in literature, was paramount, the Impressionists and Debussy being welcomed. Wilde knew little about either and had said nothing to indicate what must be avoided.

Small wonder that Rudyard Kipling became the most popular poet in England closely followed by A. E. Housman whose *A Shropshire Lad* was taken for open-air poetry of the healthiest kind. The moon became a part of the night-scene and not a disquieting symbol of one didn't quite know what, and William Watson forged ahead towards the knighthood he would receive. The Open Road school had been set hiking up Olympus by Stevenson and soon came into their own, while Masefield's verse, the open sea *and* the open road, was obviously healthy. Not for nearly twenty years, when there was a disturbing whiff of dead leaves in the early poetry of Rupert Brooke, could anything like decadence be detected in English poetry and Swinburne went out of print. Fitzgerald's *Rubaiyat of Omar Khayyam* was the favourite poetic work of the age and it was supposed to be a rumbustious drinking song.

With the new century came a demand for 'daring' books. 'Frankness' was wanted, an escape from Victorian hypocrisy, not the kind of escape that Swinburne and 'that beast Oscar Wilde' and 'all that gang' had created but virile stuff which would have been considered bawdy by critics of the 1870s and 80s. Shaw used the word 'bloody' on the stage and a dashing *avant garde* writer named John Galsworthy produced a novel with the theme of adultery, while Elinor Glyn broke all bounds—healthily, of course. No one minded a bit of smut but not foetid morbid stuff like *The Picture of Dorian Gray*. Wilde was out.

Wilde said that he put only his talent into his work and his genius into his life. If he is to be taken at his word, and his life considered as a drama which he wrote, he must be counted a pornographer in writing it. It took a pornographer to see in his drab little one-night-stands a splendid drama of the artist fulfilling his high density. To inflate, to boast in selfconscious phraseology of adulteries and aberrations, to dramatize and exalt them, is to be pornographic. If we could feel that we owe *The Importance of Being Earnest* to Wilde's idiotic amours with blackmailing valets there would be nothing more to be said, but those amours produced in him instead of the will to write a kind of lewd magniloquence which dominated his outward life. To talk of feasting with panthers was pornography. To make great literature of that feasting, consciously or unconsciously, perceptibly to others or not, would have been genius.

It took genius to write *Dolores* from the inspiration of the two 'rouge-cheeked women' who used to birch Swinburne in St John's Wood, and genius to compose *Leaves of Grass* encouraged by the hairy embraces of some predecessor of Whitman's Irish tram-conductor. But to gain from his hiring of catamites only the conviction that he was a Lord of Life, to achieve no more than a few boastful quips to his friends, showed that Wilde was right in saying that as a creative writer he had no more than talent.

It is not for the artist himself to disclose the sources of his impulse, whether they are mean little vices or a great love. We have seen that it was only a chance find of Symonds's in the Buonarroti archives which told the world the actual name of the young man to whom Michelangelo wrote his love-poetry and if it had not been for the secret essay Gosse wrote to excuse his lack of frankness about Swinburne, and Swinburne's own letters, we might never have known of a great poet's masochistic practices. But it is the duty of the critic, the biographer or the editor to reveal what he knows, not because these things affect the merit of a work of art but because they are supremely interesting to those who care about the artist and his achievements. That we owe some of Swinburne's greatest rhythms to the survival of the flogging-block at Eton, or *Alice in Wonderland* to Dodgson's urge to ingratiate himself with little girls, or Fitzgerald's *Rubaiyat of Omar Khayyam* to his helpless devotion to a young sportsman called Kenworthy Browne, or the later volumes of Symonds's *History of the Italian Renaissance* to the Swiss peasant Christian Buol, or for that matter Shakespeare's Sonnets to Mr W. H., has no bearing on the quality of these works. Nor do similar inspirations, worthy or unworthy, which have been discussed in this book detract from or add to the merit of the books that we may owe to them, like Lear's *Nonsense Rhymes*, Pater's *Marius*, Cory's *Ionica*, but knowledge of them is of perpetual and vital interest. Or why study the lives of the artists at all?

Then, in learning so much about the men who wrote we learn something of their period, for the life of the artist, told with details irrelevant to the life of the statesman or scientist, is a mirror in which the contemporary scene is reflected, and it is for us to judge how much of it is of its time and how much is eternal. Houghton in his vast library on a Sunday morning showing the choicest of his erotic books to his week-end guests till a footman enters to announce that the carriages are waiting to take the party to church, Symonds fleeing to streets more brightly lit from that dim passage near Leicester Square in which he was accosted by a soliciting redcoat, Edward VII as a middle-aged Prince of Wales coming to the first night of *An Ideal Husband* and telling Wilde not to alter a word of the script, Simeon Solomon reading the account of Wilde's conviction in a work-house and Wilde bemoaning in prison nearly two years later that he had lost his painting by Solomon, Lewis Carroll buying packets of safety-pins to offer on the beach to small girls who wanted to paddle, Wilde taking Fred Atkins to a fashionable hairdresser in Paris to have his hair curled, Angelo Fusato making his first date with Symonds and losing him because the poor young Venetian knew too well what was expected of him, Swinburne drunk but dignified falling on his face as he alighted from a hansom cab or Oscar Browning inviting blue-jackets to drink beer and shout songs in his rooms at Brasenose, these are the sights and episodes which reveal an age and so in a sense all ages. They reveal, too, its men, not as their daguerreotypes did, a set of startled features surrounded by whiskers and a bearing saintly and stiff, but as human beings with their share of eccentricity and lust, their deference to public opinion or their—scarcely less weak—noisy defiance of it, their deep or shallow loves, their sufferings, fears and triumphs.

It may not be true that to know what Shakespeare had for breakfast, how often he got drunk and with whom he slept is more important than to read the most scholarly dissertation on his plays, written in the complicated lingo of modern literary criticism, but it will probably tell us more about Hamlet.

Bibliography

IT will be appreciated that a complete bibliography, in a book which touches on so many persons and periods, is an impossibility. I have not listed, for instance, the titles of works by all the writers chiefly discussed because each would need a bibliography of his own, but have attempted rather to give sources of information and suggestion in the books of others.

Adlard, John, *Stenbock, Yeats and the Nineties* (1966)

Angeli, Helen Rossetti, *Pre-Raphaelite Twilight.* The Story of Charles Augustus Howell (1954)

Annual Register (1860)

Atherton, Gertrude, *The Adventures of a Novelist* (1932)

Beddington, Mrs. Claude, *All That I Have Met* (1929)

Benson, E. F., *As We Were* (1930)

Bibelot, The (1911)

Blyth, James, *Edward Fitzgerald and 'Posh'* (1908)

Brome, Vincent, *Frank Harris* (1959)

Brown, Ivor, *Masques and Phases* (1926)

Browning, Oscar, *Memories of Sixty Years* (1910)
Memories of Later Years (1923)
Burdett, Osbert, *The Beardsley Period* (1925)
Carpenter, Edward, *Days with Walt Whitman* (1906)
Cecil, David, *Max: A Biography* (1964)
Walter Pater (1955)
Charlesworth, Barbara, *Dark Passages*: The Decadent Consciousness in Victorian Literature (1965)
Charteris, Hon. Evan, *The Life and Letters of Sir Edmund Gosse* (1931)
Cory, William, *Extracts from the Letters and Journals* (1897)
Crackanthorpe, Hubert, *Last Studies* (1896)
Davidson, Angus, *Edward Lear* (1938)
Doughty, Oswald, *A Victorian Romantic* (1960)
Douglas, Lord Alfred, *Autobiography* (1929)
Dowson, Ernest, *Poetical Works* (1934)
The Poems of (1905)
Ellis, Havelock, *Studies in the Psychology of Sex* (1901–1910)
My Life (1940)
Esher, Lord, *Ionicus* (1923)
Falk, Bernard, *Five Years Dead* (1937)
The Naked Lady: Biography of Adah Isaacs Menken (1934)
Ford, Julia Ellsworth, *Simeon Solomon* (New York 1909)
Gallienne, Richard le, *The Romantic 90's* (1926)
Gannon, Patricio, *Poets of the Rhymers' Club* (1953)
Gaunt, William, *The Pre-Raphaelite Tragedy* (1942)
The Aesthetic Adventure (1945)
Gernsheim, Halmut, *Lewis Carroll, Photographer* (1949)
Gill, Wilfred Austin, *Edward Cracroft Lefroy* (1897)
Gosse, Edmund, *The Life of Algernon Charles Swinburne* (1917)
Father and Son (1907)
From Shakespeare to Pope (1885)
Gower, Lord Ronald, *Old Diaries* (1902)
Gray, John (Editor), *The Last Letters of Aubrey Beardsley* (1904)
Gray, John, and Raffalovich, André, *The Blackmailers* (1893)
Two Friends (Essays concerning) (1963)
Grosskurth, Phyllis, *John Addington Symonds*: A Biography (1964)
Harris, Frank, *Oscar Wilde His Life and Confessions*, 2 vols. (New York 1918)

Harte, Walter Blackburn, *Meditations in Motley* (Boston 1894)
Holiday, H., *Reminiscences of My Life*
Hough, Graham, *The Last Romantics* (1949)
Hudson, Derek, *Lewis Carroll* (1958)
Hyde, H. Montgomery, *Cases That Changed the Law* (1951)
A History of Pornography (1964)
Jackson, Holbrook, *The Eighteen Nineties* (1927)
Jepson, Edgar, *Memories of a Victorian* (1933)
John, Augustus, *Chiaroscuro* (1952)
Johnson, Lionel, *Complete Poems*, ed. Iain Fletcher (1953)
Some Winchester Letters (1919)
Kermode, Frank, *The Romantic Image* (1957)
Lafourcade, Georges, *Swinburne*: A Literary Biography (1932)
Lear, Edward, *Letters* (1907)
Later Letters (1911)
Lennon, Florence Becker, *Lewis Carroll* (1947)
Lhombreaud, Roger, *Arthur Symons*: A Critical Biography (1963)
Longaker, Mark, *Ernest Dowson* (1945)
Mackenzie, Faith Compton, *William Cory*: A Biography (1950)
Mason, Stuart (Christopher Millard), *Bibliography of Oscar Wilde* N.D. (1914)
Maurier, Daphne du *Young George du Maurier* (1951)
May, J. Lewis, *John Lane and the Nineties* (1936)
Millais, John Gulle, *Life and Letters of Sir John Everett Millais*, 2 vols. (1899)
Muddiman, Bernard, *Men of the Nineties* (1920)
Murdoch, W. Blaikie, *The Renaissance of the Nineties* (1911)
Noel, Roden, *The Collected Poems* (1902)
Essays on Poetry and Poets (1886)
Nordau, Max *Degeneration* (1895)
Pater, Walter, *Studies in the History of the Renaissance* (1873)
Pearson, Hesketh, *The Life of Oscar Wilde* (1946)
Plarr, Victor, *Ernest Dowson 1888–1897* (1914)
Pope-Hennessy, James, *Monckton Milnes*: The Flight of Youth 1851–1885 (1951)
Praz, Mario, *The Romantic Agony* (1951)
Rhymers' Club, First and Second Books (1892 and 1894)
Rhys, Ernest, *Everyman Remembers* (1931)

Richmond Papers, The, ed. A. M. W. Stirling (1926)
Ross, Margery, *Robert Ross, Friend of Friends* (1952)
Ross, Robert, *Aubrey Beardsley* (1909)
Rothenstein, William, *Men and Memories*, 2 vols. (1931)
Roughead, William, *Bad Companions* (1930)
Russell, Lord Francis, *My Life and Adventures* (1923)
Santayana, George, *The Middle Span* (1947)
Sherard, Robert H., *Oscar Wilde: The Story of an Unhappy Friendship* (1902)
Twenty Years in Paris (1905)
The Real Oscar Wilde (1915)
Sims, George R., *Sixty Years of Recollections of Bohemian London* (1917)
Solomon, Simeon, *A Vision of Love Revealed in Sleep* (1871)
Catalogue of Exhibition of Paintings (New York 1966)
Stanford, Derek, *Poets of the Nineties* (1965)
Stenbock, Count Eric, *The Shadow of Death* (1893)
Studies of Death (1894)
Swinburne, A. C., *The Swinburne Letters*, ed. Cecil Y. Lang, 6 vols. (1959–1962)
New Writings, ed. Cecil Y. Lang (1964)
Novels Love's Cross-Currents. Lesbia Brandon (1962)
Symonds, John Addington, *In the Key of Blue* (1893)
Walt Whitman (1896)
A Problem in Greek Ethics (1883)
A Problem in Modern Ethics (1891)
Symons, A. J. A., *An Anthology of Nineties Verse* (1928)
Symons, Arthur, *Dramatis Personae* (1925)
Aubrey Beardsley (1898)
Studies in Prose and Verse (1904)
Terhune, Alfred McKinley, *The Life of Edward Fitzgerald* (1947)
Tynan, Katherine, *Memories* (1924)
Vaughan, Herbert A., *The South Wales Squires* (1926)
Whitman, Walt, *Calamus*: A Series of Letters Written during the years 1868–1880 to a Young Friend (Peter Doyle) (New York 1897)
Whittington-Egan, Richard and Smerdon, Geoffrey, *The Quest of the Golden Boy* (1960)
Wilde, Oscar, *Oscar Wilde Three Times Tried* (Christopher Millard) (1911)
Trials of Oscar Wilde, The, ed. H. Montgomery Hyde (1948)
Letters, ed. Rupert Hart-Davis (1962)

Winwar, Frances, *Oscar Wilde and the Yellow Nineties* (1940)
Wortham, H. E., *Oscar Browning* (1927)
Wratislaw, Theodore, *Caprices* (1893)
Wright, Thomas, *Life of Edward Fitzgerald*, 2 vols. (1904)
Life of Walter Pater (1907)
Yeats, W. B., *The Trembling of the Veil* (1922)
Yellow Book (1894-1897)
Young, G. M., *Victorian England*: Portrait of an Age (1953)

Index

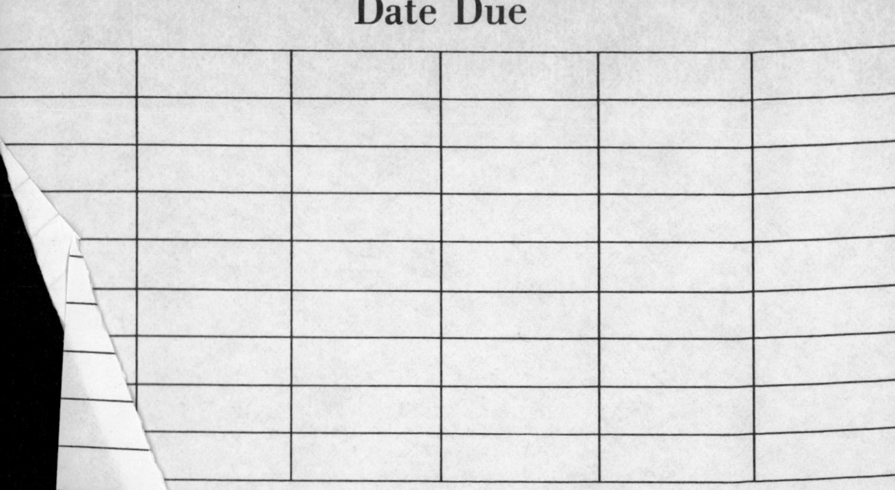
Date Due
PRINTED IN U.S.A.
CAT. NO. 23 231